The CINEMA of
STANLEY KUBRICK

The Cinema of
STANLEY KUBRICK

Third Edition

Norman Kagan

CONTINUUM · NEW YORK

2000

The Continuum Publishing Company
370 Lexington Avenue
New York, NY 10017

Printed in the United States of America

Library of Congress Cataloging-in-Publication Data

Kagan, Norman.
The cinema of Stanley Kubrick / Norman Kagan / foreword by
Andréa Staskowski.— Third ed.
    p.   cm.
"Kubrick filmography": p.
Includes bibliographies.
ISBN 0-8264-1243-2
1. Kubrick, Stanley—Criticism and interpretation. I. Title.
PN1998.3.K83K3 2000
791.43'0233'0924—dc19   88-39530
                                                              CIP

To My Brother,
Steven J. Kagan

I would not think of quarreling with your interpretation nor offering any other, as I have found it always the best policy to allow the film to speak for itself.

—*Stanley Kubrick, to F. Anthony Macklin*[1]

CONTENTS

FOREWORD

THE HISTORY of both film criticism and film studies could be written in terms of the changing status and attention accorded the *auteur,* or director of a film. American critics have, historically, valued *films* which could be identified as the work of an individual director, generally European—Dreyer, Renoir, Bergman, Fellini, Truffaut, Resnais—who worked outside the constraints of a commercial studio production system. Insofar as a film was received as the expression of an individual, an artist, a film was accorded the serious treatment otherwise reserved for literature and the fine arts. Popular cinema, the *movies,* regarded as mass-produced-genre fare of an industrial machine rather than the unique creation of an individual sensibility, were criticized from a sociological perspective. Today certain popular/commercial films are marketed with the director's name—Kubrick, Scorsese, Woody Allen, Coppola, Spielberg, even Oliver Stone—looming above the title on the marquee and in print advertising. And a generation of cine-sophisticated reviewers and viewers find pleasure in following the development of a director's career, detecting stylistic and thematic nuances in much the same way aficionados of musical or horror or science fiction films assess each film's reworking of the genre's conventions.

The emergence of the American *auteur* was facilitated by the introduction of European films and European film theory *(la politique des auteurs)* into the economically unstable American film market after World War Two. The big studios were losing both their audiences and their exhibition outlets while European governments were subsidizing film production for export to the American market. The European "art cinema," featuring serious themes (alienation, lack of communication), adult subject matter (sexuality), an open-ended narrative structure and a non-classical visual style (disruptions in spatial and temporal continuity), announced itself as the work of a particular director. Authorial presence was, in fact, one of the marks of the film's coherence. In lieu of Hollywood's illusion of reality, art cinema presented an individual's expression of, or encounter with, reality. Rather than identifying with the goals of a character within the narrative to achieve resolution of the narrative's enigma and fulfillment of the protagonist's desire, the art cinema offered identification with the teller of the tale, the director. Visual style, the marks announcing the presence of a narrator, characterized these films.

While America was discovering European film, French critics were discovering American movies. Godard, Truffaut, Rivette, Chabrol, and Rohmer, who were to become the key directors of the New Wave in the late 1950s and early 1960s, reveled in the artistry of American directors: praising Howard Hawks's genius; analyzing Alfred Hitchcock's moral philosophy; and finding poetry in John Ford's westerns. In the movies made within the studio system they discovered the marks of individual expression in what had previously been considered an undifferentiated mass of impersonal, profit-motivated entertainment. The *politique des auteurs* was a polemic for popular cinema which used the rhetoric of "high" art, citing instances of the creative genius of a unique individual, to substantiate its claim to value.

Andrew Sarris adapted the *politique des auteurs* to the American context and formulated the *auteur* theory in 1962. A method for evaluating films, the auteur theory bases an assessment of a director's greatness on the director's technical competence, the presence of a distinct visual style, and an interior meaning that arises from the tension between the director and the conditions of production (usually a studio) within which the director worked. His reassessment of popular Hollywood cinema asserted its superiority over the European art cinema. Sarris later established a pantheon of great directors through whom the history of the art of the film could be told. Therein he thoroughly discounted historical, economic, and ideological factors that affect film production, again grounding his theory on the notion of individual genius.

The validity of *auteur* studies was challenged with the introduction of structural and semiotic theories into film studies. These theories have had far-reaching effects in many disciplines—from linguistics, literature, art, and music to anthropology, psychoanalysis, philosophy, and politics—and they were not assimilated into film studies without controversy. In addition to obliterating the distinctions between "high" and "low" art, these theories did away with the concept of art itself and jettisoned the notion of the author. Art cinema, characterized by the marks of authorial presence, was no longer the focus of the now theoretically oriented academy. Questions of structural effects, ideology, and history became the issues of insistent concern. Yet, the notion of the author dies hard. Although the concept of an individual genius creating unique expressions in a historical vacuum is no longer tenable and a director's responsiveness to ideological and economic pressures requires consideration, certain film practices—and Stanley Kubrick's is an excellent example—demand that we attend to the *directorial* presence. If evidence of personal involvement and consistency of theme and style over an apparently heterogeneous range of projects distinguishes the true *auteur*, then Kubrick certainly qualifies.

Kubrick began making films in the 1950s when American independent film production was on the rise, enabling American directors to exercise control over their films in a manner resembling the European mode of production. Kubrick's notorious obsession motivated his, and a number of other directors', migration out of the chaos of the American film scene in the 1960s to the more congenial production conditions in England. And, not unlike other directors of independent feature films, the kinds of films he made resembled films made in the art-cinema tradition—a distinctive visual style and an open-ended narrative structure. Nevertheless, Kubrick's films are not so difficult as to be out of reach of the general audience. On the contrary, Kubrick's reclusiveness has not mitigated his ability to engage the popular imagination.

Norman Kagan's book will serve the cine-enthusiast as well as the film student as an indispensable guide through Kubrick's oeuvre. Comprehensive and thoroughly up-to-date, it provides information on early films that are no longer available in commercial distribution, background production information culled from interviews with Kubrick and his collaborators, glimpses into Kubrick's personality, and details of his working method. By including a survey of critical reactions at the time of a film's release, Kagan historicizes the process of interpretation and offers a range of possible meanings of each film, which allows the reader to participate in the construction of meaning for him or herself. Kagan's analysis of Kubrick's recurrent thematic motifs, which concludes each chapter, provides a structure for assimilating the material, and remains a welcome feature of this new third edition.

ANDRÉA STASKOWSKI

ACKNOWLEDGMENTS

I WOULD LIKE to thank those who contributed to the compilation of this material, and to the viewing of certain films.

Individuals include: Michael Kerbel, Professor Donald Staples, Dr. Alfred Roman, Ruth Kagan, Mary Corliss, Melinda Ward, Regina Cornwall, Janis Siegel, Chris Resnais, John Exter, Edwin D. Goldwasser, Mort Engleberg, Ray Ettore, Linda Eigner, Rajendra and Jaisri, Diane Solomon, and my editors, Sig Moglen and Evander Lomke.

Organizations include: United Artists Corporation, The Museum of Modern Art, The New York Public Library, Metro-Goldwyn-Mayer Corporation, Universal Education and Visual Arts, Films, Inc.

The CINEMA of
STANLEY KUBRICK

1
Beginnings

I don't think that writers or painters or filmmakers function because they have something they particularly want to say. They have something that they feel. And they like the art form; they like words, or the smell of paint, or celluloid and photographic images and working with actors. I don't think that any genuine artist has ever been oriented by some didactic point of view, even if he thought he was.

—*Stanley Kubrick, 1960*[4]

THE DIRECTOR Stanley Kubrick has stated: "Your own style, if you get a chance to make a film, is really the result of the way your mind works, imposed on the semicontrollable factors that exist at the time you start, both in terms of time, or the way the set looked, or how good the actors were that day." Kubrick, in fact, has little use for film aesthetics. I will show, however, that film aesthetes will have much use for Stanley Kubrick.

Stanley Kubrick was born in July, 1928, of a middle-class Bronx family. He got his first camera at thirteen, a present from his physician-father, who introduced him to still photography. He was class photographer at Taft High School, but an "F" in English and a 68 average lost him his place in college to some returning veteran. "Out of pity," he recalls, *Look* magazine hired him as a sixteen-year-old photographer, after buying one of his candid stills.

Kubrick stayed on the staff of *Look* until he was twenty-one. He describes himself at the time as a "skinny, unkempt kid who carried his cameras in a paper bag so he wouldn't be mistaken for a tourist."[5] The job was a good opportunity to learn and experiment with the photographic aspects of cinema: compositions, lighting, location, and action shooting, but all Kubrick knew about filmmaking was photography and Pudovkin's *Film Technique*. He still agrees with Pudovkin that editing is the basis of film art. "The ability to show a simple action like a man cutting wheat from a number of angles in a brief moment, to be able to see it in a special way not possible except through film—that is what it is all about."[1]

Kubrick had always been interested in films, and since he was nineteen he'd been obsessed with them, spending five evenings a week at the Museum of Modern Art looking at famous old movies, and weekends looking at all the new ones. Kubrick recalls that *PM,* the long-gone New York daily, would list every single movie in New York City in four-point type, and weekends he might even take the ferry to Staten Island to catch something he'd missed.

Kubrick now believes that those trips, and particularly the long screening sessions at the Museum of Modern Art, were the finest training in directing he could have had. Paying extremely close attention to a very few good films was of much greater value. Even the poor films had their uses, encouraging Kubrick: "I'd keep seeing lousy films and saying to myself, 'I don't know anything about moviemaking, but I *couldn't* do anything worse than this.' "[1]

The fluid camera technique of Max Ophuls was one effect that particularly entranced Kubrick: "In films like *Le Plaisir* and *The Earrings of Madam De . . .,* the camera went through every wall and every floor." This same fluid, or perhaps inertialess camera, appears in his later work, most prominently in *2001: A Space Odyssey.*

Kubrick's first film was sparked by a talk with an old high-school friend, Alex Silger, who was working as an office boy for *The March of Time,* and told Kubrick the company spent $40,000 making a one-reel documentary. Kubrick calculated he could do the same thing for $1,500.

Thus in 1950, at twenty-one, with $3,800 saved from his salary, he made *Day of the Fight,* based on one of his photoseries for *Look,* "Prize Fighter." He used a daylight-loading simple 35mm camera, an Eyemo, spending a morning at Camera Equipment Company learning how to load and operate it. Burt Zucker, a C.E.C. employee, also taught him splicing, how to do cutting, and the use of the movieola and synchronizer as he rented them. He found the technicalities of moviemaking not difficult.

Day of the Fight, a documentary about prizefighter Walter Cartier, is distinguished only by its crisp photography and straightforward structure. Kubrick's optimistic budget and proven photographic talents were what gave him the confidence to push the project through, and what probably sold it: "Even though the first couple of films were bad, they were well photographed, and they had a good look about them, which did impress people."[2]

Day of the Fight cost Kubrick $3,900, and he sold it to RKO-Pathe for $4,000, the most, he was told, they had ever paid for a short. *The March of Time* was going out of business, but Kubrick went ahead on one more short for RKO-Pathe, *The Flying Padre,* which he accurately describes as "a silly thing about a priest in the Southwest who flew to his isolated parishes in a small airplane."[1] *The Flying Padre* just barely broke even, because of the costs of location shooting.

In both films, Kubrick did everything himself—he was scenarist, director, cameraman, soundman, editor. With this comprehensive knowledge of all the aspects of filmmaking, and his two small successes, he formally quit his job at *Look* magazine to devote himself to filmmaking full time. He persuaded a poet friend, Howard Sackler, to write a dramatic screenplay, *Fear and Desire,* and began raising money.

Despite some denials, Kubrick had formulated both opinions and ideas about film aesthetics and theory, as well as working rules of his own. As noted, he considered Pudovkin's idea that the manipulation of the plastic material in editing is the basis of film art. He still recommends *Film Technique* to anyone interested in films.

Kubrick read Eisenstein at the start of his career, but thinks he did not, and does not, really understand him. What Kubrick likes about Eisenstein's films is the editing and the visual compositions of the shots. But in terms of content: "His films are silly, his actors wooden and operatic."[1] Kubrick thinks Eisenstein's acting style derives from his desire to keep the characters in the fixed frame of each careful composition, so they seem to swim or drift through each shot. Kubrick would contrast Eisenstein and Chaplin: the first he considers all form and content, the second all content and no form.

In terms of directing actors, Kubrick read all of Stanislavski's work as well as Nikolai Gorchakoz' *Stanislavski Directs,* which includes a lot of useful illustrative material. The acting in his first films, *Fear and Desire* and *Killer's Kiss,* he feels was not especially good, but he learned a great deal making the films.

Kubrick directing *Fear and Desire*. Shooting on location, Kubrick used a 35mm Mitchell, post-syncing his sound. *(The Museum of Modern Art Film Stills Archive)*

Left: Kubrick directing *Fear and Desire*. Kubrick was his own technical crew as well as writer and director. *(The Museum of Modern Art Film Stills Archive) Right:* Kubrick directs Kirk Douglas in *Paths of Glory*. At thirty, Kubrick had yet to make a dollar from filmmaking. *(United Artists Corporation)*

Kubrick checks a shot for *A Space Odyssey*. A film about the ultimate limits of technology, the director spent four months shooting its live action and eighteen months shooting the special effects. *(Metro-Goldwyn-Mayer, Inc., 1968)*

Kubrick prepares to film the attack of Alex and his droogs on the old drunkie. As *Space Odyssey* was characterized by extravagant special effects, *A Clockwork Orange* utilized carefully selected existing architecture. (*From the motion picture* A Clockwork Orange *copyright © 1972 by Warner Brothers, Inc.)*

Kubrick stresses that "the best way to learn is to do." He has, however, formulated a few general working principles.

In an interview in the London *Observer,* after the completion of *Spartacus,* Kubrick commented that the best plot to him was no apparent plot: "I like a slow start, the start that goes under the audience's skin and involves them so that they can appreciate grace notes and soft tones and don't have to be pounded over the head with plot points and suspense hooks."[4]

A real film, a film that deals with characters and a sense of life, is particularly difficult to end successfully, Kubrick believes. Most endings seem to be false, and the audience can sense the gratuitousness of an unhappy ending. Alternately, if a character triumphs, Kubrick feels the ending has a kind of incompleteness about it because that seems to really be the beginning of another story. He very much enjoys the anticlimactic endings of John Ford: "anticlimax upon anticlimax and you just get a feeling that you are seeing life and you accept the thing."

Kubrick feels unhappy endings are also hard to take because a good movie engages you so much that an unhappy ending is almost unbearable. "But it depends on the story, because there are ways for the director to trick the audience into expecting a happy ending, and there are ways of very subtly letting the audience be aware of the fact that the character is hopelessly doomed and there is not going to be a happy ending."[4] Some of these ways will be noted in later chapters.

Kubrick, in terms of his characters, is not interested in Freudian theory, nor does he believe in romantic heroism. For example, the true case histories of Humbert Humbert and General Jack D. Ripper are never really given. Kubrick puts it this way: "I think it is essential if a man is good to know where he is bad and to show it, or if he is strong, to decide what the moments are when he is weak and to show it. And I think that you must never try to *explain* how he got that way or why he did what he did." These ideas come up often, particularly in the earlier, less stylized films.

In directing actors, Kubrick states his task is always to know the emotional statement that he wants, then to use taste and judgment to get that performance. The real center of his job is to keep asking himself: Is it believable? Is it meaningful? Is it interesting? hundreds of times a day.[1]

Finally, Kubrick has usually edited his films himself, marking every frame and segment, doing everything exactly the way he wants it.

Nearly all of Kubrick's films began as adaptations of novels. Their subject matter and quality have differed enormously: *The Killing* started as and ended as a paperback robbery thriller; *Paths of Glory* hewed pretty close to the "touchy" Hollywood property about corruption in a World War I chain of command; *Spartacus* retained the plot and treatment of Howard Fast's historical novel; *Lolita* was greatly revised, perhaps for the better, by Nabokov himself; *Strangelove* was a satirized, stylized, tightened-up, and much-improved version of *Red Alert,* a paperback predecessor to *Fail-Safe; 2001: A Space Odyssey* was written at the same time as Clarke's book. Only *The Killing* and *A Clockwork Orange* were adapted by Kubrick working alone.

Kubrick's ideas about adaptation are pleasantly unorthodox. In an article in *Sight and Sound,* written while he was filming *Lolita,* the director commented: "The perfect novel from which to make a movie is . . . the novel which is mainly concerned with the inner life of its characters. It will give the adaptor an absolute compass bearing . . . on what a character is thinking or feeling at any given moment . . . from this he can invent actions which will be an objective correlative of the book's psychological content, and will accurately dramatize this."[5] In contrast, many filmmakers adapt only "plotty," scriptlike novels.

Kubrick feels a movie must make its point obliquely, the viewer's conclusion derived from the sense of life that the film conveys. Even more to the point is his comment that a great book's quality is "really a result of the quality of the writer's obsession with his subject, with a theme and a concept and a view of life and an understanding of character. Style is what an artist uses to fascinate the beholder in order to convey to him his feelings and emotions and thoughts. These are what has to be dramatized."

These two qualities, obsessiveness and extreme stylization, increase in each film Kubrick has made. Kubrick discusses a third factor which has become more and more prevalent in his works—intellectual detachment, a disinterested concern with ideas and form over dramatic content: "I think it is the [director's] duty to be one hundred per cent faithful to the author's meaning, and to sacrifice none of it for the sake of climax or effect."

Finally, Kubrick stresses the dynamic and developmental in the creation of film: "Any art form properly practiced involves a to and fro between conception and execution, the original intention being constantly modified as one tries to give it objective realization . . . in making a movie this goes on between people."

2

Fear and Desire

Its structure: allegorical. Its conception: poetic. A drama of "man" lost in a hostile world—deprived of material and spiritual foundations—seeking his way to an understanding of himself, and of life around him. He is further imperiled on his Odyssey by an unseen but deadly enemy that surrounds him; but an enemy who, upon scrutiny, seems to be almost shaped from the same mold. . . . It will, probably, mean many things to different people, and it ought to.

—Stanley Kubrick, 1952[5]

FEAR AND DESIRE WAS BASED on a screenplay Stanley Kubrick persuaded a twenty-three-year-old poet friend from Taft High School, Howard O. Sackler, to write. It was made at a total cost of $40,000, of which $9,000 Kubrick borrowed from a druggist uncle. The rest came from his father and several friends.

Kubrick shot the film in the San Gabriel mountains outside Los Angeles. His "crew" consisted of three Mexican laborers to carry the equipment; Kubrick did all the technical work himself. He shot in 35mm with a Mitchell camera, and added the sound later (this process, called "post-synching," is usually more economical than recording sound while shooting the picture). In this case it proved a mistake. Shooting *Fear and Desire* cost just $9,000, but it took $30,000 more to complete the soundtrack. Kubrick admits several more errors out of ignorance, but is proud that he did manage to finish the film.

Though *Fear and Desire* is no longer commercially available, I was able to obtain a print for critical screening.

The film, in black and white, begins with a pan across a wooded mountain valley, B-picture emotional music, and some lines of poetry by an unseen narrator:

> *There is war in this forest*
> *Now a war that has been fought, nor one that will be*
> *But any war*

And the enemies that struggle here do not exist
Unless we call them into being
For all of them, and all that happens now
Is outside history
Only the unchanging shapes of fear and doubt and death
Are from our world
These soldiers that you see keep our language and our time,
But have no other country but the mind.

A light plane roars overhead, and four such "abstract" soldiers sprawl or plunge into cover. From the beginning, the film is photographed well, the shots crisp black and white compositions of figures or faces dappled by the sunlight through the forest leaves, a little like *Rashomon*.

Lieutenant Corby is a slim, handsome, part-time philosopher with riding trousers, an officer's cap, and the only pistol. The three men with him possess just their baggy, camouflage-dappled coveralls: Mac is a tough, angry primitive; Fletcher an agreeable but weary Southerner; Sidney an impossibly naive, dependent youth. Resonances with straightforward war movies are unavoidable, particularly when the Lieutenant begins drawing maps in the dirt, showing how they will build a raft, and drift out from behind the enemy lines where their plane has crashed on a convenient river. In the rush to set up the symbols, the film becomes a little simple, almost corny. Lieutenant Corby: "By my calculations . . ." Mac: "*Brilliant* figuring!" But the tension is serviceable (patrols are out), and the group is soon crashing through the brush toward the river.

The trek is subjective. While the men stumble along we hear their disjointed thoughts—Corby's responsibility, Sidney's rising hysteria, Mac's anger, Fletcher's weariness. The voices are confused, desperate: "Hurry home, baby, I'm getting old." "Nobody's safe!" "Don't *be* here!" As proof of their fears, they see an enemy truck rumble past. The screen darkens.

By the river, their shirts off, the men are finishing their raft. (Why don't they build it under cover?) Lieutenant Corby struts and talks while the others work: "There's nothing so refreshing as a day outdoors in enemy territory. It's too bad the sun doesn't turn us green instead of brown—camouflage, you know." The handsome, dreamy officer and the obedient laboring men might lead a Marxist critic to mutter of class oppression. For me they suggest "high-school intellectuals at play."

"How far is it to the lines?" Mac asks truculently.

"Only a short distance—the distance between life and death," Corby answers.

"Why do you look at everything like you were seeing it through a window?"

"Naturally, I prefer to remain alive," Corby responds, "but I'm sure I don't know why. My hobby is collecting reasons—it's sort of like collecting butterflies."

Alone, Fletcher comments: "Some people just talk that way—the way a preacher talks."

"Don't let anybody kid you," another remarks significantly. "Everybody's got a reason for living."

Through field glasses, Mac spots a small airstrip and an enemy command post, from which a figure is addressing some troops. Now he has a focus for his fury: "A general!"

The raft is completed. (Corby: "All we need is Huckleberry Finn.") But at that instant, a light plane dives overhead toward the landing strip and Corby orders them all into the woods, not even hiding the raft.

"Maybe the generals are having a convention."

They stumble into the woods.

Next, the four encounter a shack among the trees, spying out two enemy soldiers, their dinner, and rifles. In a tense action sequence they rush the shack, killing the enemy at dinner with trench knives (Kubrick has them stab the camera), the dying men twitching and clutching among the splashed stew meat, a series of powerful grotesque images. While Mac wolfs the dead men's food, Sidney stands shocked. Corby reflects: "If we could just live inside our skins, and never feel alone in a crowd . . . now we're all islands." Dead faces stare at us; war rips open the unspoken convention of brotherhood. A third enemy enters, is blasted with rifle fire, and the soldiers flee again. Darkness.

The men sprawl on the ground, frightened, confused: "The woods must be crawling with patrols." (In the rapid alternation of terrorized flight, idle waiting, disjointed conversations, obsessions and speculation, *Fear and Desire* is very dreamlike.)

In the water nearby, a lovely young girl is wading and fishing. (The photographic quality is and always remains near Salem commercial level.) The men hear her coming and duck for cover. She stops in the clearing, wanders purposely toward a bush where one is concealed. The camera alternates points of view. Suddenly the man leaps out, seizes and gags her. The others come out of hiding and surround them.

"She's quite nice, don't you think so, boys?" Corby says in a "sophisticated" voice. (Scenes like this destroy Corby as a serious character.) "I must admit I've had worse-looking guests," he says with a touch of lechery, of perversity.

Mac grunts ironically at him: "Let's remain civilized."

The men stand around the frightened, helpless girl, themselves bewildered and wary. Using two of their belts, Corby lashes her to a tree. The boy Sidney wants to let her go. The obsessed Mac thinks she is bringing fine fish and strawberries to "his" general.

Corby decides to reconnoiter the raft, and leaves Sidney his pistol to guard the pinioned girl. Always on the edge of hysteria (perfect man for a solo mission!), he accuses them of deserting him. Fletcher tells him: "Jes' relax an' don' get panicky." Here, as at several other points, there is a feeling of improvisation.

In double exposure, we now see quickly cut images of the marches, the slaughter in the shack, the girl's capture. We see Sidney's face now, then a twoshot of him on the ground, squatting and moaning and rocking back and forth, while the lovely girl is lashed helplessly to the tree beside him.

He babbles on: "I'm really glad they let me stay. They thought you'd like me. It's not my fault." Shots of their two faces: frightened, gibbering.

Sidney begins a clumsy jape of the General to entertain her, gobbling and slurping his dinner, then strutting pompously. "Quite frankly," he shrills, "the situation is desperate! I don't think I can cope with it alone." (Shades of HAL-9000!) "The General—I am the General! I'm lost, I'm lost, lost on this terrible island." He hugs her. "I know you hate me. Please try to like me, also."

On the beach, the three other men find neither a destroyed raft

Lieutenant Corby, Fletcher, and Sidney rest. Kubrick has stated that his purely technical skill, as demonstrated here, gave him the confidence to make films. *(The Museum of Modern Art Film Stills Archive)*

Sidney embraces their fettered captive. His uncontrolled assault recalls the final assault on the writer's wife in *A Clockwork Orange. (The Museum of Modern Art Film Stills Archive)*

The ghostly shape of the drifting raft. The eerie image suggests the characters' "terminal" mental states. *(The Museum of Modern Art Film Stills Archive)*

nor an ambush. "They must have been reading a magazine in that plane," someone says. When asked if he thinks the raft is too small, Corby mystically describes an immense ark he'd like instead, full of animals, trees, and other things worth preserving, and flying a white flag of truce. A few feet away, Mac obsessively scans the command post with his binoculars: "There he is again! God, if this was a rifle sight!" He turns to Corby.

In the woods, the girl twists and turns, trying to get free. The boy Sidney brings her some water in his cupped hands. Eyes closed, she plays up to him, licking the moisture from his palms, smiling shyly. "You like me, don't you?" The girl says nothing. He kisses and hugs her, clumsily reaching around the tree to untie her, his eyes unfocused.

The men are coming back.

With one hand, Sidney squeezes her mouth and jaw, twisting the delicate flesh erotically, while with the other he paws for the belts holding her helpless. "I'll get you loose—you'll have your arms around me," he moans, pressing himself against her slim form and light summer dress with hysterical lust. She finally twists free and stumbles away, but is brought up—one wrist is still secured, and he holds the end of the belts as a tether. Erotic hysteria flashes into fear and the anger of betrayal: "You're going to tell the General!"

In flashes we see her lovely terrified face, her slim body running, the screaming, gibbering Stanley bringing up the pistol. He fires, and collapses moaning, as Mac dashes into the clearing.

We see the girl, who has never said a word, face down in the dirt.

Sidney, his face split in a bizarre grin, cries: "The Magician did it—Monstro the Magician. Before I was a general, now I'm a fish. I'm going for a swim—coming in, Mac?" Laughing, he dashes off through the trees.

The others come into the clearing. They look at the girl on the sun-dappled ground beneath the wind-stirred leaves.

Mac: "Sidney must have gone out of his head—something about a magician . . ."

"There's gonna be more room on that raft than I thought," Fletcher remarks.

For the third time we see the view from the beach where the raft was constructed. As they wait for nightfall, Mac, now completely engrossed with the idea of slaying the General, argues Corby and Fletcher into the plan. He will take the raft and draw the sentries from the house with his fire, while the other two kill the General and escape in the plane.

Mac tries to justify his compulsion: "I'm thirty-four years old, and I've never done anything important. When this is over I'm going to fix radios and refrigerators. . . . This is something for me. They dangle a general in front of you, you know it's only for this once." Fiercely: "What are *you* living for?"

Corby replies: "The only reason is to hunt for a reason. But how can I stand in the way of a man with a reason to die?"

After a moment, he agrees to the plan: "All we have to lose is our future."

A wipe crosses the screen.

Corby and Fletcher scout out the plane, then move toward the enemy command post, a nondescript two-storied house, in the gloom. With his binoculars, Corby gets his first real look at the General and his aide—the General is played by Kenneth Harp (Corby), his aide by Steve Coit (Fletcher)—the two men coming to kill them.

Meanwhile, Mac drifts and poles his way downriver on the raft. Kubrick continues to get fine visuals despite the darkness: the defiant, furious figure upright on the raft; the marsh grass and purling waters; fronds and branches passing overhead. Mac's mind is a burning chaotic jumble of hatred and self-hatred: "You try every door because you like the voices you hear inside, but the knobs come off in your hand. . . . It's better to make your life all in one night—one night, one man, one gun! Nobody is going to cry now, or cheer later. Nobody else is me! Nobody else is buried under the chains of everything I said and did. What a trade—me for him! Thanks, General!"

At the command post, Corby and Fletcher see that the General and his aide are drunk. The two commanders, in dress uniform, sit around a guttering candle at a plain table and sip whiskey. The aide grins as the old General talks regretfully of wars he has fought before: "waiting to kill, waiting to die . . . I find myself confused. I cannot quite believe that it was me who ordered the slaughter."

Outside Corby and Fletcher approach the *CP* through the trees, rifles ready.

On the river, Max raves to himself: "I'll get him. Clay pigeon on a slow rack. They'll shoot me like a fish in a barrel. . . . The only way to finish up. Even the river is helping me out!"

The General mumbles to himself and his aide in the darkness: "Sometimes . . . when I look at these battle maps . . . I think my grave is marked . . . I dream that it's planted here, or here."

Mac, drifting on the river, clutching at his rifle: "It's like kissing my great-grandmother when I knew she was dying." He begins to fire. "C'mon out of your tents!"

The enemy soldiers run toward the river, dropping into the grass and firing at Mac, leaving the command post deserted. They fire and fire at him.

From behind the command post, Corby and Fletcher leap onto the porch.

Inside, the General speaks: "I wonder what those last few moments feel like."

Corby stands watch while Fletcher races to the window and shoots both men at close range. The bullets blast them out of their chairs, flinging them along the floor.

"He's only wounded," pants Fletcher. "We have to finish him off."

The General crawls out the front door on his stomach. "I surrender," he croaks.

Corby fires point blank. The General's head slams forward, banging the porch. Corby stares at him, recognizing his own face below the white hair.

Moments later, the plane takes off.

The firing from the river has stopped. Mac groans and rolls across the raft, badly wounded. He floats down the river in the moonlight. Like an apparition, the mad Sidney appears before him, a black shadow on the silvery water: "You're going back . . . can I come?"

"Hop on. There's plenty of room."

"You rest. I'll be quiet."

The raft drifts on.

Shot of an anonymous military airport.

Corby and Fletcher have apparently just told their story. The two go down to the river to watch for the raft in the dawn mists. Fog shrouds them as they wait patiently on the river bank. They talk to each other sporadically, answering slowly.

Fletcher says wonderingly: "I'm all mixed up . . . I wish I wanted what I wanted before."

"Head bother you?"

"No . . . it's something else."

They hear the voice of someone crooning wordlessly in the fog. Fletcher begins again: "I'm not built for this."

"Nobody ever was," says Corby in a flat voice. "It's all a trick we perform, because we'd rather not die immediately."

Silence for a moment.

The raft floats out of the fog. Mac lies sprawled, perhaps dead, upon it. Sidney, crouching on all fours, stares into the mist, singing incoherently. The four are together again. The music swells up in triumph.

Recently, Kubrick described *Fear and Desire* as "a very inept and pretentious effort."[2] In general, most reviewers were more sympathetic. *Variety,* the film trade paper: "a literate, unhackneyed war drama, outstanding for its fresh camera treatment and poetic dialogue."[9] *The New York Times* thought Kubrick and Sackler had turned out "a moody, often visually powerful study of subdued excitements."[10] James Agee told Kubrick, with a very pained and strained expression on his face: "There are too many good things in the film to call it arty."[1] It's noteworthy that *Fear and Desire* was released by Joseph Burstyn, who brought *Open City, Paisan,* and *Bicycle Thief* to the United States.

Reviewers particularly singled out Kubrick's photography for praise; the lights and shades of the forest are compared to those in *Rashomon* by several writers. One reviewer notes that it is the photography that makes *Fear and Desire* good poetry: "He has artistically caught glimpses of the grotesque attitudes of death, the wolfishness of hungry men as well as their bestiality, and in one scene, the wracking effect of lust on a pitifully juvenile soldier."[9]

Other reviewers complained that Kubrick overworked his close-ups of faces with animal-like expressions of terror, hatred, lust, and rapacity. One also gets the feeling, especially in the first few discussions between the castaways, that the original shots had to be supplemented later, and then worked together in the editing. Dissatisfaction was expressed mainly with the film's uneven poetry, causing some to dismiss it as a simple antiwar polemic, others as a "curiosity." A sour *New Yorker* reviewer writes: "Mr. Kubrick, setting out to demonstrate that he disapproves of war . . . proceeds to talk his prejudice to death."[7] The New York *Herald Tribune,* on the other hand, acknowledges something more subtle and complex was being attempted: "Often they are carried away on the wings of their own zeal into images too revolting for useful dramatic purposes, into hyperbole too elliptical to grasp in the form of movie dialogue and action."[4]

To me, *Fear and Desire* is a fascinating effort containing a host of ideas, images, and themes which continue to appear in Kubrick's later films. Indeed, since Kubrick made *Fear and Desire* completely on his own, with no obligations to adapt another work or satisfy studio backers, working with a writer who was both a peer and close friend, *Fear and Desire* is probably his most personal film until *Lolita.* Since he made it at only twenty-two, I think his concepts and objectifications are all the clearer.

The first theme in *Fear and Desire,* stated in the poem at the opening, is that the story is made up of "imaginary worlds": each man's "war," "enemies," and "conflict" are his mind's way of dealing with the enigmatic events and inconsistent behavior that surround him. This is objectified throughout the film: in the powerful shocking images of animal-like passion, in the dreamlike retreats, chaotic killings, idle and absurd "philosophical" conversations. The images of the dead men are grotesque, eerily back-lighted—they are no longer real men, but "pure enemies"—corpses stylized into ideas. In the end, Corby sums up life this way: "It's all a trick we perform, because we'd rather not die immediately." It recalls T. S. Eliot's "Human beings cannot stand very much reality."

Two other linked ideas are the futility of intelligence and the distrust of the emotions. The most intelligent man, Lieutenant

Corby, is so detached he doesn't know why he is alive, but just collects reasons ("like butterflies"). He uses his brain mostly to make "intellectual jokes" nobody else gets. His contribution to survival, the raft, must be abandoned because a plane may have spotted it by chance. If the raft is finally used, it is out of luck that an enemy patrol has not booby-trapped or destroyed it. It should be noted that the emotion-obsessed man, Mac, comes up with a better escape plan, and Corby can't logically argue him out of his desire for self-destruction, and in fact doesn't even try.

The emotions are equally useless to everyone in *Fear and Desire*. The boy, Sidney, is driven to assault and murder by his fear and lust. Kubrick's treatment of eroticism is embarrassingly grotesque and perverse, but not unrealistic—an attitude that persists through all his work, though the next few films are relatively sexless. Mac, obsessed by his desire to justify himself by killing a general, and the most effective soldier, is driven half-consciously to self-destruction. This pair of homicide-suicides—Sidney and Mac—is typical of nearly all of Kubrick's films: *Lolita* (Humbert Humbert, Quilty); *Dr. Strangelove* (General Ripper, Major Kong); and *2001: A Space Odyssey* (HAL-9000, Astronaut Bowman). But the portraits of such characters, driven by passions and compulsions they only half understand, are never so clear.

All these concepts—the world as a dream, intelligence as futile, emotion as suspect—are rather pessimistic. There are two more ideas in the film that are more encouraging.

One is the notion of a journey to freedom, an Odyssey. It is possible to move toward knowledge and safety, and though the men flounder and run in circles, their concern is always such an escape. Individually, each man travels along the road to self-knowledge. Lieutenant Corby realizes that he plays with ideas all day because it helps him survive in a hostile world. The boy, Sidney, passes beyond his fear and hysteria, even though they destroy him. Mac becomes aware of his hatreds and self-hatred, works through a purge of them, and is finally at peace. Even the stoical Fletcher knows that he wants something new. In a way, the four soldiers are like the exploded fragments of a personality: intellectual thought and playfulness, emotional drives like lust and fear, emotional control and self-discipine, and the self-maintaining functions. At the end, they have triumphed, survived, and rejoined each other. The other positive theme is the triumph of an obsessed, dedicated man. Mac, in the last analysis, is a hero. He thinks up the plan to kill the General, takes the riskiest assignment, and carries it out successfully. If his motives are not purely societal—he is hardly a patriot!—they are pure in a larger, aristocratic sense: He is purging himself, redeeming himself, through a socially approved act, a *katharsis*. Of the four, Mac seems in the end the one with the greatest self-knowledge. He knows what he is, what he must do, the price he will pay—and never hesitates.

Some of the more explicit ideas in *Fear and Desire* are less successful. The conceit that the enemy general and his aide are only older versions of Lieutenant Corby and Fletcher, so they are really killing themselves, doesn't come off. There is little effort to make the enemy officers sympathetic, so their deaths are not even as upsetting as that of the speechless young girl. Nor is it likely that a dreamer like Corby would stay in the army any longer than he absolutely had to. Finally, the desperate plight of the four castaways is not at all similar to the fatalistic musings of the smug enemy officers.

Fear and Desire failed to pay back the investors, though Kubrick subsequently was able to return all the money. Different people backed his next film, *Killer's Kiss.*

3
Killer's Kiss

I haven't come across any recent new ideas in films that strike me as being particularly important and that have to do with *form*. I think that a preoccupation with originality of form is more or less a fruitless thing. A truly original person with a truly original mind will not be able to function in the old form and will simply do something different. Others had much better think of the form as being some sort of classical tradition and try to work within it.

—Stanley Kubrick, 1960[2]

KILLER'S KISS IS certainly the most untypical of Kubrick's films. It is a weak, naturalistic thriller, shot from Kubrick's own screenplay. The story line shows Kubrick's early errors as a dramatist: It wavers and lacks the obsessional drive and energy of the later films, as do the characters. *Killer's Kiss* is most successful at creating the ambiance of lower-class New York life, realistic touches and urban types.

Killer's Kiss begins in Pennsylvania Station in the afternoon. Chugging of a locomotive, a clanging bell. A cheerful, tough-looking young man waits patiently under the glass roof: "Crazy how you can get yourself in a mess sometimes. Maybe it began with taking it easy, just before my fight with Rodriguez . . ."

Transition to Davy Gordon's plain furnished rooms. He puts down his paper, shaves. Stuck around the frame of the mirror are photos of a farm, a pretty girl, cows, a smiling old man with a dog. He glances out the window, conscientiously feeds his fish, nervously looks out again. Kubrick has quickly sketched his character.

A phone call. Cheerfully Davy takes it, dresses, goes out. The pretty blond girl across the courtyard watches him, starts to go out too. (Thus Davy's voyeurism is alluded to, and neutralized. She is looking, too.) Gloria and Davy meet in the shabby lobby, separate outside, the big dirty brick building behind them. The heavy-set man, Vince, who picks her up, murmurs: "You're doing all right for yourself. He's a pretty good fighter."

Times Square, a grubby portrait: sidewalk photographers, a bobbing plastic bird drinking water, wandering derelicts, a dime-a-dance parlour, Pleasureland. Gloria somnambulates around the floor. A fatigued girl pulls her sweater off. Gavin Lambert notes that "it is not only the sardonically glimpsed hostesses and their partners, but a series of vivid, casually related images—signs, advertisements, objects, that create the *milieu*."[2]

In the subway, banging downtown, Davy reads a letter. His family wants him to come out to Seattle and visit.

In the gym, Davy gets an alcohol rub and massage. We hear the bell ending a round. Twisting and ducking, Davy works out. His manager shouts advice. Kubrick's shooting of *Day of the Fight* was useful here.

Vince, the dance-hall owner, smokes and drinks in his office, turns off the lights. On the television screen, Davy jabs, counterpunches, goes in again while the crowd roars. On the dance floor a drunk clumsily punches another. The girls draw back, annoyed. In the ring, Davy is shown on his back, a dark silhouette between the brilliant fluorescents, shot from above.

Outside, the counterpointed drunken brawl is over. One man is down, the other staggers off. Later, in his office, the gross, aggressive Vince makes out with Gloria on the couch in front of the dead eye of the television. Gloria's tawdry, humiliating position and milieu is now perfectly clear.

A long pan follows the dispirited Gloria down Broadway, past the honky-tonks, dirty book stores, cheap movies, toward the subway, emphasizing her entrapment.

Davy lies in darkness. Across the court, Gloria switches on the lights and radio. Because of the positioning and lighting of her rooms, the young girl moving about and undressing to the music of the radio seems to be part of a bright, surrealistic vision of peace and warmth and sensuality floating before Davy. The shot has enormous power. Davy stares with wonder and longing at this romantic tableau, entranced with the girl. She continues to remove her clothes.

Davy's phone rings.

"Hello, Uncle George," Davy strains. The phone cord is just too short to let him see the girl. As always, Kubrick's sex is sardonically spiced.

"Yes, yes, thank you, it wasn't an easy fight!"

The girl circles lazily around behind her bed.

"Sure, see you soon! Thanks a lot for calling!"

Davy slams the phone into its cradle.

The girl switches off her lights. . . .

Later, in the dark, Davy lies staring at the ceiling.

Suddenly, in negative, we plunge down a city street lined with apartments, screaming and wailing in terror, the white buildings with their black windows whipping past. This rapid, prolonged tracking shot, typical of Ophuls, continues to appear in Kubrick films, but this one best prefigures the eerily violent penetration into otherness at the end of *2001: A Space Odyssey*.

Davy wakes, but the screams continue. "What's going on there?" He runs out into the corridor, over the dark roofs. Vince hides on the stairwell. The music brays melodramatically.

In her bedroom, Davy comforts Gloria: "There, that's better. What happened?"

Gloria's voice quavers: "About an hour ago . . ."

In a flashback, over Latin music, Vince struts through her apartment.

Gloria: "What do you want? Get out!"

The dancehall owner approaches her angrily, pleading: "I've always spoiled the things that meant the most to me . . ."

"You're just an old man . . . no thanks!"

"No chance? Nothing?" He seizes her.

"Let me go or I'll scream." She screams. . . .

Davy soothes her: "Just close your eyes . . ."

Asleep, Gloria is a small, helpless, almost childlike figure on the bed.

Davy wanders around the room. He runs his hand along the silky sheen of her nylons, smells her perfume, glances at a letter with a touch of guilt.

She is asleep. Dissolve.

Davy stands at her door. We hear his voice: "First thing in the morning, I went back to see how she was. . . ." (The review in

Davy prepares for the televised match. This sequence let Kubrick exploit the proficiency he gained making *Day of the Fight*. (United Artists Corporation)

Above: Davy comforts Gloria. The end of this sequence may have been dropped by U.S. distributors. *(United Artists Corporation) Below:* Davy threatens Vince with a pistol. The firing of a pistol in Kubrick's films is often preceded by a long monologue, e.g., *Fear and Desire, Lolita, Dr. Strangelove. (United Artists Corporation)*

Davy holds Vince and his men at bay. With little money, Kubrick made do with real locations in lower Manhattan. *(United Artists Corporation)*

The bizarre battle using dress dummies. It recalls the toga-draped last moments of Quilty in *Lolita,* and the Beethoven versus phallic sculpture death duel in *A Clockwork Orange. (United Artists Corporation)*

Sight and Sound by Gavin Lambert suggests that in the European version they make love that morning.[2])

Gloria tells him the story of her life, starting with a picture of her older sister, Alice (Ruth Sobotka, Kubrick's first wife). For the length of the story, the sister performs elaborately alone on an evocatively lit stage. The ballet and photography are excellent, and may even detract from Gloria's autobiography, but her story, beside being cookbook Freud, has little to do with the rest of the film. (Her talented sister made a loveless marriage to pay for father's doctors. When father dies, Gloria taunts her, and Alice slashes her wrists. "Afterwards," Gloria explains, "I took the job in the dance hall, and started to feel less unhappy.")

Davy and Gloria go out for a walk in the bright sunlight. Again Kubrick uses weather and lighting to create a hopeful ambiance. Davy dismisses the girl's story: "I was already in over my head, and couldn't have cared less." They embrace. "I love you."

In Pennsylvania Station, Davy reflects: "She agreed to come out to Seattle with me. She was so scared she'd grab at anything."

In the dance hall, Vince, on the phone, smashes a mirror in a jealous rage.

At the gym, with a background of panting fighters and leather striking canvas, Davy calls Gloria: "Hello there, baby . . . I want to cash my check . . . meet you at Pleasureland. . . ."

At Pleasureland the floor is full. The camera pans down Broadway to Gloria as she runs upstairs. Vince, raging, confronts her: "I understand you're going away someplace. I could kill you right here and now."

"Somebody's waiting downstairs," he's told.

"You'll spend the rest of your life grubbing for money," he rants.

"Can happiness buy money?" she quips. She's not afraid of him any more.

Outside, Davy waits at the entrance to Pleasureland, surrounded by drifting pedestrians and dirty neon. A Times Square denizen, a sort of street musician, dances up, grabs his scarf, and runs. Davy dashes after the urchin.

Moments later, Davy's manager shows up with the money. He and the girl wait together. Suddenly, two toughs appear: "Vince says go upstairs to collect your money," one announces darkly. From the top of the stairs, we see her wearily ascending, the three men below, neon pulsing their shadows. The cheap dance music drifts down the stairwell. Suddenly the two turn on Davy's manager and back him into an alley. The passage is narrow, dark, backlit; it's hard to see what's going on. The manager cries out as the two smash him to the ground. They start silently out, then stop. One man goes back and picks up his hat. *Film Daily* considers this little scene one of the film's most effective, though for Gavin Lambert it inevitably recalls *The Set Up*. The snatched scarf is a bit gimmicky, but not important at the time, and the actual killing does not lack verisimilitude. The little touch of ominously returning to the victim only to reclaim a hat works nicely.

In his room, Davy packs for Seattle. He leaves a note: "Please feed the fish once a day." To poignant music Davy picks up his bags, goes over the roofs to Gloria's rooms. They're empty, barren. He looks back through the window at his own place, as the landlord switches on the lights and lets in two cops. "He's in big trouble—they found his manager in an alley about an hour ago with his head bashed in."

Downstairs, Davy sees Vince watching the building in his car. He drives off, and Davy simply follows in a taxi all night. Toward dawn the cars pull up, and among the squeals of sea birds the two men face off, as plausibility fades out.

Davy: "Good morning, Mr. Rapallo. That was my manager you knocked off. The girl—where is she?" He pulls out a pistol. "I'll count to three, and then blow your brains out."

"She's on ice."

Davy gets in Vince's car, and they go off through the grimy deserted streets of lower Manhattan. Rapallo takes him to a loft building, where the two criminals are holding Gloria; they are playing cards.

"Everyone up!" yells Davy. "Lean on your hands—against the wall."

The two hard guys use Gloria to start a fight, smashing Davy in the face and taking his pistol. Desperately, Gloria tells Vince: "I'll do anything you say, anything, on my honor."

Vince embraces her, muttering: "You and lover boy ain't gonna put me on the hot seat." Davy, making a desperate break, throws himself through a window, then runs away, hands to slashed face.

The mobsters pursue Davy through the deserted loft district. Kubrick uses the pitch-black shadows and doorways as masks for his lens, so Davy and the killers flee and lurk in small panels of lit screen, the rest blackness. Davy, in a dead end, goes up a fire escape and over the roofs once more. Vince and a henchman follow. Davy, injured, moans to himself. The viewer becomes aware of the dreamlike, eerie quality of the pursuit—men running across the tops of the city, leaping and soaring across wide unnatural planes amidst the urban verticals. Only the melodramatic music tries to sustain the mood of menace, recalling a similar sequence in *Naked City*.

Fatigued and wounded, Davy hides in a storeroom full of dress shop dummies. Vince tussles with him, losing his handgun. The killer searches for Davy amid the abstract, featureless heads and torsos. He creeps behind a group of them with exaggerated delicacy. An assortment of hands strung on a cord swing gently, pointing out his hiding place with their rigid index fingers. Suddenly, Davy bursts from cover, using a torso as a club; Vince chases him, puffing, with the loft's fire axe. Davy throws the manikins in his way, Vince chopping them. In the distance, a police siren begins to wail. Vince turns to flee, but Davy grabs a crowbar and begins swinging it, hissing, in broad arcs. Vince falls clumsily. Davy desperately jams the pole into him, as he screams. . . .

In Pennsylvania Station, Davy concludes his story: "When the cops came, I picked up Gloria . . . I wondered if she thought how I must have felt, running away. . . . Five hours later they chalked it up as self-defense. I cashed my check, sent flowers to Albert's widow, cleaned up, and here I am. . . . "

A voice announces the Seattle train. Davy picks up his bags and goes toward the tracks, looking, looking . . .

Outside the station, a taxi rolls up. Gloria runs inside the station, down the stairs. "Davy, Davy!" As the music comes up, they kiss. . . .

The critical reception of *Killer's Kiss* was not enthusiastic. *Variety* commented: "The yarn too frequently is reminiscent of old-fashioned melodramas which have the hero dashing up in the nick of time to save his beloved from the villain."[1] *Film Daily* thought the film tried to use stale avant-garde film conventions on a melodrama: ". . . the film drowns its characters in the kind of strangeness which is liable to irritate the average audience and lead more sophisticated patrons to laugh in the wrong spots."[4] Gavin Lambert's review in *Sight and Sound* was enthusiastic but unconvincing: "a melodrama too full of familiar and not always skilled contrivances, it has a simplicity of outline, an atmospheric power, a directness in its characterization, that suggests a maturing and distinctive personality."[3]

There are clearly good reasons for Kubrick's choosing an action-thriller format for his second film. Commercially, though he again lost money, he was able to sell *Killer's Kiss* to United Artists, where it remains in distribution. ("It is always instructive to view the early works of a director, who, in later years, goes on to bigger and better things."—from *United Artists 16mm Film Library Catalogue, 1970.*) Most of the film is shot outdoors or without sets, uses a very small cast, and is economically post-synched. Once more Kubrick acted as a one-man production unit, writing, coproducing, directing, photographing, and editing the film.

Aesthetically, *Killer's Kiss* is for Kubrick a step backward. The photography remains excellent, catching the flavor of lower-class New York life: tawdry Broadway vistas, gloomy massive apartment piles, shabby lofts and tenements. Occasionally, as in the shadow theater vision Davy has of Gloria, it is brilliant. Kubrick also knows his way around a gym, a boxing ring, and some of the grotesqueries of Times Square.

The great weaknesses of *Killer's Kiss* are in the story. Since we're shown and told that Davy and Gloria survived, free and unhurt in the prologue, the subsequent action-chase scenes lose much of their menace. The real question: Will Gloria go with Davy? is touched only at the last minute. Gloria has been going with the unsavory Vince all along. She only shows affection for Davy once, and he himself admits: "She was so scared she'd leap at anything." Later, threatened, she goes back to Vince. Hardly a basis for a romance.

There are several holes in the plot: Why does Vince bother to wait downstairs after he's kidnapped Gloria, so Davy can follow him? Why doesn't he just kill Davy in the loft? Who called the cops?

The two short flashbacks within the flashback seem pointless. Couldn't Gloria just *tell* Davy of Vince's assault? And why tell her family story? One suspects that the long ballet sequence was inserted to bring the film up to a bare sixty-seven minutes to qualify as a feature.

Slices of action in *Killer's Kiss* look as if they are from other thrillers—the murder in the alley, the chase across the roofs. The same holds for stale bits of dialogue: "I'll count to three, and then blow your brains out."; "You and lover boy ain't gonna put me on the hot seat." *Film Daily* remarks that the understated delivery of such lines makes them unconsciously comic. They also suggest that Kubrick's heart may not have been in the project.

An interesting aspect of *Killer's Kiss* is that, although straitjacketed by his genre, Kubrick still included his major themes:

The imaginary worlds. Though *Killer's Kiss* deals in the shabby details of lower-class life, the characters give little attention to their economic and social plights. They focus on dream worlds which provide specious relief. Vince doesn't work, but spends his time obsessed with Gloria. Gloria is dominated by the personal traumas of her past. And it is the dreamlike vista of Gloria's room that motivates all Davy does.

Futility of intelligence, errors of emotions. Alice, the brilliant artist, kills herself. Vince's passion drives him to self-destruction. Davy almost dies for his love. His manager is destroyed by a coincidence. Gloria, who thought she could hurt her sister, degrades herself in remorse.

The journey to freedom. The train trip to Seattle is hopefully such a journey, but so is Davy's search for Gloria through shabby New York.

Triumph of obsessional dedicated hero. Davy's winning of Gloria.

The pair of suicide-homicides. Vince has the manager killed, then dies, and Davy (who kills Vince) is allowed to live on for a "happy ending."

In *Fear and Desire* and *Killer's Kiss,* these murders and suicides have some vague social context. Later, this context fades out completely. In general, Kubrick ignores and ridicules society the way he does intelligence.

Killer's Kiss was Kubrick's last privately financed film. Soon after, he met James Harris, a man with his own money sources, persuasive powers, and desire to get into movies. Kubrick and Harris formed a production company. Their first property was another crime thriller, this one based on Lionel White's novel, *Clean Break,* which they called *The Killing.*

4

The Killing

In a crime film, it is almost like a bullfight: it has a ritual and a pattern
which lays down that the criminal is not going to make it, so that, while
you can suspend your knowledge of this for a while, sitting way back in
your mind this little awareness knows and prepares you for the fact that
he is not going to succeed. That type of ending is easier to accept.

—Stanley Kubrick, 1960[3]

THE KILLING IS Kubrick's first big picture, a well-made
crime-documentary of a track robbery timed to coincide with a
big horse race. Kubrick rewrote Lionel White's *Clean Break* as a
screenplay, then he and Harris approached Sterling Hayden to star
in the project. When Hayden agreed, United Artists came through
with $200,000, and Harris raised an additional $120,000 on his
own. With $320,000, a very low budget by Hollywood standards,
even in 1955, Kubrick was able to get, for the first time, professional actors and a full professional crew.

Though he was working for a major studio, the young director
was able to maintain full artistic control. Kubrick has admitted he
lacked the real stature as a director to insist on this; he persisted
because "it seemed inconceivable that I could work any other
way."[4] In the end, all parties agreed to a given budget, to securing
the Motion Picture Production Code Seal, to approval by the
Catholic Legion of Decency, and to a maximum length. Otherwise,
Kubrick and Harris were on their own.

Titles and tense theme music. Behind them the underground
stables of the Bay Meadows Track, the horses trotting out into
the sunlight. From inside the rail they move toward the starting
gate. Finally, they're ready to go!

Behind the grandstands, the weary, alcoholic Marvin Unger
emerges into the big, paper-strewn betting area, and moves to the
bar. He passes a note to bartender Mike O'Reilly.

The gravel-voiced, omnipresent narrator gives the time and place, identifies Unger, and tells us he is one of three men who know the vast sum of money ultimately at stake. From outside, cheers. The horses run around the far turn. Unger speaks with the barman. Narrator: "Now the addition of the others, like fragments to a picture puzzle."

Cut to a cocky young policeman, Kennan, entering a sleazy club, greeting an impatient debtor. Narrator, dead pan: "About an hour later, Patrolman Randy Kennan had some business to attend to." Kennan has gambling debts he's anxious about but unable to pay off. Val Cannon, a tough pretty-boy, looks on.

A big shabby apartment. The tough, knowing Johnny Clay drinks beer while his frail fiancée looks on with an attitude of supplication. Narrator, remorseless: "Johnny Clay had finished his design. . . ."

"None of them are rich," Clay murmurs, "all of them got little problems." Apparently he's just free, after five years in prison. "I'm not pretty and I'm not very smart, don't leave me," the girl pleads. "I want you to stay out of the way," Clay tells her. The elderly Unger comes in, and the two begin planning.

Another apartment, smaller but no finer. A tired-looking man greets his invalid wife. Narrator: "Half an hour earlier, Mike O'Reilly came home."

In another domestic scene, George Peatty, the colorless little track cashier, comes home. "Honey, I've got a hole in my stomach," he whines. His big, brassy, trampish wife Sherry: "That's nothing to the one in your head." "Hurry up with that drink," he tells her. The big woman dominates the frame, taunts him. "If I had big money, hundreds of thousands . . ." he sniggers. The woman is instantly alert, pries without success, complains: "My own husband doesn't trust me . . ." They bicker, threaten, make up.

The same sleazy club. The now submissive, coquettish Sherry makes up to the smooth Val. "Don't bug me," he swaggers, "I got to live my own life a certain way." In his bedroom, she whines: "I'm not creepy, I'm in love with you." He walks toward her as the screen darkens. Breathless, later, she cries: "Georgie has stumbled onto something big! They're gonna knock over the track for the day's receipts!" Lit from below, their expressions are ghoulish. "We gotta find out more about the plan. . . ."

From below, we see the five principals examining a map on an oilcloth-covered table, surrounded by darkness: Johnny Clay, Unger the alcoholic, Kennan the indebted cop, little George Peatty, O'Reilly the bartender. Clay, puffing a fat cigar, shot so his face dominates the frame, rumbles that two more hoods must be hired and paid off. He sways and gestures as he discusses the plans, moving in and out of the light. "I figure the loot at two million bucks," he tells them. There is a noise outside.

All start, push back their chairs. Clay goes outside; they hear a slap and a woman's gasp. George Peatty is shocked: "It's Sherry!"

"You little clown," the frightened men snarl. "Tell us what you told her!"

"She must have found the address in my pocket . . . thought I was two-timing her," he explains ironically.

Clay, angrily: "I'll just slap that pretty face into hamburger!"

The others leave silently, passing the treacherous Val lurking outside.

Alone, Clay confronts the woman: "A mighty pretty head . . ."

She smiles at him sluttishly: "Maybe we can compromise and put it on your shoulder."

Clay: "You're a no-good tramp. . . . ! You've got a big dollar sign where others have a heart. . . ."

At home, the mild George Peatty is dressed in oversized pajamas, like a child. His wife, in mules, gown, and silk robe, listens to him sulk.

"Some friends . . . they've offended me plenty. Sherry, did Johnny try anything?"

His wife shrugs, looks away.

Petulantly: "I'm afraid, this business tonight, I realized the kind of guys I'm getting in with . . . you'll love me, Sherry— *always?*" Poisonously and desperately, the two embrace.

Dissolve to the rumbling narrator: "Three days later, Johnny Clay began the final preparations."

Johnny Clay is in deep conversation with Maurice, a massive bald Greek ex-wrestler who now runs a chessplayers' retreat. Sunlight slants in through the dusty second-story windows on the

Brassy Sherry and her mild husband. The composition suggests their sado-masochistic relationship. *(United Artists Corporation)*

Above: Johnny Clay (Sterling Hayden) outlines the robbery. The lighting and camera placement recalls Kubrick's treatment of the Hayden character (General Ripper) in *Dr. Strangelove. (United Artists Corporation) Below:* Maurice creates a bizarre diversion. The struggle has surrealistic elements—what if wrestlers didn't stay inside their shabby rings? *(United Artists Corporation)*

The pathological sharpshooter Nikki Arrane. This sequence has an element of fantasy—murdering a horse from a parking lot—that hints at Kubrick's increasing use of stylized shocks in his films. *(United Artists Corporation)*

Above: Clay in a cartoon mask threatens the track clerks. Note the realistically harsh afternoon sunlight. *(United Artists Corporation) Below:* The sprawled corpses of the gang. Like the dead men in *Fear and Desire,* they are backlit to appear grotesque and unreal. *(United Artists Corporation)*

hunched, concentrating players. In this and the next few scenes, Kubrick chooses a few more obscure, interesting city settings.

Clay wants the wrestler to start a fight as a diversion: "twenty-five hundred is a lot of dough. Part of it is for not asking questions." Clay stares at him. "I want somebody who is absolutely reliable."

Outdoors, on an abandoned farm, Johnny talks with Nikki Arane, a strange, long-jawed, psychopathic gunman. Clay watches the man knock over a series of targets, cardboard 1930s mobsters with cigars and black hats, then gives him the proposition: "For five thousand you shoot a horse, a special kind of horse . . ." Clay never smiles: "It isn't even murder, I don't know what it is . . ."

Finally, Clay rents a shabby motel room. . . .

Dissolve to the Peatty home. Narrator: "Four days later, at seven A.M., Sherry Peatty was wide awake."

The big brassy woman comes up to stand over her tense, hunched husband: "You can't fool me. Today is the day!"

"If you don't stop pestering me . . . !"

The two sit facing across the breakfast table. The alarm clock ticks on. Both faces show tired alertness. Sherry probes, George prickles suspiciously.

"If you let people beat me up and then take their side . . ."

"What were you gonna tell me that night?"

"I tried to stop him, I struggled . . ."

George Peatty switches sides in a moment: "All that matters is how I feel about you . . ."

We see the stables at dawn. Narrator: "At the track, the favorite, Red Lightning, was given only half a portion of feed."

Johnny faces Marvin Unger, the weary alcoholic.

Narrator: "Johnny Clay began what might be the last day of his life."

Johnny: "You've done your part. We'll probably never see each other, but you're a stand-up guy." The old man looks up pleadingly: "You remind me of my kid. Wouldn't it be great just to go away . . ."

"The seventh race starts at four-thirty," Johnny tells him emotionlessly. "Keep away from the track. Go to a movie. . . ."

In a few flashes Johnny gets his getaway plane tickets, confirms the motel rendezvous, buys a big box of flowers, puts a rifle inside instead, finally checking the box at the bus station. . . .

At home, the bartender Mike O'Reilly exults to his bedridden wife: "We're gonna be rich, and soon! You're gonna have a fine house, and doctors that'll make you well again!" He leaves her, picks up the flower box with the rifle, and catches the Race Track Special. Narrator: "At twelve-ten, as was his custom, he arrived at the track."

"Blowin' your money on dames!" another employee jeers, as O'Reilly stows the box in his locker. Outside, the guards hoist a strongbox of receipts into the track's business office.

Shots of the loudspeakers, flags, horses, crowds. Narrator: "After the first race, Mike was in business." The bartender cautions a heavy drinker.

At a suburban street corner, Officer Kennan calls headquarters. "I think my set's a little on the blink."

A woman wails toward him: "Officer, come quick, they're killing each other!" Kennan snorts, and roars away toward the track without a glance at the woman. Narrator: "Ten seconds too late would be fatal." Officer Kennan parks his patrol car just below the track business office. He stands beside it with arms folded, as if on watch.

At the chess club, the old wrestler listens to the track broadcast.

Kubrick repeats the first three prologue shots: the horses moving up into the sunlight, round the track, lining up at the gate. Radio: "The horses are approaching the starting gate!"

Behind the grandstand, the wrestler swings his massive arms and shoulders as he moves up to the bar. . . .

Maurice drinks a moment, quietly. He notes Johnny standing beside the "No Admittance" sign on the employees' entrance.

Maurice suddenly smashes the bartender! Two policemen close in. He lifts one to his shoulders, spins him, throws him at the other. Two more cops approach, but Maurice simply bangs their heads together. The scene has little verisimilitude, but nevertheless a strange power: a shabby Samson holding off everyone in a big, paper-strewn arena. Finally, six policemen seize the old battler and drag him off. But Johnny Clay is already inside. . . .

Narrator: "At eleven forty-three Nikki Arane left his farm in his sportscar. He arrived at the parking lot at one thirty-five."

An eager-to-please black attendant puts Arane and his MG in the first row, overlooking a big drop down to the track. The psychopathic gunman pulls out his binoculars and watches the horses come out through the haze.

Shots of the running horses, cheering crowds.

Once more, the three-shot prologue: out into the sunlight, past the inside rail, up to the starting gate.

The overfriendly black, hanging around, is now a threat to the gunman. Nikki, querulous, desperate, pleads: "Be a nice guy! Go on about your business!"

They're off! In extreme telephoto, the horses pour toward us through Nikki's gunsight. He slams the windshield flat to the hood, grabs up his rifle, fires. Red Lightning stumbles, falls (these shots are certainly stock footage of a track misfortune). Nikki tries to drive away, as a guard pulls his pistol: "Stop or I'll shoot!" A moment later Nikki is dead, his lucky horseshoe shattered. . . .

We see Johnny in town, easing past George Peatty at his window, nodding to Maurice to start fighting, go inside. Cops pellmell down from the track business office to the fight. Johnny runs up the corkscrew stairs of the locker room, pulls the gun out of the locker and puts flowers in the box. He quickly adds rubber gloves and a sad-faced Emmett Kelly clown mask, then ducks into the business office: "Get your hands up, all of you!"

The clerks rush to fill his enormous duffle bag. Next he tricks the passive, balding, elderly men out of the room. In a moment, alone, he shoves mask, gloves, and gun into the sack, then throws it all out the window to the waiting Patrolman Kennan. He leaves as the policemen march Maurice off.

In Unger's shabby apartment, the four other members of the gang are waiting for Johnny Clay, sitting exhausted or nervously pacing back and forth. The radio brays: "In a daring and methodically executed robbery—" Patrolman Kennan turns it down. The querulous policeman tells them: "No one saw the duffle bag come out . . . the captain was convinced I was holed up, drunk . . . he'll get here, he had to pick up the dough at the motel . . ." The doorbell sounds.

Val, Sherry's boyfriend, and other men appear at the door:

"Everybody, hands up!" Someone moves, and a barrage of bullets drops them all as little George Peatty simultaneously shoots the intruders. Kubrick's camera tracks silently round the sprawled corpses, their eyes staring upward, eerily lit.

Narrator: "At six forty-five, Johnny had reached the motel."

Clay almost goes into the wrong room, but finally picks up the waiting duffle bag. As he approaches the rendezvous, he sees the bleeding, stumbling George Peatty emerge from the apartment house, and drives swiftly past without stopping.

Narrator: "Johnny had no choice but to save himself and the money. Ten minutes later he bought the largest suitcase he could find." Behind a billboard, Clay jams the haul into a big squarish case, locks it, drives on.

In the drab Peatty apartment, Sherry is also packing. She hears the door, and cries excitedly: "I'm back here, packing." George Peatty, his suit bloody, comes through the door in a stiff-legged stumble, zombielike, bullet holes torn in face and chest. Sherry stares up at him, her parrot moaning in its cage. "Why'd ya do it," he gasps, and fires. "I never loved anyone but you." Peatty collapses, pulling the bird cage down.

At the airport, Fay waits for Johnny Clay, hugs him as he arrives. His slitted eyes drift past two plainclothesmen while a fat lady and her poodle keep the clerk busy. The clerk won't let Clay take the enormous case into the cabin.

"Let me talk to your supervisor!"

"Mr. Grimes, over here."

"It's quite a bit too large . . . those are our flight regulations for comfort and safety."

"All right," Clay snarls. "Check it through!"

Johnny and Fay watch the enormous shabby case as it is hurled atop the baggage wagons, which are pulled across the field by a little tractor. Suddenly, the fat woman's little dog runs yipping into the tractor's path, as the woman screams. The tractor swerves, the old case falls and bursts. The money, a sudden storm of dollar bills, swirls across the runways in some propwash; Johnny stares at it, stunned, till Fay leads him off.

Supervisor Grimes, at his desk, answers the phone: "Oh, you're not serious? . . . right out on the runway!"

Johnny and Fay stumble past the detectives to the taxi ramp, calling for a cab. Through the glass doors, we see Grimes whispering urgently to the detectives. They come through the doors with their guns drawn, Johnny and Fay turning to face them, as the theme music swells up and out.

Pauline Kael, more than a decade later, considers *The Killing* the real start of Kubrick's career: "an expert suspense film, with fast incisive cutting, a nervous edged style, and furtive little touches of character."[2] Kubrick's cinematography, now by Lucien Ballard, remains excellent and almost documentary, keeping the rifle-concealing flower-box always screen center, or catching the dark, poisonous, self-deceptive ambiance of the Peatty home. The ghoulishly lit corpses are standard Kubrick, while the stark style of shooting lacks a single self-conscious camera angle. The wise use of track stock footage solves the problem of Red Lightning's "murder."

Most of the 1956 reviewers agreed with Miss Kael, praising *The Killing* in terms of its genre, with particular plaudits for the casting. The New York *Herald Tribune:* "an excellent portrait of a crime, unusually taut, keenly directed and acted, and with a sharp, leanly written script."[1]

Variety judged it "sturdy fare for the action market, where it can be exploited for better than average returns."[9] (*The Killing* broke even.) *The New York Times* reviewer, a trifle cooler, commented: "Though *The Killing* is composed of familiar ingredients and it calls for fuller explanations, it evolves as a fairly diverting melodrama."[8] The reviewer compared the preparations for the crime unfavorably with *The Asphalt Jungle,* which he thought they resembled.

Kubrick's script is methodical and terse. The very first shots are of the critical race, and Kubrick returns to them again and again to orient the audience throughout the film. Next, we see the scene of the crime; the narrator suggests its scope; we meet the five principals, and see the problems which led to their involvement: medical bills, a demanding, shrewish wife, gambling debts, Unger's alcoholic dependence, Clay's criminal nature. The rumbling narrator, like the voice of fate, ironically introduces each man in a moment of shabby vulnerability. Their weaknesses, especially the fickle sluttishness of Sherry, seem to shout the inevitable defeat of their plans. As Kubrick says in the introductory quote, the film subtly prepares us for failure almost from the first.

There is almost no romantic interest, and few encouraging elements of any sort. Fay's loyalty to Johnny, like Unger's, is the dependency of the weak and defeated. Mike O'Reilly cares hopelessly for his comatose wife. Sherry, the only person to display any passion, is a sly sado-masochist, tormenting her husband but fawning over a worthless young punk. Those with tender feelings, like O'Reilly, George Peatty, or the elder Unger, are destroyed. The mood of the film is unrelentingly pitiless.

The eavesdropping and third degree of Sherry at the planning session are a little muddled. George Peatty's rationalization of her snooping is too fast, and she should be the one to say it. Clay's dressing down of her seems very weak and romantic. The reasons for Peatty's and Unger's taking part are not made clear: perhaps Peatty is the inside man who knows how and where the money is handled, and Unger was the middle man between Clay and the rest. But the film doesn't say.

While the preparatory actions are all methodically worked out, the editing of the actual crime is more complex. The bartender and cop making the pickup are shown getting into position early. Then Maurice the wrestler creates his diversion, his timing made clear by the introduction of the three-horses-into-position shots. Next Nick the sharpshooter's role is played out, his scheduling likewise indicated by the placing of those three shots, and Red Lightning's collapse. Finally, the actual robbery, carried out by Johnny Clay, is clocked in and out by shots of the start and end of Maurice's diversion. Kubrick's editing thus keeps the viewer oriented with a minimum of repetition and almost no narration, while he goes over the same few minutes from three different viewpoints. In the last few shots of the sequence, Clay escapes, O'Reilly leaves anonymously, and Maurice is hustled away in a clump of track police.

The weakest parts of this sequence are the two scenes of crim-

inal violence. Maurice's wrestling diversion, despite its eerie intensity, would certainly have been stopped sooner—by billy clubs,
brass knuckles, a blackjack, the threat of a pistol, or judo tactics—
Kubrick's track police pour into the bar like fumbling Keystone
cops who've never dealt with a violent drunk. Likewise, the professional criminal sharpshooter, Nikki Arane, even if a psychopath,
wouldn't be so stupid as to fire at the track in plain sight of the
police, with no clear getaway. Psychopaths are amoral, not
suicidal, and Nikki's MG argues for a man who likes living. Firing
from a well-guarded parking lot is clearly asking for a police
bullet in the back, which Arane gets.

The rest of *The Killing* holds up, allowing for dramatic license.
The walk of the bullet-torn George Peatty back to confront the
treacherous Sherry seems unlikely, and the ending is also improbable: A cool customer like Johnny Clay would more likely hide
the money, mail it to himself, or have a special getaway plan in
case of betrayal. The swirling disposal of the swag is a nice touch,
reminiscent of *The Treasure of the Sierra Madre,* though of course
without any warm philosophical chuckles.

Kubrick's direction is always adequate, often very effective. He
depends strongly on fast cutting for the action sequences (fast by
pre-*A Hard Day's Night* standards), and for the more dramatic
portions uses long, well-framed takes, expecting his professionals
to handle their not-quite-stereotyped roles, which they do. Some of
Kubrick's own words describe his style well: "At its best, realistic
drama consists of a progression of moods and feelings that play
upon the audience's feelings and transforms the author's meaning
into an emotional experience. . . . Writers tend to approach the
creation of drama too much in terms of words, failing to realize
that the greatest force they have is the mood and feeling they can
produce in the audience through the actor."[5] Kubrick keeps his
dialogue sparse and banal, and concentrates on eliciting facial
expressions, bodily actions, and tones which convey his drama.

In *The Killing,* the Kubrick techniques of obsessive, driving
development and consistent stylization (in this case melodrama)
are apparent, along with a clear intellectual detachment: until the
last moments, causality is as systematically arranged and inevitable

as the packing of a parachute. Even the ironic ending seems built in.

A discussion of themes in *The Killing* is also valid, but here is as good a place as any to admit the limitations of such analysis. Themes, being general ideas, can easily be restated into Hollywood scenario cliches. The theme of the journey or Odyssey to freedom, for example, is often just a cheap way to give a film a story—making it a series of bloody or humorous wandering encounters, changing nothing. Likewise, Kubrick's homicide-suicide pairs can be "found" in many films, usually as a fast way to set up a Hollywood morality play—the Bounty Hunter, or Spy, or Commando destroys someone who is also dangerously unstable, then perishes himself to no real purpose. Nevertheless, I believe the frequency, interior variations, and most important—real significance—of these and several other themes in Kubrick's work, worth following.

While straitjacketed by his genre, and more so by a source novel, the characteristic ideas can again be seen:

The imaginary worlds. In *The Killing,* the imaginary worlds of the characters take the form of bold robbery with its enormous payoff. Except for Clay, all involved are marginal men, losers. Their thoughts are centered not on their mundane problems, but the split-second plan that will "solve everything." They want to see their colleagues as effective; while in fact they are such bunglers and potential squealers that the chances of success are negligible.

The distrust of emotions, errors of intelligence. Though the brilliant plan succeeds, everyone dies or is caught. The super-logical Clay cannot respond adequately to Sherry, whose hysterical emotions likewise doom her. Maurice survives perhaps because he neither emotes nor plans.

The journey to freedom. Clay's getaway, from the crime itself. As circumstance blocks him again and again, Clay is freed of friendships, loyalties, and finally his lover and wealth.

Triumph of obsessional, dedicated hero. Clay, of all the men, come closest to success. His plan does succeed, and he is only caught through circumstance, and perhaps the imposition of Hollywood morality.

The homicide-suicides. These are Sherry Peatty and husband. Mrs. Peatty is fickle; her submission to Val a sort of bid for passivity; her tormenting of her childish husband and the catastrophic double cross she plots are the courting of destruction. Mr. Peatty, obsessed by his wife, destroys her with his last reserves of strength, then dies himself, rather than prudently seeking aid for his wounds in the first place.

The Killing broke even on its investment, and brought from United Artists one million dollars for a Harris-Kubrick production of Humphrey Cobb's novel of World War I vainglory, *Paths of Glory.*

5

Paths of Glory

The soldier is absorbing because all the circumstances surrounding him have a kind of charged hysteria. For all its horror, war is pure drama, probably because it is one of the few remaining situations where men stand up for and speak up for what they believe to be their principles. The criminal and the soldier at least have the virtue of being against something or for something in a world where many people have learned to accept a kind of grey nothingness, to strike an unreal series of poses in order to be considered normal. . . . It's difficult to say who is engaged in the greater conspiracy—the criminal, the soldier, or us.
                  —Stanley Kubrick, 1958[7]

HUMPHREY COBB'S *Paths of Glory* was a best-selling novel in 1935, a grisly account of a French World War I tactical disaster due to the vanity, ambition, and incompetence of a few officers, and the vengeful "cover-up" court martial—execution of three privates for "cowardice." Twenty years later, with a minimum budget and a script by Kubrick, Calder Willingham, and Jim Thompson, Kubrick–Harris Films Corporation could stir up little interest in a *Paths of Glory* film.

Finally, Kirk Douglas saw the script and was impressed. With his willingness to star, and the Kubrick–Harris track record, United Artists Corporation was willing to advance $1 million, actually still a very low budget. The gamble the two young men had made was paying off.

Paths of Glory was produced entirely in Germany, perhaps partly to liquidate some UA blocked assets. The interiors were shot in the Geiselgasteig Studios in Munich, with the chateau and battle lines about forty minutes away. Kubrick used about six hundred German police as his extras—they'd had three years military training.

The director spent a month on the terrain of the disastrous assault, digging in and blasting up the field, putting a great number of props around—ruined guns stuck in different holes, bits of soldiers' tunics. "You couldn't see them, but you could feel them."[7] Explosive charges were carefully planted for the battle sequence. Kubrick found it impossible to tell each of his six hundred soldiers where to fall. Instead, he split the battleground into five zones and five groups of the assaulters, announcing: "Every man die in his own zone, and try to get killed by an explosion near you." The men in zone five went all the way.

The performances Kubrick gets are extraordinary, especially from Kirk Douglas as the sober, intelligent, courageous Colonel Dax whose illusions are gradually destroyed, and Adolphe Menjou as the wily, urbane, incalculably corrupt and finally enigmatic General Broulard. Menjou said of Kubrick at the time: "The greatest director was Chaplin. Stanley works more like him than anybody I've ever seen—in that the actor is always right and the director always wrong. . . . He'll be one of the ten best directors."[7]

In the treatment which follows, two visual elements should always be emphasized: the terrible intensity of the images, of men screaming and dying or waiting terrified to die, and the constant ironic cutting between the delicate, ornate chateau and the dirt and blood of no-man's-land. . . .

Paths of Glory begins with exteriors of the fragile, stately chateau, the attack's command center. Within, amid snowy marble, gilt and brocade, a nattily dressed General Broulard circles arm and arm amidst the Louis XVI tables with the young, pantherlike General Mireau. Kubrick tracks dreamily, Ophuls-like, behind them, as the generals stroll, grinning foxily at each other. Broulard has orders to take a citadel called the "Ant Hill."

"That comes pretty close to ridiculous," Mireau replies skeptically.

Broulard thinks only Mireau can handle it.

"Out of the question. You know my troops' condition. We'll be torn to pieces."

But Mireau is being considered for a promotion. Carefully, with a wordly smile, Broulard wheedles and probes, plays on his pride and arrogance.

"Those men know I would never let them down . . . nothing is beyond them, once their fighting spirit is aroused."

Mireau's voice echoes in the high-ceilinged chamber, convincing himself: "We might just do it, by God!"

Broulard smiles: "You are the man to take the Ant Hill. . . ."

Explosions, concussions. Through a slit Mireau studies the hulking formation called the Ant Hill.

Now, in an endless tracking shot, he marches down the trench, braying to each man he encounters: "Hello there, soldier—ready to kill more Germans?" "Yes-suh!"

Behind him, explosions along the parapet, snare drums, clicking heels.

"You married, private? Well, I bet your mother's proud of you!"

"Looking over your rifle, soldier? Good—a soldier's best friend. You be good to it, it'll be good to you!"

Encountering a shell-shocked man, the ever-eager General rages: "There's no such thing as shell shock! Get him out of here; I won't have brave men contaminated!"

Beside him, his sycophantic aide murmurs: "These tours of yours have an incalculable effect on the fighting spirit of the men. Their spirit derives from it."

Mireau smiles dubiously.

Mireau arrives at the shabby trench quarters of Colonel Dax. "Pretty little spot you've got here." He laughs nervously.

Dax, washing, a stocky, plain-speaking man, greets him courteously.

The General, chary of breaking the news, laughs at desk officers: "Afraid a mouse'll run up their leg."

"With a choice of mice or Mausers, I'd take the mice every time," Dax says sensibly.

General Mireau laughs, but "an officer has got to fight!"

All of them study the Ant Hill. "I've seen much more formidable objectives," Mireau blusters, as machine guns roar ominously. Explosions. Shells rush over, whining evilly.

Mireau chatters about recent casualities: "Stupid. Inexcusable. All swarmed together like a bunch of flies."

"Herd instinct." His aide grins cruelly. "Lower animal sort of thing . . ."

"A kind of a human sort of thing, or don't you make a distinction?" Dax responds loudly, looking the man in the eye.

Details of the trench system. A smug Mireau inspects the troops. *(United Artists Corporation)*

The assault on "Ant Hill": The sculptured and detailed terrain of no-man's-land, and the sweeping line of soldiers. *(United Artists Corporation)*

The three soldiers at their trial. Placement of the camera makes them small, passive, dominated by the massive and sinister yet gossamer architecture of the chateau. *(United Artists Corporation)*

ft: Dax confronts General Broulard. Even in the magnificent chateau, Dax's stance is atter-of-fact, while Broulard's reaction is stylized, calculated. *(United Artists Corporation)*
ght: The first German in the film, the frightened refugee farm girl. Out of the trenches, the en respond harshly at first, but soon are deeply moved. *(United Artists Corporation)*

"Yes indeed, very regrettable," Mireau jitters. "Your regiment is going to take the Ant Hill."

Dax stares at him—

"Men are going to have to be killed. Possibly a lot of them. Absorb bullets and shrapnel. And by doing so allow others to advance."

Mireau marches back and forth in the dugout while Dax hunches on the bunk. Kubrick lets him shift in and out of frame, as he reels off a wild estimate of the casualties. Mireau appeals to Dax's patriotism.

Dax quotes Johnson: "Patriotism is the last refuge of a scoundrel, General."

Mireau changes tactics: "You're tired, Dax. You've accomplished so much. I'm putting you on indefinite leave."

Dax hesitates. "We'll take the Ant Hill!" he sneers. "If any soldiers can, we can."

"And when you do," Mireau placates, "you'll be relieved, and your men will get a long rest."

When darkness falls, a patrol is organized. Again, a tough, realistic underling regards a nervous, effete commander who tells him: "Send up flares to guide us at five-minute intervals!"

"I told him ten minutes—or they'll draw enemy fire!" says Corporal Paris.

"Quite a strategist!" Lieutenant Roget tells the men to wait outside for him.

"He's fortifying himself," Corporal Paris says bitterly. "I can always tell when he's had a few."

"At least he could pass it around," says the lighthearted Lejeune. "What's he got against you?"

"We went to school together. He thinks I don't have enough respect for him," grits Paris. "He's right!"

Dax wishes them luck, and they crawl into the darkness of no-man's-land. Tense music throbs threateningly in the background. The terrain is jagged and broken, full of shell holes, corpses, twisted wire, old trenches, pits full of water, rubble. The patrol goes under the wire, clumsily lurching forward on alternate knees. The camera tilts and scuttles after.

"What's that?" Roget cries. "Lejeune! Look it over, we'll cover you!"

"Split a night patrol?" Paris snarls. They glare at each other. "Move out, Lejeune!"

Paris and Roget wait in the darkness. There is a drumbeat, clouds, the wind.

Suddenly, a flare hisses and blooms silently, illuminating ghastly corpses, smashed fortifications, barbed wire. Machine guns go bump in the night.

"Let's get out of here!" Roget cries, terrified.

"We've got to wait." Paris lashes him.

"He must be dead . . . where is he?"

Another flare tears the night open. Terrified, Roget sees a soldier move, and destroys him with a bomb. In the last light of the flare, the ripped-open body is seen to be Lejeune. . . .

In the bunker, Roget is finishing his report. Out of the darkness comes the bitterly smiling Paris: "Surprised to see me, Lieutenant?"

Now all brisk, chuckling maturity, Roget: "Yes, I am indeed, happily surprised. I thought you'd been killed."

"You ran like a rabbit," Paris cries, face twisted. "An officer wouldn't do that. A man wouldn't. Only a thing would. A sneaking, boozing, yellow-bellied rat with a bottle for a brain and a streak of . . ." Paris grins. "You got yourself into a mess, Lieutenant."

Roget back-paddles, lists some charges against his corporal. Circling him, Paris names the worse ones he faces: "Drunk on duty, wanton murder of one of your own men, cowardice in the face of the enemy . . ."

Roget grins slyly: "Have you ever tried to bring charges against an officer. . . ? I'm sorry. It was an accident. I'd give anything if it didn't happen."

"What kind of man do you think I am?" Paris cries, then suddenly deferential: "Oh, good morning, Colonel!"

Dax puts them at ease. Paris, resigned, leaves Roget to complete the report. . . .

In his own narrow bunker, Dax addresses his officers. They

stand around him, some in profile, some half-lit, some just shadows. "Artillery starts at zero five-fifteen. . . . Last wave out no later than zero five-forty."

A few questions. Dax nods: "Well, gentlemen, good luck. I'm sure you'll get through, as you always do."

In a set of tiered bunks, two privates, mostly hysterically, discuss their chances and fears:

"I'm not afraid of dying, only of getting killed."

"Most of us are more afraid of getting hurt than of getting killed."

"High explosives tear you up worse than anything . . ."

"If you were always afraid of death you'd live in a funk. Why should you care what it is that kills you."

Now in the silent dawn we once more view the enigmatic Ant Hill. . . .

In the command post, General Mireau waits.

"All units report themselves ready," an officer reports.

"Gentlemen, may I offer you some cognac," Mireau murmurs. "To France . . ."

Down the center of the trench, inspecting his men in a grotesque contrast with Mireau, Dax strides confidently, nodding and staring gamely. Kubrick tracks from behind, then from ahead, seemingly for minutes as Dax sees his men into battle, the reinforced walls to right and left sliding behind him. The tracking shot of Dax goes on and on as the bombardment increases, the air full of whining bombs, explosions, the thump of machine guns. Gradually the trench begins to fill with dust and smoke, the men's faces grown terrified or frozen, as if they were already penetrating enemy territory. Snare drums hiss. The tension is terrific . . .

Crouched with his squad, pistol in one hand, whistle in the other, Dax studies his watch: ". . . four, three, two, one. Go!"

The troops pour out in a line into the smashed, twisted lunar landscape of no-man's-land, as the barrage roars. They stumble and run after Dax blowing his whistle, waving his pistol, running on. Men begin to fall. Kubrick shoots in medium and long lateral tracking shots: the landscape, jammed with blasted fortifications, old corpses and trenches, barbed wire, pits full of water, pits full of dead, pits full of living, the smaller props of ruined guns, torn tunics, ruined weapons, and running, twisting, crouching and collapsing figures, the flash of explosions, the thumps and roars and dim battle cries—all have a terrible jammed-together cubist intensity.

Dax runs on, pitifully blowing his whistle, men falling all around him. Smoke drifts across the phantasmagoric landscape. The action occurs all over the longshots in little incidents: Two men hide behind an old fortification—one edges out and is cut down; another falls, twisting, into a pool of water; an explosion snares one more. The sound of shells falling is like a giant tearing yards and yards of cloth. Dax finds himself alone. And slowly, softly, the faint battle cries we have heard all along become faint wails and moans, voices of defeat and agony. . . .

In the command post, Mireau is hysterical: "Where are they? They're still in the trenches, they're not advancing! Miserable cowards!" The General orders the batteries to fire on his own positions.

The battery commander, haggard but coolly confident behind his bristling mustache, refuses without signed orders: "Suppose you're killed, where'll I be?"

"You'll be in front of a firing squad," Mireau squeals. . . .

Dax finds that many men are still in the trenches, and hysterically begins pushing and yelling: "Get these men out of here! Aren't you ready for another try? Get these men—" He climbs the parapet, is blown off. The barrage thunders, the men huddle. "It's just impossible," squeaks a sergeant, "just impossible!"

Kubrick cuts to the quiet command post. Mireau's bland-faced aide tells of the failure of the attack.

Mireau has the men relieved, orders a general court martial for three o'clock that day. "If those little sweethearts won't face German bullets," he lashes as the camera zooms in on his face, "they'll face French ones!"

In the chateau's gilt and brocade salon, among the spindle-legged chairs, crystal chandeliers, porcelain cherubs, Mireau, Broulard, and Dax face each other.

"Half of your men never left the trenches!"

"A third of my men were pinned down because the fire was so intense."

"I'm going to have ten men from each company," Mireau cries vengefully, "tried under penalty of death for cowardice. They've skimmed milk in their veins instead of blood."

"It's the reddest milk I've ever seen," Dax returns fiercely. "My trenches are soaked with it."

The two men quarrel: Mireau sullenly and vengefully, Dax angrily and faintly hysterically—for the lives of his men are at stake. "I did not intend to be insubordinate. My only aim is to remind you of the heroism these men have shown on every occasion in the past."

For a moment, General Mireau speaks with the cold, remorseless logic of war: "It was their duty to obey that order . . . we can't leave it up to the men to decide when an order is possible or not. If it was impossible, the only proof would be their dead bodies lying in the bottom of the trenches."

He pauses, and sadistically spits: "They're scum, the whole rotten regiment. A pack of sneaking, whining, tail-dragging curs."

Dax is stunned: "You really believe that!"

"Yes, I do. That's exactly what I believe. What's more, it's an incontestable fact."

Dax throws up his hands: "Why not shoot the entire regiment? Or take me, one man will do as well . . . the logical choice . . . the officer responsible—"

Broulard chuckles: "This is not a question of officers." He turns to Mireau. "Paul, we don't want to overdo this thing. Supposing we just make it a dozen."

They haggle, and Mireau tells them: "I'll settle for this—have each company commander select one man in his first wave—three in all."

Broulard radiates approval: "Well, that's very reasonable of you, Paul! Then the court martial meets at three o'clock."

Dax, previously complimented as a criminal lawyer, is allowed to defend the accused. "Consider it settled!" Broulard announces cheerfully.

Outside, the nervous Mireau stops one of his officers in the echoing marble hallway, and asks that his battery commander, whose shells fell "dangerously short," be transferred to another outfit.

A moment later he faces Dax, who refuses to drop the matter. General Mireau tells him in an intense murmur: "When this affair is cleaned up, I'll break you. I'll find an excuse and I'll break you to rank. I'll ruin you and it'll be just what you deserve, showing such little loyalty to your commanding officer."

Dax faces his battalion commanders, and tells them each to choose a man. The charge is cowardice in the face of the enemy.

Moments later, the Colonel faces his three human sacrifices. Each quickly tells his story.

Corporal Paris: "Lieutenant Roget killed Lejeune on that patrol, then blackmailed me into keeping quiet. That's why he picked me."

Dax nods: "Corporal, I understand your feelings, but that story has nothing to do with the charges you're being tried for . . . I believe you, but no one else will. Such charges against an officer would only antagonize the court."

Private Arnaud, an earnest bearded man: "Sir, in my case, Captain Renoir had us draw lots. I was picked merely by chance."

Private Ferol, a tall whiner: "You're luckier. Look at me. I was just picked because Captain Sansee said I was a social undesirable. Me—a social undesirable!"

The three men, small figures in the background, face a tall, somber, faintly disgusted Dax: "You've all got to understand the reason you were picked is immaterial. Whatever the reasons, you're on trial for your lives. . . . Stick to the stories you told me, and act like soldiers—and brave ones at that!"

The trial takes place in another of the ethereal, high-ceilinged, marble-floored rooms of the chateau. The voices of the court and defendants echo majestically at first, but become eerily distorted as the trial progresses. The indictment is not read or recorded, and Private Ferol, the whiny social undesirable, is quickly browbeaten into agreeing that he retreated. It's clear that there will not be the slightest pretense at fair play.

The quiet, intelligent Private Arnaud, his voice echoing weirdly, his feet shuffling the tiles, tells his story: "Most of us were dead or wounded before we got three feet beyond the trenches. . . . I didn't urge them on."

Dax tells the court: "You were designated a coward simply because you drew a slip of paper marked X."

General Broulard laughs: "I don't see that is significant."

"This soldier has distinguished himself in the past."

"We're not trying him for his former bravery, but his present cowardice."

Corporal Paris, knocked unconscious at the start of the attack, has no defense.

Dax paces back and forth between the three prisoners and the three judges, as he gives his final defense. He condemns the court's methods, then concludes emotionally: "To find these men guilty would be a crime to haunt each of you to the day you die. I can't believe that compassion for another can be completely dead here. I humbly beseech you. Show mercy to these men."

The head of the court announces: "The hearing is closed."

Ironic cut to the squad preparing for the execution. The officer in charge marches back and forth, announcing the schedule, the weapons, and so on. The chateau hovers in the background, delicate and unreal.

Cut to the prisoners. A guard comes in with an immense tray. "Compliments of General Mireau!"

But the men can't eat it; they've been forbidden knives and forks. Arnaud and Paris shudder; they know it's their last meal. The ex-con, Ferol, digs in: "This is terrific!"

Ferol thinks he can escape somehow, while Arnaud says Colonel Dax will see them through. Paris wonders if they have friends among the guards.

Ferol laughs at him: "Right now, we have no friends."

Arnaud points to a cockroach: "Tomorrow morning we'll be dead and it'll be alive. I'll be nothing and it'll be alive."

Ferol casually mashes it: "Now you've got the edge!"

The door slams, a priest enters. "Colonel Dax asked me to tell you that you must prepare yourselves for the worst." The holy man tries to comfort them. "Have faith in your Creator—death comes to us all."

Arnaud makes an ugly sound. "Really deep! Death comes to us all." He holds up his bottle. "This is my religion . . . get out of here, you sanctimonious—" He struggles with the others. "What're you hanging around here for, to torture us?"

Ferol tries to escape as the priest leaves, with serious results. The bland military doctor tells them to strap him to a stretcher in the morning so he won't fall, pinch his cheek so he's awake. "The General wants him conscious!"

After nightfall, Dax calls Lieutenant Roget to his quarters. The Colonel speaks casually, Roget with calculated ingenuousness.

"I've got to pick someone—for the firing squad." Dax explains about putting a bullet in each prisoner's head afterward.

"I request that I be excused!"

"Request denied!" Dax tells him savagely.

"Colonel, I beg of you . . ."

"You've got the job! It's all yours . . . that's all . . ."

Captain Rousseau, the artillery officer during the attack, comes in. "I have something which may have a great bearing on the court martial . . ."

Cut to the chateau, where a dress officers' ball is in progress. The light chamber music continues as Dax and General Broulard retire to his book-lined study. Amiably, the General tells Dax: "From the records of the casualities, the efforts of your regiment must have been considerable."

Dax asks how he can let the men be shot if this is true.

His eyes hooded, Broulard replies: "We think we're doing a good job running the war. The General Staff is subject to all kinds of unfair pressures from the press, from politicians. Perhaps it was an error of judgment to attack Ant Hill. But if your men had been a little more daring, you *might* have taken it. Why should we have to bear more criticism than we have to . . ." The commander's eyes glitter.

"There's the question of the troops' morale. These executions will be a tonic for the entire division. There are few things more fundamentally encouraging and stimulating than seeing someone else die. Troops are like children. Just as a child wants his father to be firm, troops crave discipline. And one way to maintain discipline is to shoot a man now and then."

Dax is shocked: "Do you sincerely believe all the things you've just said . . . ?"

The General ushers Dax toward the door, while Dax tells him sweetly: "By the way, sir, have you heard that General Mireau wanted his batteries to open fire on his own positions during the attack?"

The door *slams!* With Dax and the General inside.

". . . the General insisted he commence firing on his own trenches in front of witnesses." Dax pulls out sworn statements, and wonders what the newspapers and politicians, Broulard's pressure groups, would make of them. Broulard asks if he is being blackmailed.

Dax stares at him impassively. "You are in a difficult position. Too much has happened. Someone has got to be hurt. The question is, who? His attempt to murder three innocent men could be prevented by the General Staff."

General Broulard stares at him, and asks to be excused. Dax waits alone. . . .

A rooster crows. A squad marches into the prisoners' room. Ferol is strapped to the stretcher, Corporal Paris is silent, but Private Arnaud is breaking down, crying and pleading.

"Dignitaries and newspapers will be there," the sergeant barks. "How do you want to be remembered?"

"I don't want to die," Arnaud gibbers. "Save me."

In longshot we see the chateau, the troops drawn up before it. Broulard, Mireau, even Dax are in full dress uniforms, as if on parade. Two sets of drums never stop. The three prisoners are marched up to the posts and lashed: Ferol unconscious, Arnaud moaning and shambling ("I don't want to die!" "Brace yourself!"), Paris silent. Lieutenant Roget offers them blindfolds, murmuring a manly little "I'm sorry" to Paris. Drums, drums, drums. Coffins wait in an open cart.

The firing squad raises and aims, and there is a twitter of birds.

They fire! The three dance, twitch, collapse. Kubrick holds the shot. . . .

Generals Broulard and Mireau are having breakfast, smiling slyly.

"I have never seen such an affair handled any better. The men died wonderfully!"

Dax comes in, and Broulard congratulates him: "Your men died very well." He turns to Mireau, his voice turning impassive: "By the way, Paul, it's been brought to my attention that you'd ordered your artillery to fire on your own men during the attack . . ."

Mireau looks up, thunderstruck, at his friend. Broulard indicates Dax.

Mireau rages: "I've always known that you were a disloyal officer, but I never dreamed you'd stoop to anything so low as this."

Broulard cheerfully informs him of the public hearings—a chance to clear his name!—and smiles at the man he's destroyed.

"So that's it! You're making me the goat! The only completely innocent man in this whole affair." He takes a breath. "I've one last thing to say. The man you stabbed in the back is a soldier!" He strides out.

Broulard sighs. "Had to be done—France cannot afford to have fools guiding her military destiny." Broulard smiles at Dax, and offers him Mireau's job. After all, he's been after it from the start!

Dax only gradually understands. When he does he's almost crying: "Would you like me to suggest what you can do with that promotion! I apologize for not revealing my true feelings . . . that you're a degenerate, sadistic old man. And you can go to hell before I apologize to you!"

Broulard does not fall down. He regards Dax coolly, his feelings, if any, well hidden. "Colonel Dax, you've spoiled the keenness of your mind by sentimentality. You really did want to save those men, and you were not angling for Mireau's command. You're an idealist, and I pity you, as I would the village idiot, for fighting in a war that we've got to win. Those men didn't fight, so they were shot. You bring charges against General Mireau, so I insist that he answer them. What then have I done wrong?"

Outside, alone, Dax wanders the streets of the town, passes by an inn. The keeper, like a carnival pitchman, introduces a frightened German girl refugee: "A little diversion, what's life without a little diversion? (the men cheer) I give you our latest acquisition from the enemy . . . no talent except a little natural talent, eh! (the men stomp, whistle) "And she can sing like a bird." The girl begins singing a sweet German folk song. The men hum along, weep into their beer. Dax recognizes companions of the executed, the men who saw Mireau's madness.

Outside, an officer tells Dax to get the men moving, it's time to return to the trenches.

"Let them have five minutes more," Colonel Dax says, his expression impassive, watching and listening. Drums and the brassy military theme rise and drown the folk song as Dax stands alone.

The complete auteur, Kubrick released his pitiless film on Christmas day.

The reviews were uniformly very favorable, particularly of Kubrick's direction. Bosley Crowther of *The New York Times* spoke of *Paths of Glory* having "an impact of hard reality . . . a frank avowal of agonizing, uncompensated injustice is pursued to the bitter, tragic end."[3] The reviewer speaks of the film's shattering candor: "The close hard eye of Mr. Kubrick's sullen camera bores directly into the minds of scheming men, and into the hearts of patient, frightened soldiers who have to accept orders to die." Zinsser of The New York *Herald Tribune* calls *Paths of Glory* "a good hard movie . . . powerful in design and execution."[8] It's interesting that both these important reviewers instinctively rejected any larger meanings in the film. Crowther sums up: "It is grotesque, appalling, nauseating . . . but so framed and isolated that . . . you are left with the feeling that you have been witness to nothing more than a horribly freakish incident." Likewise, Zinsser concludes: "You may not believe that two such evil men could wield this power, or that French military justice could be so polluted. In this case, *Paths of Glory* will strike you as a narrow and unlikely drama."

The review in *Time* magazine typifies many other popular evaluations. While praising the technique and performances, it uses the last scene to dismiss the content: ". . . and so the men are executed. To what effect? Within an hour of the execution, the regiment is watching a pretty girl in a *boîte,* and has apparently forgotten that the three men ever existed."[5]

Gavin Lambert's lengthier analysis in *Sight and Sound* does justice to some of the film's tough subtleties. Lambert compares *Paths of Glory* to *All Quiet on the Western Front,* to the former's great advantage: "*Paths of Glory,* by showing the gulf between leaders and led, fatally widened by the fact of war, shows war itself as an extended struggle for power, internal and external. . . . The visual contrast of, say, a 'Summit' conference and a hydrogen bomb exploding on a city, is only taking *Paths of Glory's* contrast of the chateau and the trenches a stage further."[4]

Lambert points out that more frightening than the physical horror of combat is the social structure of the war: ". . . The world seems cruelly divided into the leaders and the led. The officers conduct their foxy intrigues in the elegant rooms of a great chateau, and the setting somehow emphasizes their indifference to human life. The men go to the trenches and into battle, as in peacetime they went to offices and factories."

A comparison between Humphrey Cobb's original novel and the Kubrick screenplay is also of some interest. The novel introduced the three doomed soldiers at the beginning and ends with the bullets of the firing squad. Most of the scheming and collusion of the officers does not appear. Colonel Dax remains in the background: He doesn't defend his men at the trial, or threaten to blackmail Mireau. Of the three soldiers, one is a sly blackguard, but the other two are heroic and sensitive individuals.

In Kubrick's *Paths of Glory,* the men are not introduced until the last third of the film, as three semiciphers of dubious worth, after the audience has surely identified with Dax. The treacherous and scheming staff officers, and Dax's struggle to save the three and learn with whom he is fighting and why, become the center of the story. The doomed soldiers are in the background, passive.

There are several critically rewarding ways to approach *Paths of Glory.* First, it may be examined as a construct of ironic devices and effects. The cutting between the ethereal, lovely chateau with its pettiness and vanity and the grim trenches full of blood, mud, and death is clearly a taunting sarcasm on the nature of society. The three men on trial will be shot by their own side because they were not shot by the enemy, a bitter irony indeed. The visuals are full of ironic cuts: from the judge telling the prisoners "the hearing is closed" direct to the firing squad getting their orders; from Dax brooding on the trial to the frivolous officers' ball the same night; from the executed men slumping against the posts direct to Generals Broulard and Mireau eating a luxurious breakfast. Identical activities are repeated in bitter contrast: Mireau pompously and hypocritically reviews his men in the trenches, as Dax does the same quietly and sincerely before zero hour; Roget slyly talks Paris out of telling the truth about the patrol, so does Dax, later, for the same reasons. Ironies arise in role reversals: Lieutenant Roget should have been shot for what he did on the patrol, but is put in charge of the firing squad instead; the honorable Dax is forced to blackmail to save his men. The title itself is ironic: There are no "paths of glory," all paths lead almost inevitably to ruin. Mireau's choice of such a path dooms them all, including Mireau himself. Dax, who seems to have walked the Glory Road, is condemned and hated when he tries to assert the principles he lives by.

A second interesting approach to *Paths of Glory* is to look at it as an intellectual period piece of the mid-fifties, an unconscious compendium of ideas then in fashion. As such, it has astonishing similarities to the novel *Catch-22,* by Joseph Heller, which was outlined and begun around 1955, too. Like Captain Yossarian in the Heller novel, Colonel Dax begins as an innocent member of a power-mad bureaucracy engaged in a brutal, dehumanizing struggle (neither work justifies its war in the slightest). Yossarian and Dax both have simple, decent subordinates who are inevitably destroyed; small-minded or self-serving compatriots who prosper more or less according to their degree of callousness; and childish, power-hungry superiors who live only to rule. In the end, Yossarian and Dax face their two superiors, one of whom slyly controls the other. The men on top admit their viciousness and offer the heroes a deal to "be their boy." Dax and Yossarian both refuse, denounce them, and depart.

In the perspective of the seventies, both *Catch-22* and *Paths of Glory* can be seen as products of the stifling anti-intellectualism, smugness, and paranoia of the Eisenhower-McCarthy years. Both are full of pointless brutalization, absurd and arbitrary power, and smothering conformity. Criticism of *Catch-22* (both the book and the film) suggests the less obvious absurdity of Kubrick's hero: trying to stay always within the limits of the military system, Dax winds up arguing the defense of his men against the judge who arranged the trial so they would be put to death. You can't become more of an absurd hero than that! For better or worse, Dax can be seen as an absurd, impotent character who won't or can't rebel, even staring into the face of evil itself.

A third heuristic critical approach is to see *Paths of Glory* as a dramatized model of society (clearly created by a brilliant nihilist). Gavin Lambert has pointed out the class structure of this society. Its cruel, dehumanizing, and pointless "work" is production in a consumer economy, allegorically intensified. The lives of its citizens are "mean, nasty, brutish and short"; they tend to advance in proportion to their wits, endurance, aggression, and tolerance for inflicting pain. The closer to the top, the worse they are. But the men on the bottom have no nobility—of the three chosen to die, the shrewd, vengeful hater endures the wait; the brave man chosen at random cracks up and becomes a babbling child; the criminal destroys himself in a clumsy escape attempt. There is no law or justice, of course, and the trappings of civilization—the exquisite chateau—are used for displays of vanity, ambition, treachery, and monstrous "public relations stunts" like the trial.

Looking at *Paths of Glory* as a model of a Hobbesian state, General Broulard becomes a darkly ambiguous and enigmatic figure. His seduction of General Mireau into attacking Ant Hill, his decision to sacrifice the three men "as an example," his outfoxing of Dax's blackmail plan and betrayal of the vain Mireau, all "make sense" in this dog-eat-dog reality. Again, his sly half-retracted statements about the childishness of the troops seem more than half true. At the last, when he says he pities Dax for fighting idealistically "a war we've got to win," General Broulard reveals himself as what novelist George Mandel calls a "super realist," a ruthless hero of the dark uncertain world where most issues, like the attack, can never really be resolved; a world the liberal Dax will not accept. If the life of the soldier, of each of us, is at heart a conspiracy, as Kubrick suggests,[7] only General Broulard is shrewd, devious, and powerful enough to have his conspiracy triumph.

Using these various approaches in turn, *Paths of Glory* becomes a complex, multi-faceted work, the ideas "sunk into" its sense of life. Consider the last scene: Dax stands outside the *boîte* as his men drink and hum along with the German peasant girl; after a moment he allows them a few minutes more.

The scene is ironic in several ways: Broulard's "example" seems already forgotten; the first "enemy" shown in the film is accepted and cheered; finally, all Dax can do for them is offer a little more diversion before they're killed for nothing, practically as "diversion," themselves.

Simultaneously, the scene bears the stultifying stigmata of the Eisenhower years: The bureaucracy rules forever; and with all his new dark knowledge, Dax remains impotent.

Finally, the cruel and pitiless world is on full display: Existence for the soldiers is blood and death punctuated by a "little diversion"; Dax can do nothing to help them or himself, for he is now one of them, doomed and controlled; the great war and the horrible enemy is shown to be another fraud, one more conspiracy.

Along with all of this, Kubrick's themes are present in full force:

The imaginary worlds. Mireau and Broulard live in a world of fabulous ambition and vainglory. The men in the trenches see themselves as passive creatures who can only follow their leaders through a slaughterhouse universe. The "brave" condemned soldier realizes his self-delusion too late, and experiences a mental collapse.

Futility of intelligence, errors of emotions. Corporal Paris, cannier than the weak, alcoholic Lieutenant Roget, is destroyed by him. Dax, thoughtful and resourceful, cannot save the men. Mireau's pride and vanity lead to his hysterical orders to the gunners and the destruction of his career. Dax's idealism and thirst for justice lead to the ruin of his career. Broulard, who flourishes, lives by power, not feeling or thought.

Murder-suicide pair. Mireau kills the three men, along with many others, and threatens Dax with the destruction of his career. But his hysterical behavior provides the weapon which will destroy him. Dax initiates Mireau's destruction, but ruins his own career by showing his true feelings to Broulard.

Odyssey to freedom. Colonel Dax travels an intellectual odyssey, slowly learning the truth about his superiors, how and why the war is really fought, and the meaning and consequences of his own beliefs in this context.

Obsessed hero. Colonel Dax, it will be recalled, took part in the attack on Ant Hill because General Mireau threatened to take him from his men. Dax, obsessed by his loyalty, labors always to do justice to and remain with his men. His obsession leads to his destruction as a career officer, but it is clear from the last scene that he has been allowed to retain his command, possibly to die with them, advancing in another vainglorious attack.

6

Spartacus

Then I did *Spartacus*, which was the only film that I did not have
control over, and which I feel was not enhanced by that fact. It all
really just came down to the fact that there are thousands of decisions
that have to be made, and that if you don't make them yourself, and
if you're not on the same wave length as the people who are making
them, it becomes a very painful experience, which it was. Obviously I
directed the actors, composed the shots, and cut the film, so that, within
the weakness of the story, I tried to do the best I could.

—*Stanley Kubrick, 1968*[8]

AFTER COMPLETING *Paths of Glory* in 1957, Kubrick
found himself in a remarkable situation. At thirty, he had directed
four feature films, the last two Hollywood productions, and *Paths
of Glory* with a budget of a million dollars. He had a considerable
reputation as a skilled and talented professional. But he had yet
to make a single dollar from directing. (A lesson here for aspiring
filmmakers.) His first two films lost money, and for *The Killing*
and *Paths of Glory* he had worked on 100% deferred salary—
and since neither film made any money, neither did he. Meanwhile,
Kubrick subsisted on loans from his partner.

Kubrick wrote two scripts the next year that no one in Hollywood wanted, then worked for six months with Calder Willingham (from *Paths of Glory*) and Marlon Brando on a script for
One-Eyed Jacks, which he hoped to direct. Kubrick's script apparently wasn't used, nor did he direct *One-Eyed Jacks,* but reportedly he got $100,000 for the job anyway, and began to dig
himself out of debt. A number of abortive projects followed, and
so another year coasted by.

Then, after a week of production, Director Anthony "Abby"
Mann resigned from Universal's *Spartacus,* and Kubrick was hired
for the job. Kubrick's contract was such that he did not have
complete control: "although I was the director, mine was only one
of many voices to which Kirk listened. I am disappointed in the
film. It had everything but a good story."[6] Nevertheless, Kubrick

apparently worked the story over several times while in production, and did control the other elements of the film.

Kubrick found the making of *Spartacus* confirmed many of the ideas he'd already formed about moviemaking. In an article written shortly after the spectacle's completion, Kubrick noted his approach: "You have to figure out what is going on in each scene and what's the most interesting way to play it. With *Spartacus,* whether a scene had hundreds of people in the background or whether it was against a wall, I thought of everything first as if there was nothing back there. Once it was rehearsed, we worked out the background."[10]

Kubrick felt that the wide screen was simply a new shape to compose his shots within: "For some scenes it just doesn't make too much difference. Instead of having the people stand two feet apart, sometimes you have them standing four feet apart; or you throw up a prop in the corner or something . . . a big screen from the back of the house is a small screen, and a normal screen is a big screen from the front rows." Nevertheless, *Spartacus* strongly demonstrates Kubrick's talent for visual composition, both static and dynamic, including many ideas which appear for the first time in his work.

Kubrick found working out of doors or in real locations very distracting, and preferred the tight control to be achieved only in a studio. A sound stage, he felt, is better for films where the actor must use his full concentration and resources, such as psychological stories where the characterization and inner feelings are the key. During the making of *Spartacus,* Olivier and Ustinov confirmed to him that: ". . . they felt that their powers were just drifting off into space when they were working out of doors. . . . They preferred that kind of focusing-in that happens in a studio with the lights pointed at them and the sets around them. Whereas outside everything fades away, inside there is a kind of inner focusing of psychical energy."

Despite his dissatisfactions, Kubrick was aware that *Spartacus* was his biggest project to date: a real Hollywood super-spectacle with a $12 million budget, and a cast that included Kirk Douglas, Lawrence Olivier, Jean Simmons, Charles Laughton, and Peter Ustinov. Total cast was 10,500 (including 8,000 Spanish soldiers as extras). The battle scenes were shot outside Madrid, the rest on and off the sound stages in California. Total shooting time: 167 days.

Kubrick's real unhappiness lay with Dalton Trumbo's script. Ignoring for the moment the director's own themes, ideas, and devices, the original treatment's weaknesses and embarrassments were succinctly summed up by the British critic Peter John Dyer: ". . . Dalton Trumbo's highly emotional brand of Left-thinking goes back to Roosevelt and the New Deal. The result . . . is preordained. Freedom is represented by eve of battle visits to the troops, nude bathing scenes, babies, aged peasant faces, trysts in forest glades, Super Technarama-70 rides across sunset horizons, and a heroine shot in romantically gauzy close-ups; its intercommunication with art by one of those noble brotherhood relationships between the poet Antonius and Spartacus which can only be sundered by death and a fervent kiss; and Rome by a bisexual dictator who inquires of the body slave bathing him whether his taste runs to both oysters and snails."[4]

Because *Spartacus* is not truly Kubrick's creation, my treatment will stress the composition, direction, and cutting rather than story line and characters.

Kubrick begins directing at the gladiator's school run by Batiatus, a brutal and sly coward. He tries to wheedle Spartacus into attacking him, unsuccessfully: "You're not as stupid as I thought, you might even be intelligent . . . that's dangerous, for slaves."

The script fills in the detail, makes the ambiance clear as the future combatants meet. "I don't want to know your name. You don't want to know my name." Spartacus and the lovely Varinia meet.

Kubrick delights in the visul exposition of the school: the gladiators exercising, running, dueling, practicing, jumping and ducking a spinning ball with blunt projections in the dusty courtyard, a pre-Christian "gym." In a lecture on combat, Batiatus dapples Spartacus with colored dyes: "Go for the red first!" Spartacus watches Varinia from the slaves' common room. In the dim morning, she dishes out food to the gladiators. Kubrick uses very little voice-track, just grumbles and clatter and romantic music.

The cruel, sardonic General Crassus arrives with depraved friends, watches the practicing gladiators, and demands a fight to the death. The canny Batiatus looks out at the hundreds of strong bodies and refuses. The slaves wait in their dark, dungeonlike quarters, only their faces silhouetted.

Two predatory, degenerate women choose the gladiators, including an Ethiopian and Spartacus. Kubrick zooms and tracks in on the bars of their cages, showing their helplessness. On the veranda over the small arena, Crassus's effete companion twists Varinia to him.

Spartacus and the Ethiopian sit jammed face to face in a little anteroom to the arena, the first combat visible through a tiny slit. Neither of these men look. They stare agonized at the ground, the fight traceable only from cries, scuffles, shouts, moans. In the box the women gossip, hardly watching the murder they've commanded.

In the arena, the Ethiopian in the foreground holds his net so it covers Spartacus. The two slash and chase each other with net, trident, and shortsword, their eyes bulging. The editing cuts from rush to feint to a pinned, helpless Spartacus. "What's the matter now—kill him!" With a cry the black turns, throws his trident at the box, leaps and clings. From above Crassus slashes his neck tendons, splattering blood. Kubrick zooms in on the dazed, wondering Spartacus.

Cut to the dead Ethiopian, eyes staring, hung by his feet over the gloomy gladiators' common room. "He'll hang till he rots," Batiatus grins. Spartacus looks at his friend once more. Again, Spartacus sees another depart: Varinia, sold, leaves in an oxcart.

At a morning meal, a gladiator strikes a brutal guard, and the whole room bursts into violence. Another master is drowned, writhing, in a kettle of boiling stew (shades of *Fear and Desire*); more are struck down. The gladiators seize dinner knives, slash and smash, Kubrick's camera laterally tracking across the jailbreak, Spartacus at the fore. A wall is broken and, shouting, the men pour outside, hacking and stabbing so an ornamental fountain purls red. Kubrick's camera, liquidly smooth and swift, tracks around the break for freedom. Spartacus climbs the barbed fence

Batiatus uses Spartacus as model opponent. The director's use of visual aid in ancient military training is another mockery of intelligence. *(Universal Pictures)*

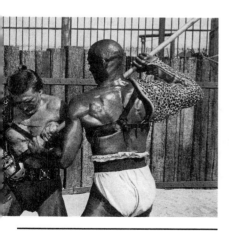

The savage duel of Spartacus and the Ethiopian. These early scenes in the film seem closer to the director's personal style than the later pageantry. *(Universal Pictures)*

Spartacus leads the slave revolt. This chaotic murderous fight is similar to the terrifying confusion of combat in *Fear and Desire*. *(Universal Pictures)*

of bars so it falls toward us, him atop it. The slaves pour out of the training school, cheering and smashing. . . .

Kubrick's Rome is marble halls on many hills, the great Senate in session ("The garrison of Rome stands ready!"), the shrewd jowly Gracchus with a chicken for sacrifice. As the meeting goes on, the Senate remains lit, but the powerful figures conspiring in the foreground are sunk into darkness. . . .

In a "liberated" villa, Spartacus silently watches the revels of his fellow gladiators, as they set two fat, middle-aged, balding patricians to "fight to the death." Spartacus, his face determined, strides out and tells them: "I promised I'd never see two men fight each other to the death." The men boo, throw junk, but he goes on: a plan to free everyone with a big army—"we can beat anybody." He starts a speech . . .

Kubrick cuts to a mountainside. Utilizing his big screen, Kubrick has the ragtag freemen come down it, the vanguard plunging ahead yelling as the stragglers are still breaching the top. A romantic theme is heard amid cries of rejoicing. Spartacus rides ahead, his figure richly colored in the sunset, the newly freed watching with mingled joy and reverence. Varinia appears with some refugees and the big man rides to her. . . .

In Imperial Rome, the gnawing Gracchus remarks: "The nastiest people are invariably thin," describing himself as "the most treacherous man in Rome." His guile and spite are counterpoint to Spartacus' faith when the Senator justifies an act: "Why do I do this? To annoy Crassus, and help you."

Cut to the bisexual dictator Crassus, who points out of a great window in his villa, a frame within a frame, at the towering bastions of the city, and tells the delicate poet Antonius with double-edge imperiousness: "That, boy, is Rome! The might, the majesty, the terror that is Rome! You must bow before her. You must love her. . . ." Kubrick zooms in on his revelry of power, then his confusion. Antonius has fled. . . .

A long shot of shabbily clad horsemen pounding along a cliff edge. Martial music. Kubrick tracks continuously with them: past ballistae aimed at the valley below, other weapons abuilding, sword practice in groups, the twirling teaching machines from the gladiator school, slaughtered sides of meat—the renegade camp, wordlessly exposited. Next are children at play, a dunking bath, work-hardened but carefree old and young laughing peasant faces. Spartacus reviews his chuckling, mildly rebellious band, including Antonius. "You know magic? Maybe you can make the Romans disappear, ha!"

Meanwhile, the Imperial legions slog toward the outlaw stronghold. Some are drunk on wine, others on empire—officers on horseback pound down the middle of the road, so the marching troops must leap aside.

Kubrick cuts back to the ex-slaves practicing on their horses, without uniforms or saddles, but with swords out and swinging. A freeman gallops past a gourd on a post, slashes it in half. The shot is repeated, a second man chopping another gourd, and again, and again, and again. Spartacus asks for volunteers, and every man steps forward.

Later, the ex-slaves sit around the campfire while Antonius entertains with magic and songs. Spartacus and Varinia go off to lie in the grass, head to foot, seen dreamily through dappled leaves. . . .

Now Spartacus and Antonius greet a swarthy trader in a terrible downpour, the first time the weather has played a part in a Kubrick film. In his dimly lit tent, Spartacus throws back a trunk lid revealing sparkling treasure. In the low-key lighting, the flames from the braziers beat like unspoken fears against their faces, darkness surrounds them. Yes, with enough money the slaves can buy passage out of Italy. Spartacus pulls up the tent flap. The screen is split—the right side is the warm red of the shelter, the left the cold roaring blue of the rainstorm. The swarthy captain departs.

Later, the horses of a slave patrol thunder across the screen, past a gorge which spews more horsemen that follow, breaking up the action. The blue soldiers race to the red Spartacus: "The Romans!"

In the blue evening light, Spartacus' troops, spears high, ride off. Kubrick's camera lifts liquidly from behind the tent to see them go. . . .

In the dark Roman encampment, a flame lights the darkness. It is a rebel attack! Fire runs along the line of tents, as the Romans stumble out into slave swords. Tents turn to torches. The Imperial standards blaze as they tumble to earth. Kubrick tracks laterally through the maze of combat. In moments the Commander of the garrison stands in shadow, encircled by Spartacus and his men, all devilishly lit by their own flaring brands. The ex-slaves, laughing, throw him on a horse and send him back to Rome.

The routed Commander, his face stricken, addresses the Senate, who pose questions to him in short static shots which reflect the legal body's repression and hypocrisy. Gracchus, his eyes twinkling, announces: "Crassus sponsored this young man. Let *him* pronounce sentence."

In longshot, Spartacus moves his army across the rugged, weathered Italian terrain, the long lines curving with the eroded hills and empty watercourses, all in tones of brown and dusty yellow. Again there is no voice track, only stirring music and a parade of simple, emboldened faces. The slave army splashes or drifts through a green stream, tearing its yellow scum; over a snowy pass; laboriously up a vertiginous slope. . . .

Varinia swims a lilied and reeded pool: "Spartacus, you frightened me!" The two speak as lovers. He wraps her in his robe, lifts her: "Spartacus, put me down! I'm going to have a baby!"

Across a burned brown plain, the slaves advance to martial music.

In the Senate, debate rages: "Can Spartacus be intercepted and destroyed?"

Spartacus appears in a port, his army's ranks filling the streets, marching proudly. Varinia puts his hand on her waist—he can feel his child.

In a steamy Roman bath, Crassus speaks intimately with Caesar: "Why have you left us for Gracchus and the mob?" The bath is tiled in blue and white, with red-fleshed men wandering in and out. The crafty General smiles lasciviously at the ruler as the screen darkens.

In longshot, a rider plunges, half out of control, down a sandcliff to the slave encompment by the sea. Chanties are wailed dimly in the background. Young and old couples prance to the tunes; one couple poignantly kisses against the clouded sunset.

Spartacus, intense and eager, faces the Semitic merchant captain. Is the fleet ready to carry them off? There is no escape.

Crassus has bribed and threatened the merchantmen not to evacu-
ate the slaves. The gladiator studies his maps, the camera placed
behind them; all are silent beside the burning braziers. The answer
is plain: They can only turn back to face the might of Rome.
Kubrick cuts from Spartacus in profile, tanned, in crude robes, to
a profile of General Crassus addressing the Senate, all in Imperial
red and white, the sycophantic senators nodding. Cut back to a
browned Spartacus against a blue sky, addressing his people in
their coarse garments the color of earth. Spartacus stares over his
loyal followers at the triumphant conclusion of their march, the
lovely sea coast they have won, touches Varinia and feels his child.
But it can never be . . .

A great, empty, green valley. Along the very bottom, a thick
rope of legions jerks forward. We see close-ups of the cavalry,
foot-soldiers, seige weapons—now the rope is jerked apart into an
array of mustered squares which advance ponderously and clumsily up the green, against the thin lines of Spartacus' men, a ponderous ballet of power. There is martial music, no speech. The
lines close in, a diagonal across the screen. Dwight MacDonald
sees these battle scenes as subtle derivations from Eisenstein's
Alexander Nevsky.

Suddenly, from the leading edge of the slave forces, rollers of
flaming straw half as high as a man race toward the enemy, pulled
by pairs of slaves. Kubrick moves in closer only slowly, so we
hardly understand what the spinning, blazing weapons are before
we see the panic: fleeing soldiers who stumble are mowed down
and set aflame, screaming; the horses rear and plunge; more
soldiers are roasted black on the great twirling burning spits. But
slowly, in the gaps between, and behind the first ranks, the legions
regroup, advance and meet the slaves . . .

The battlefield is a primal chaos. Kubrick's camera sweeps
effortlessly over the hacking, spearing, bloody combat. Smoke
from the burning straw drifts on the wind, obscuring the fray.
Kubrick lingers over a close-up of a soldier methodically pinned
and butchered against a great boulder; another's arm is chopped
free. The camera shoots a struggling cluster from the right, then
the left. Two swords and their owners' hands cover the bottom
third of the screen, changing the shape of the frame. Again the

camera tracks endlessly across the struggling, killing mass of bodies, as the battle goes on and on . . .

Corpses. Endless tumbled corpses, staring. General Crassus strides across this sea of dead flesh. On the rim of the valley, wagons collect the highest ranking dead. Beside a great boulder, the few hundred slave survivors are collapsed, Spartacus among them. Crassus offers a deal for a betrayal. In reply, each man cries bitterly: "I'm Spartacus!" "I'm Spartacus!" "I'm Spartacus!" "The prisoners are to be crucified!" cries Crassus. A little beyond them, Varinia with her newborn child is salvaged by the specter-faced Crassus. They travel toward Rome, the road lined with crosses.

At Crassus' villa, the plucky Varinia bullies and frightens the mighty but hollow Crassus.

After they reach Rome, Crassus sets Spartacus and Antonius against each other beside the highway of agonized slaves; Kubrick's camera hangs godlike overhead. The guards, wraithlike, ring them, while Crassus looks on rapaciously. The poet vows: "I won't let them crucify you, Spartacus!" But out of love he lets himself be destroyed.

"Now crucify him!"

The witty demagogue Gracchus knows that with Crassus in command, his own days are numbered. He gives Batiatus, who has somehow survived, money and safe conduct passes for himself, Varinia, and the infant. Alone, he wanders abstractedly the length of his bed chamber, passing behind the veiled divan to take his own life.

The girl and child stare at the crucified Spartacus, then climb into Batiatus' cart. It rolls away from us down the road lined with crosses.

Some of the nicest things about *Spartacus,* Hollis Alpert points out,[1] are the clichés it omits: Christian martyrs being devoured by lions, homicidal chariot races, orgies of semi-nude girls and fat, lascivious nobles. In general, the reviewers found both negatives and virtues, and were well disposed to the epic. *Variety's* professionally cautious appraiser commented: ". . . let's come right out with it, sheer pictorial poetry that is sweeping and savage, intimate and lusty, tender and bittersweet." As for Kubrick, he had "out

DeMilled the old master in spectacle."[11] Even *Time*, the sarcastic scold, complimented: "In intimate scenes his camera follows the action with delicacy and precision; but he also knows when to let the frame stand grandly still and the audience stare, as if through a huge picture window, at a magnificent landscape or a ponderous ballet of legions that precedes a battle."[13]

Spartacus reveals other new directorial skills. Kubrick's techniques for moving compositions is much more complex than the "five zones for dying" of *Paths of Glory*. Shots like the laggards of the slave army breasting a hill while the vanguard plunges to the foot, show a real feel for moving masses about on the screen. The almost geometric mustering of the Roman legions in the climactic battle, and the tidal paths of the slaves through the rugged, eroded terrain, are likewise skillfully arranged.

A second debut is Kubrick's use of color: the contrast of the Imperial red and white banners with the earth-colored freemen under their rich Mediterranean blue sky; the leathery, dusty ambiance of the gladiator school; the symmetry of the warm tent hearths open to chill blue storm.

Third, Kubrick works very creatively with his sound track. *Spartacus* probably has the lowest word count of Kubrick's films, after *2001: A Space Odyssey*. Grim muscular gladiators; glib, dissembling knots of senators; liberated slaves on the march; legionnaires hacking at their foes; anxious desire for a loved one or power—all these are evoked from martial or cloying music and the permutations of groups of querulous or triumphant voices.

Interestingly, many of the reviewers agree with Kubrick that the major weaknesses of *Spartacus* are in the story. Beckley in the New York *Herald Tribune* calls the first half hour almost a new kind of spectacle, with the emphasis on "intimate skin-close sinewy concentration on the matters at hand"[2]—murderous combats, brutal yet fascinating killer training, slashing gladiators in revolt.

But with the break-out of the gladiators, the film's own intensity seems to flatten, lose impetus, and "resorts to rhetoric, sexual innuendo, pageantry of empire." The passages in the slave encampments along the march are increasingly tedious, too—full of the old Left clichés of happy traumaless rustics; an ignorant yet skillful leader; "innocent" lovemaking; pure ideology and simple trust perfectly uniting thousands under great stress—pathetically naive notions in 1970. Even in 1960, Crowther found the sequences pretentious and tedious.

The climactic battle is an eyefilling abstract and then suddenly murderously real spectacle, but Crowther and several other critics attack the end as very unsatisfactory: ". . . a great deal more is made of Miss Simmons' post-war predicament than of the crucifixion of 6,000 captive slaves." Though she carries away Spartacus' line and ideology, it hardly seems a fair trade for all the slaughter of the last thirty minutes, as if a sour Kubrick wanted to make his own disgust plain.

It is interesting to speculate how Kubrick would have written and shot *Spartacus,* given full control. He supposedly did rewrites at several points, and one can peer for Kubrick themes stillborn or contorted to fit the structure: Spartacus and Crassus as the suicide-homicide pairing (Crassus enduring a living death), or Spartacus obsessed by freedom. But they're weak and uncertain recitatives.

At heart, the character Spartacus is to me incompatible with Kubrick's films, for he is a man who undergoes a profound personal transformation, from good bright tough to heroic democrat-general. Such a character shift is unknown in all the director's films: The very most a person can change his point of view is to fall in love, and that is almost always fatal. (Sidney in *Fear and Desire,* Vince in *Killer's Kiss,* all the couples in *The Killing*). Kubrick's characters are driven or passive. They cannot change. It takes extraterrestrial intervention before a Kubrick person is significantly altered.

A second trouble with an all-Kubrick *Spartacus* is that the story violates his vision of human relations. Human relationships in Kubrick's films are rarely satisfactory, and never warmly democratic. Spartacus and his fleeing comrades, living in a sort of ideal socialism, are an optimistic comment on human community, a topic Kubrick always approaches with distrust, pessimism, and futility (the natural confluence of reason and emotion).

7
Lolita

I've got a peculiar weakness for criminals and artists—neither takes life
as it is. Any tragic story has to be in conflict with things as they are.
—*Stanley Kubrick, 1957*[11]

AFTER THE SUCCESS of *Spartacus,* Kubrick teamed up
once more with James Harris to make *Lolita* for M-G-M—in
England because of blocked M-G-M funds (profits), which could
not leave the country, and anticipated censorship problems. As a
film, *Lolita* had three special production difficulties: the casting of
Lolita herself, the writing of a satisfactory screenplay, and, related
to these, the likelihood of censorship.

Casting Lolita was an interesting business. Kubrick was
swamped with letters from American mothers eagerly offering up
their teen-age daughters for whatever the screenplay of the notorious novel required. Kubrick's final choice was blonde, blue-
eyed, fourteen-year-old Sue Lyon. He had spotted her on *The
Loretta Young Show,* let her read with James Mason, and decided: "She is a natural actor. Also, she has a beautiful figure
along ballet lines."[9]

Nabokov at first refused to write the screen adaptation, but re-
considered after dreaming that he was actually reading the screenplay. "Almost immediately after this illumination, Mr. Kubrick
called me again, and I agreed. . . . The screenplay became poetry,
which was my original purpose."[9] Kubrick's own attitude toward
the problems of adaptation of the highly subjective, sophisticated
novel was noted in an article in *Sight and Sound,* written while
shooting *Lolita* at ABPC Studios: "To take the prose style as any
more than just a part . . . is simply to misunderstand what a great
book is. . . . Style is what an artist uses to fascinate the beholder
in order to convey to him his feelings and emotions and thoughts.
These are what have to be dramatized, not the style."[7]

In a recent interview,[4] Kubrick disclosed that he and Nabokov
agreed at the time that the main narrative tension was in Humbert's pursuit of the nymphet. After he got Lolita into bed halfway

through the book, interest sagged. To keep the audience attentive to the very end, they agreed to have Humbert murder Quilty at the start, bizarrely and for no apparent reason. Kubrick thought the revision sacrificed a great ending, but served a worthwhile purpose, maintaining tension to Lolita's final confession.

In the same interview, he faulted himself for some aspects of the screenplay, the results of giving in to the Production Code and other pressures. Because he couldn't dramatize Humbert's erotic relationship with the nymphet, and could only hint at his sexual obsession, Kubrick thinks a lot of the audience assumed Humbert was simply in love with Lolita from the beginning—thus their last, poignant encounter, with Humbert's revelation of real love for the girl, lacks emotional force.

The censorship problems were tied up, certainly, with Kubrick's desire at the time for his films to reach the widest possible audience, the resulting success hopefully allowing him maximum artistic independence. Kubrick decided that he must produce as well as direct his work to attain creative freedom, a position he's achieved in *Dr. Strangelove, 2001: A Space Odyssey, A Clockwork Orange,* and the planned *Napoleon.*

The surmounting of censorship problems in the making of *Lolita* is discussed in Alexander Walker's *Sex in the Movies.*[12] Sue Lyon's sometimes teen-age appearance was perhaps the only real sop to the censors. In other respects Kubrick and Nabokov skillfully circumvented trouble. The collaborators shot in Britain to decrease the chances of harassment, cleared the screenplay with the authorities ahead of shooting, and began with a visual metaphor of the adult Humbert's pathetic enslavement by a sullen child—the professor giving her imperiously-thrust-out leg a self-debasing pedicure. Such undertones of irony and pathos keep turning up all through the film, but this humiliation scene was apparently of particular importance in the strange game of moral arithmetic called movie censorship. Right at the start retribution is meted out, before sin is even committed.

More retribution appears in the next scene, Humbert's agonized execution of a dissipated Quilty for casually seducing Lolita, among empty liquor bottles, sheeted furniture, and marble statuary in a dilapidated mansion. Quilty's twitching, bouncing, wisecracking death throes (Walker: "leaping up and down like a ticklish kangaroo") were also pleasing to the censors. The logic was that such a surrealistic, improbable scene was unlikely to stimulate any imitations.

Kubrick scored more points on what he left off the screen. The details of the "game" Lolita proposes to Humbert are left out, but his contrasting excitement suggests this isn't the first time she's played it. The grotesque marriage of Humbert and Mrs. Haze is short and down-pedaled, and the idea that Quilty as well as Humbert has slept with both mother and daughter is never explicit. Nor can traditional Hollywood morality be denied: Humbert and Quilty get their just deserts; Mrs. Haze is put out of her misery just as she learns that she's married a contemptuous degenerate; and the accessible innocent Lolita becomes a premature matron stuck in a tedious, hand-to-mouth, lower-class marriage.

Walker quotes an industry source who claimed only one interesting difficulty was found with the screenplay: the depiction of Humbert Humbert's theory of nymphets. In the novel *Lolita,* a passage begins: "Now I wish to introduce the following idea. Between the age limits of nine and fourteen there occur maidens who, to certain bewitched travellers, twice or many times older than they, reveal their true nature which is not human, but nymphic (that is demoniac); and these chosen creatures I propose to designate as 'nymphets.' "[8]

In the original screenplay, Walker believes, James Mason's Humbert begins: "Now I wish to propose the following idea . . ." and as he goes on, Kubrick cuts quickly through a series of nymphetlike girls: very young students, cinema usherettes, adolescents at play . . .

The censors apparently found the proposal sequence both too direct and too generalized. Nabokov's stimulating theory is offered with a suggestive, illustrated delivery worthy of a public service message encouraging child molesting. The implication is that Humbert has a universal drive that in his case went too far, rather than a rare crippling pathological condition. The sequence was dropped.

Kubrick believes that the treatment could certainly have been more erotic. But in 1960, things were different: "At the time I made it, it was almost impossible to get the film played. Even after it was finished, it laid around for six months. And then, of course, the audience felt cheated that the erotic weight wasn't in the story. I think that it should have had as much erotic weight as the novel had. As it was, it had the psychology of the characters, and the mood of the story."[6]

We hear arch notes and purple chords, what a critic calls: "A false, sweet forties sound track piano concerto theme throbbing like an embarrassed wound."[3] Behind the credits, a lovely imperious young leg is thrust into the frame, and Humbert Humbert, a handsome, somehow weak middle-aged satyr cushions the little sole while painting each nail with degrading devotion. . . .

Shot of a station wagon rushing down a country turnpike.

Humbert in a mouton coat enters a dusty mansion, cluttered with dust-sheeted furniture, marble statues, a harp, a piano, empty liquor bottles. The ambiance is opulent and unreal. He picks his way, does a run on the harp strings, calls: "Quilty! . . . Quilty!"

A bleary Bronx voice: "Wha'? wha'?" Still wrapped in a dust cloth, a figure rises wraithlike. He drapes it around him: short, soft, wide-hipped, intelligent but flaccid-faced, dissolute: "No, 'm Spartacus! You come to free the slaves or somethin'?"

"Are you Quilty?"

An assent. Humbert begins putting on leather gloves. Coolly: "Shall we have a little chat, or die before we start?"

"Wow!" Quilty says slowly. "All right, all right . . . listen. Let's have a lovely little game of Roman ping-pong, like two civilized senators." He serves: "Roman ping . . . you're supposed to say Roman pong!" Humbert pays no attention. "Kinda tricky serve to handle, eh, Captain?"

Humbert, slowly: "You really don't remember me, do you? . . . Do you remember a girl—" he almost sobs—"named Dolores Haze?"

Quilty chatters, Humbert barks for his attention: "*Lolita!*"

Quilty, grinning casually, in Bronxese: "Lo-lee-tuh . . . yeah, yeah!" Seeing Humbert's pistol: "Gee, you're sort of a bad loser, Captain. . . ! Didn't anyone ever tell ya, it's not whether you win

Humbert points his pistol at a togaed, bleary Quilty. The enormous, luxurious, cluttered, half-abandoned mansion suggests Quilty's own brilliance and dissipation. *(Metro-Goldwyn-Mayer, Inc.)*

Charlotte confronts Humbert with his secretly written diary. Two imaginary worlds clang together. *(Metro-Goldwyn-Mayer, Inc.)*

Humbert bickers with Lolita after the school play. Kubrick stylizes the teen-age temptress with a princess' crown, mascara, and bubblegum. *(Metro-Goldwyn-Mayer, Inc.)*

or lose, but how you play . . ." He stumbles away, silly. "Gee, I'm just dyin' for a drink . . . I'm just dyin' . . . to have a drinkee."

Humbert, pitilessly: "You're dying anyway, Quilty! . . . I want you to concentrate, you're going to die . . . try to understand what is happening to you!"

Quilty imitates a glib Gabby Hayes: "Heh, that's a *durlin'* little gun ya got there. . . ! How much do you want for a *durlin'* little gun like that?"

Humbert thrusts a paper at him.

Suddenly serious: "What's this, the deed to the ranch?" Gabby, quavering, cackling: "Can't read, Mister! . . . I never did have none of that there booklarnin', ya know!" Singsonging, cackling: "Because you took advantage of a sinner . . . because you took advantage of my disadvantage . . . when I stood Adam naked (oh, Adam Naked, you should be ashamed!) . . . before a Federal Law and all his stinging stars . . ." In moments, furious, Humbert pulls the poem away.

Quilty pulls on boxing gloves. Melodramatic: "I want to die like a champion!"

BANG! The bullet ricochets, smashes a vase.

"Gee, right in the boxing gloves," Quilty murmurs. Outside, the wind wails a little.

Quilty, peril penetrating, "Listen, Captain, why don't you stop trifling with life and death? I'm a playwright, I know all about this sort of tragedy and comedy and fantasy and everything, I got fifty-two successful scenarios to my credit, added to which my father's a policeman. . . . Why don't I play you a little thing I wrote last week . . ."

He rushes to the piano, begins Chopin's Grand Polonaise.

"We could dream up some lyrics, share the profits, it'll make the Hit Parade."

Quilty jumps up and runs for the curving stairs. Humbert fires: BANG, BANG, BANG BANG BANG. Quilty bounces and bounces on the wood.

Halfway up the stairs, he calls like a young child: "Gee, you hurt me, you really hurt me!" At the bottom Humbert reloads the Sacred Weapon, trembling.

Quilty, dazed, gasping, bantering: "If you're trying to scare me, you did a pretty good job. . . . This house is roomy and cool, you can move in . . . I got nice friends, use 'em for furniture, one guy looks like a bookcase . . . I could fix it up for you to attend executions, just you there, *watching* . . . not many people know the chair is painted yellow . . . you'll be the only guy in the know . . ."

Humbert comes up. Quilty crawls, scrambles upward, behind a Victorian portrait of a young girl. Humbert's bullets rip through the picture. "That hurt!" His legs kick, slump down.

Title: "Four Years Earlier," Humbert is to spend a peaceful summer in the attractive resort town of Ramsdale. Music to Catch Trains By. Images of a plane over Manhattan, a streamliner at a country station.

Mrs. Haze, a tall, talkative caricature of the culture-vulture matron, leads Humbert through her house. From the first, the dialogue is ironic: "Oh Monsieur, I can assure you you couldn't get more peace anywhere, ha-ha-ha. . . ."

She opens a bedroom, regards the European intellectual archly: "It's what you might call a studio . . . well, a semi-studio . . . it's very male—sigh!—and quiet . . . culturally we're a very advanced group, we're very progressive, uh, intellectually!"

Humbert, smoothly: "That is immediately apparent!"

Charlotte Haze bubbles: "Bathroom right next door . . . we have that quaint plumbing . . . should appeal to a European." Charmingly he flushes it: K-WOOOOSH! Gushing, holding it in her finger tips: "Oh, excuse the soiled sock!"

Humbert was divorced in Paris ("Ah, Paris—France, oh-la-la!"), and Mr. Haze has passed on. "He was a lovely man," Mrs. Haze says sentimentally, as Humbert studies the balding serious chap's picture, and touches the urn beneath. "Those are his ashes," she laments. Humbert jerks his hand away.

Downstairs they go. "The kitchen . . . that's where we have our informal meals," she declaims. "My pastries win prizes around here!" Humbert asks for her phone number, framing a rejection. Out to the garden ("My flowers win prizes around here."), the Lolita theme comes up, a chorus of teasing, denying nymphets "naaa-naaing."

"Voilà!" A golden Lolita, in sunglasses and little else, stares at him coolly. Mrs. Haze gibbers on eagerly: "I offer you a comfortable home . . . a sunny garden . . . a congenial atmosphere . . . my cherry pie!"

Humbert stares, stumblingly agrees.

A fade to prolonged black. . . .

Screams! Frankenstein jerkily stalks the castle!

In the Haze car, Lolita, Humbert, and Charlotte have eyes front. Shot of knees: Mrs. Haze's right hand leaps atop Humbert's left. His right hand seizes Lolita's on her knee! Lolita's free hand covers Humbert's right! Humbert's left covers that! Mrs. Haze's is an unwanted topper. A nice visual metaphor for what's going on. . . .

Humbert and Charlotte play chess, Charlotte's eyes on him, Humbert's studying Lolita. "Well, g'night," she murmurs, and goes up. Humbert immediately checkmates Charlotte, and retires. . . .

Lolita, petulant in Levis, lustily hips her hula-hoop, while Humbert leers at her over the edge of the book he's reading. . . .

A 1950s high-school dance, all billowy white frocks, shiny teen-age faces, bright-eyed chaperones. Mrs. Haze introduces the Farlows, a fun couple. ("In fact, before marrying, John and I were both—broadminded.") Humbert skims from table to table, lurking behind the flower arrangements, spying on Lolita.

Charlotte sees Quilty, glib and self-possessed, swaying with a darkhaired, zombie-faced, young woman. She bleats: "Oh, hello, *hello, again!*"

He can't recall . . . "Don't you remember, that afternoon changed my whole life!"

Smugly: "Yeah, really great!" With enthusiasm: "Don't you have a daughter with a lovely name, a lovely lilting name? Yeah, that's right, diminutive of the tears and the roses, Lolita." He smiles ingenuously.

Lolita goes to a party at the Farlows, Humbert and Charlotte go home, where she changes to a provocative dress.

Mrs. Haze turns on Cuban music, and the air is full of irony and *double-entendre:* "Oh, Humbert . . . what say you I teach you some of the new steps?"

Humbert: "I don't even know the old ones!"

Charlotte in her low-cut gown pursues Humbert, hungrily. They cha-cha: "Very good, Humbert, a little more *joie de vivre!*

. . . in certain lights you look like Harold . . . I swore I'd never marry again!"

"One doesn't always find such loyalty these days!"

Passionately (and hilariously): "Take me in your arms! I can't live in the past!" She grabs for him.

A lazy, mocking, young female voice: "Hi!"

Charlotte, recovering quickly, clucks: "Darling, come back for something?"

"No, Mona's party turned out sorta a drag." Lolita sullently slumps in a chair. "I thought I'd see what you two were doing . . ."

"We had a wonderful evening, dear," Humbert chirps and races to make her a sandwich.

"Did you have a good time with Clare Quilty?" she asks Mrs. Haze. "The girls are crazy about him, too." After a querulous exchange, Lolita retires.

A harried Charlotte: *"That miserable brat . . .* her sneaking back here and spying on us. . . . She's always been a spiteful little beast . . ." Pathetically: "Is it my fault if I feel young? Why should my child resent it? Do you think I'm just a foolish American girl?"

"No . . ." But he won't go out for a ride, and wants to sleep. His door closes. Downstairs, Charlotte begins to sob.

A fade into prolonged black. . . .

Humbert writes: "The twofold nature of the nymphet: the mixture of tender, dreamy childishness and a kind of eerie vulgarity. I know it is bad to keep a diary, but it gives me a strange thrill to do so . . ."

Morning. Lolita dawdles over breakfast, her mother cranky from last night's frustrations: "We do not eat with our table on the elbows—*elbows on the table!"*

Lolita takes breakfast up to Humbert, languorous, in a loose sweater, leaning provocatively over his desk, noting the diary he's hiding.

Lolita drawls: "Afraid I'm gonna steal your ideas and sell 'em to Hollywood?"

Downstairs, Mrs. Haze has a surprise; she's shipping Lolita to camp! "Is something the matter with your face?" Next morning, a bleary Humbert watches the females load the station wagon. Lolita rushes up, her voice casual: "I guess I won't be seeing you again huh?" They clinch: "Don't forget me!" The sentimental piano theme comes up. Humbert throws himself on her bed, sobbing, surrounded by records, pennants, dropped clothes, a poster of Clare Quilty.

The maid gives the anguished man a letter, which he reads hoarsely: "This is a confession. I love you!" He snorts! ". . . You are the love of my life, and now will you please leave! Go, scram, *departez!*" Humbert laughs hysterically. "Your remaining would mean you're ready to link your life with mine! Dear one, pray for me!" The room is full of fiendish laughter. . . !

The newly wedded husband scribbles in his diary in the bathroom, his bulkily robed wife fussing querulously outside: "Dear, the door's locked . . . sweetheart, I don't want any secrets between us . . ."

"I haven't been in here long . . ."

Wailing: "Were there a lot of women in your life before me?" Miserably groaning off key: "Oooooh, I'm *lonesome* . . ." Resolutely: "I don't care about any other woman. I know that our love is sacred . . . the others were *profane!*"

Humbert comes out. Charlotte: "Oh, you arouse the pagan in me. . . ! Just touch me, and I go limp as a wet noodle." In the bedroom, she shows him Mr. Haze's small black pistol, whining unhappily: "This is a Sacred Weapon, a tragic treasure."

The two embrace on the bed. Mrs. Haze stares upward voluptuously: "I have a most ambitious fantasy . . . a real French servant girl . . ." Humbert looks over her shoulder at a framed portrait of Lolita on the night table, adoringly.

Upstairs, Humbert, his hairy legs sticking out of his threadbare dressing gown, sips whiskey, stares down the pistol's muzzle, opens the cylinder, lets the bullets drop out, contemplating murder: "She splashed in the tub, a clumsy, trusting seal—but what d'ya know, folks? I just couldn't make myself do it!"

In the bathroom, dressed, forehead wrinkled, Charlotte studies the diary. Humbert, in his most enchanting voice: "Please, please, please . . . no, no, no."

Charlotte hisses: "The Haze woman . . . the cow . . . the obnoxious mama . . . the brainless baba . . ." SCREAMING, "You're a monster . . . you're disgusting!" Wailing, gasping: "Get out of my way! I am leaving. But you are never going to see that miserable brat again!"

Charlotte stumbles into her room, talks drunkenly to the urn: "Harold, look what happened! I was disloyal to you . . . I couldn't help it, seven years is a very long time!" Screaming: "Why did you have to die on me!" Crying: "Next time it'll be someone you'd be proud of!"

Humbert stumbles around, making a pitcher-sized drink and yelling explanations. The phone rings. He cries: "There's a man on the phone who says you've been hit by a car . . ." Thunder is heard.

Piano theme music up.

Humbert slumps in the bathtub, mostly drunk, his problems solved. The Farlows anxiously come up the stairs, spotting the pistol: "You musn't think of doing anything rash!"

Blearily, Humbert agrees.

The next visitor is the driver's father. "It was the pedestrian's fault," he instantly, tactlessly announces.

"Absolutely . . . I have no quarrel with you," the European tells him gently.

"I must say you're wonderfully sympathetic . . . maybe you'll allow me to pay for the funeral expenses."

The teasing, adolescent Lolita theme mingles with Charlotte's sexy cha-cha as Humbert drives the station wagon into Camp Climax for girls. Charlie, the only boy at the camp, summons the packed Lolita.

"It's your mother," Humbert soothes. They'll visit her at the hospital.

"I haven't missed you . . . in fact I've been revoltingly unfaithful to you," Lolita pouts. "But it doesn't matter, because you've stopped caring. . . ."

Humbert kisses her, starts talking smoothly . . .

At a big country hotel, the sardonic Quilty and his zombie girl friend are kidding with the night clerk, Mr. Swine. "She's a yellow belt and I'm a green belt," Quilty tells him. "She gets me in a sweeping ankle throw—I lay there in pain but I love it, it's really the greatest." The two retreat and Humbert comes in, observing him from behind the comics.

"Wow! This is swank!" Lolita bubbles at the desk. The clerk fusses, they'll have to settle for a single and a cot—there's overflow from next door. He points to an ominous banner: "State Police Convention."

Lolita retires; Humbert wanders through the hotel onto a terrace. A very nervous, shy, fresh-faced Quilty quavers out a hello. Humbert asks if he's with anyone.

"Heh-heh, *I'm not with anybody, I'm with you,*" Quilty stabs, then immediately contrite: "I meant, heh-heh, I was with the State Police, but right now I'm on my own . . ."

Pleading, in jittery very flat fast speech, yet energetic and somehow threatening: "No, you don't have to leave at all . . . I get the impression you'd want to leave but you don't like to leave because you think you look suspicious and I'm a policeman, heh-heh. You don't have to think that because I haven't really got a suspicious mind at all. I'm not suspicious, but other people think I'm suspicious, especially when I stand around on street corners. One of my boys picked me up the other week, he thought I was too suspicious!"

Still pleading, jittery, flat, fast, energetic, menacing, the next moments are an ambiguity breakthrough; they could mean Quilty is almost anything—policeman, nymphetophile, homosexual, sharp citizen, anything: "I couldn't help *noticing* when you checked in tonight, it's part of my job, I noticed you were an *individual,* and I noticed your face, and I said to myself when I saw you . . . that's a guy with the most *normal* face in my life . . . 'cause I'm a *normal* guy, it'd be great for two *normal* guys like us to get together and talk about *world events,* y'know, in a *normal* sort of way . . . let me say one other thing, I noticed you had a lovely *little girl* with you, as a matter of fact she was taller than little, *lovely sweet* girl . . . your daughter? I figured you might want to get away from your wife, if I was married I'd take every opportunity to get away from my wife."

Humbert tells him Charlotte was in an accident.

"That's really terrible, a normal guy's wife having an accident, is she coming on later?"

Humbert nods, Quilty stabs: *"How, in an ambulance?* Heh-heh-heh, I'm sorry, I just got carried away there. . . ."

Quilty waxes enthusiastic: "I'm friends with Mr. Swine, I can help you. I could move one of the troopers out, give you and your daughter a *lovely little bridal suite . . ."*

Humbert goes back upstairs; comically clumsy, he and a black bus boy set up the cot. Kubrick's camera lingers on Lolita's lovely face and hair, spread across the pillow in the moonlight. Humbert tries to crawl in. . . .

Lolita wakes first, hissing rapidly into his ear: "Wake up, Humbert, the hotel's on fire! Get out of that bed real quick!"

Happily alone, they compare skin colors, Lolita shows how her thumb can reach back to touch her wrist. She suggests they play a game: "I learned a lot of games . . . in camp," she tells him coyly. "I played it with Charlie . . . you sure you can't guess. . . ?"

Humbert's lament: "I'm not a good guesser."

Lolita, smiling, whispers it to him. Kubrick close-ups his excited, delighted face . . . Lolita giggles.

Later, the station wagon rolls on. "Hey, let's tell mother," Lolita announces.

"No, I don't think that'd be very funny." But Lolita wants to call her mother anyway.

"You can't . . . because . . . your mother's dead!"

Lolita bursts out laughing and giggling. When she catches her breath: "C'mon, cut it out! Why can't I call her?"

"Your mother is dead."

Lolita bursts out again, crying and sniffling endlessly. Finally she adds, with spectacular unconscious irony: "Everything is *changed* all of a sudden. Everything was so *normal. . . ."*

"Promise me something," she asks Humbert desperately, still weeping. "Promise you'll never leave me . . . I don't want to be in one of those horrible places for juvenile delinquents . . . I'd rather be with you. . . . You're a *lot* better than one of those places."

Six months later, at Beardsley, it doesn't look that way. Humbert suavely rants and raves at Lolita for staying at school late to watch a football game: "I thought we understood, no dates!"

"It wasn't!" "It was!" "It wasn't!"

"I want you to be proud of me," Lolita assuages. "They want me for the lead in the school play; a few school people and Clare Quilty."

"Out of the question!"

Scornfully she rails at him: "You don't love me. You're driving me *crazy*. You just want to keep me locked up with you in this filthy house. . . . "

That evening, Lolita's stepfather enters and switches on the lights.

"Good evening, Dr. Humbert," hisses a smooth, Dracula-like voice. In the living room is a man in suit and vest, with heavy glasses and mustache, thick hair, and a German accent. He calls himself Dr. Zemsh, the Beardsley High School psychologist, he tells Humbert, sitting in the dark to save electricity.

"Dr. Humbert, do you mind if I am putting to you a blunt qvestion? . . . We are vundering if, ah, anyvun instructed Lolita in the vacts of life . . . to those little boys at Beardsley High, she is mit the sving and her chest she has got their temperatures up, she gets a lot of notice. . . . "

Facing each other in the living room, Dr. Zemsh sketches the profile of a normal girl adolescent: "She sighs a gud deal in class, starts making zounds ah-UHHHHHH!" And concludes: "She is suffering from acute repression of the libido of her natural instincts."

Dr. Zemsh threatens a full psychological investigation: "*Vee Amerikans* (!) believe it's important to prepare for the majority successvul mating of the satisvactory children!" At last he thinks of a way to let Humbert off the hook: "You, Dr. Hombard, zhould devinitely unveto that girl's *partizipazion* in the school play!"

Backstage. Excited faces, blaring lights. Lolita, decked out as a fairy princess, smiles covertly at the ubiquitous Quilty before going on. "To the dark kingdom with him. Away, away," she annunciates in a high voice. She's been skipping her piano lessons, and Humbert drags her, sulking, from the cast party. . . .

Humbert drags Lolita, kicking, yelling, still in costume and make-up, into the house. "You've got a big fat nerve, you creep!" she cries, breathing hard.

"Shut up, Lolita!" To himself: "All these people bumping their noses into our business—*stop doing that!*" Suddenly: "We're going to leave this place . . . a wonderful trip around the country . . . get back to the way we were before."

"No! I HATE YOU! I HATE YOU!" Breathing hard: "Why don't you leave me alone!"

A neighbor rings, Lolita flees. . . .

Humbert finds her hanging up in a phone booth, contrite and apologetic: "I *want* to leave school . . . everything's going to be *great* . . . we can go for a long trip . . ." They wander off: "Oh, yes, my darling. . . ."

Humbert asks for time off for a "Hollywood engagement"—he's involved in a film about existentialism. The car climbs a turnpiked hill, Lolita holding his arm, smiling contentedly.

Humbert, to ominous music: "I cannot tell you when I first knew with utter certainty that a strange car was following us. Queer how I misinterpreted the designation of doom."

Humbert, in black shirt and trousers, drives into barren Western hills, the car swaying and careening upward. Beside him, Lolita squeals: "You want to get us killed? What's the big fat hurry?"

BANG! A tire blows, the car skews and stops. Lolita shrieks giddily. The car stops one hundred feet away.

Humbert, his voice odd: "The police wouldn't stop way back there . . . maybe he's some special kind of police . . . who're just supposed to . . . follow people."

Lolita, with relish: "Maybe it's the vice squad!"

While they gabble, the car U-turns and leaves.

Humbert decides he doesn't feel well. Lolita: "*Oh, shut up!* I feel pretty lousy myself." Lolita bets she's getting the Asiatic flu. . . .

Humbert, sweating, flushed, visits a convalescent Lolita in the hospital. He finds a suspicious note—it's from the nurse's boyfriend. Lolita, exasperated: "Do you have to *antagonize* everybody!" Sympathetically: "What's the matter, you look kinda slimy. . . ." A vexed nurse insists the trembling Humbert move his car from the doctor's parking lot: A discovery—"Since when do nurses wear dark glasses on duty?" "Mr. Humbert, please move your car!"

Humbert in bed in a narrow dark room, tossing, sweating, bleary under a fat bolster. An intimidating flat voice on the phone: "Is this Professor Humbert? Just wondering how you're enjoying your stay in our lovely little town?"

Choking, annoyed: "Who is this?"

"It's an unremarkable name . . . my department is sorta concerned about the bizarre rumors about you and that lovely, remarkable girl . . . you're classified in our files as a white widowed male. I wonder if you'd be prepared to give us a report of your current sex life, if any. . . !"

A whirlwind of frantic music. The predawn hospital, nightlights glowing, stands amid the parking lots. Humbert, sweating, coughing, agitated, bursts into reception: "Where's Miss Haze?" This entire scene is flat, grainy, dimly lit—an overtired, came-the-dawn cinematography.

The nurse says he'll have to speak to Dr. Keygee. A little alarmed: "Calling Dr. Keygee!"

Dr. Keygee is a tall, balding, confident Western doctor in rimless glasses and flapping whites: "How long have you had *that* cough?"

The nurse reads off that Miss Haze was discharged at eight-fifteen. Humbert, hysterical ("WHERE IS SHE? LET GO!"), tries to fight his way into the sickrooms.

Keygee grapples with him in the long corridor of private rooms in the half-light. Keygee: "What d'ya think you're doing!" Out leap two husky attendants. The attendants throw Humbert flat while he shouts, struggles. Grunting, they subdue him; a clumsy, slithering pile-up on the linoleum; Keygee, crisply: "Smitty, get a straitjacket!" Humbert writhes, kicks furiously. Nurse, ready to lock Humbert up: "This man must be a psychotic!"

Humbert stops, or is stopped, his eyes terrified. He probes cautiously: "Miss Haze left in the care of her uncle? That's a strange thing to forget!" The black attendant gives Humbert an out: "He's drunk, thaz whats da matter wid him!" Humbert, chirping desperately: "Yes, that's right, I've been drinking much too much, I have personal problems!" He breathes heavily as a flashlight beam jabs his eye in the dim, gritty corridor. "Want some black coffee? . . . See that he gets home all right. . . ."

Humbert, forlornly, hopelessly: "She didn't by any chance leave any message . . . ?"

Slow dissolve to dark screen, melancholy piano theme up . . .

Close-up of typewriter keys cautiously pecking, a canny tension device (one word at a time), as well as giving facts and character quickly:

Dear Dad,
How . . . is . . . everything? . . . I . . . have [and so forth] gone through much sadness and hardship. I'm married. I'm going to have a baby. I'm going nuts because we don't have enough to pay our debts and get out of here. Please send us a check.

Nervous trumpets toot his way. An industrial city. Shabby, lower-class frame houses on an overcast day. On a dead end, Humbert parks before a two-story frame house, puts the Sacred Weapon in his mouton coat, marches in the gate. The same slow, breathy, teasing voice: "Wow, gee, what a surprise!"

Shock! Lolita is now a shiny-faced matron with an upswept hairdo, black harlequin glasses, no make-up, her baby bulging, in a maternity smock. She admits the handsome, urbane Humbert to her sloppy, lower-class kitchen. Through a window, two young men in leather jackets are building something. Lolita offers a chair, coffee, a drink? With matronly dignity: "Oh, you'll have to excuse my appearance, you caught me on ironing day." Having the advantage: "I wouldn't blame you for being sore . . . me dropping out of sight for so long, then writing for a handout."

Husband Dick thinks Humbert's only her stepfather. The step-father-plus wants the man who took her from the hospital.

Lolita, all mother-knows-best bray: "Oh, there's *no point* in going into *that!* It's *all over!*"

They bicker a final time. Tightly, Humbert says: "If you're a sensible girl, if you want what I've come to give you, you'll tell me—"

Lolita takes a deep breath: "You remember Dr. Zemsh? That car that followed us around? Mother's old flame at the school dance? That guy you talked to at the hotel? And that guy that called you at the motel?"

Humbert's lament, impatient: "I'm no good at guessing."

In a patient, reproving voice: "It was *Clare Quilty*—all of them, of course!"

In a dreamy rush: "I'd had a crush on him ever since he used to visit mother. He wasn't like you and me, he wasn't a normal person. (!) He was a genius! He had a kind of a beautiful . . . oriental . . . Japanese philosophy. . . ."

Humbert, hard-eyed: "He spotted us at the hotel, and followed for the sheer fun of tormenting me?"

Ignoring him: "I guess he was the only guy I was ever really crazy about," Lolita swoons to herself. "Dick's very sweet—but it's just not the same . . .

"He took me to a dude ranch," Lolita goes on, a soft-voiced, soft-eyed cynic. "He had a bunch of weird friends staying there: painters, writers, nudists, weight lifters. But I figured I could take anything for a couple of weeks because I loved him. . . . He promised to get me a studio contract, but it never turned out that way, and instead he wanted me to, uh, to cooperate with the others in making some kind of art movie. . . ." Spitefully, biting each word: "*No, I didn't do it*—so he kicked me out. . . ."

Husband Dick comes in, a lanky innocent in work clothes, a hearing aid, a twanging Western accent: "This is a *grand* surprise! You can stay upstairs; we sleep down here 'cause Lo' likes to watch teevee." The boy sits on the couch, one leg up. Smiling, her eyes admonishing behind the ludicrous glasses, Lolita leans against Dick, legs propped along the couch beside his, baby bulging grossly against the smock—a bizarre portrait of crummy bliss.

Lolita, showing the whip hand: "*He can't stay, Dick!*"

"That's a shame!" Dick rambles politely about some vaguely marvelous Alaskan job opportunities. . . . "Lo'll make a swell mother, nuts about dogs and kids!" He goes outside again.

"Dick's awful sweet!"

Humbert turns to the girl, his voice husky, agitated, as the sentimental theme rises: "Lolita, life is very short. Between here and that old car is twenty-five paces. Come, now, just the two of us!"

Lolita, blandly cynical: "Oh, you'll give us something if I'll go to a hotel."

Humbert, husky-voiced, desperate: "*No,* you've got it all wrong! I want you to leave your husband and this awful house and live with me and die with me and *everything* with me!"

"You must be *crazy!*"

Desperate, pleading: "I've never been less crazy in my life. We'll start fresh, we can forget everything. . . . It's *not* too late! I've waited three years already, I think I could wait for the rest of my life—"

Lolita sees he means it. Hushed, staring, half to herself: "I'm going to have his baby in three months! I've wrecked too many things in my life, I can't do that to him, he *needs* me. . . ."

Humbert, finally, sobs openly.

Lolita, comforting softly: "Oh, c'mon now, don't make a scene."

In a muffled voice, sobs breaking, he gives her the financial details.

"Thirteen thousand dollars—wow!" With pleased concern: "Oh, c'mon now, don't cry . . . I'm sorry, try to understand." Slowly, passing judgment: "I'm sorry that I cheated so much. . . . But I guess that's just the way things are. . . ."

Humbert jumps up, runs clumsily out. Lolita calls from the door: "Hey, let's keep in touch . . . I'll write you . . ."

The sentimental piano theme comes up, dominates, as Humbert drives off headlong . . . lowers as his station wagon rushes down a country turnpike, and he picks his way through the same marbled statues, sheeted furniture, harp. Again he runs his fingers along the strings. "Quilty? . . . Quilty!" The theme shimmers, grows around him as he moves forward . . . it cascades through the great cluttered empty hall.

A title: "Humbert Humbert died in prison of coronary thrombosis while awaiting trial for the murder of Clare Quilty."

Lolita had a very poor critical reception. Reviewers complained that Kubrick had censored the film down to nothing, along with substituting a well-built, fetchingly vulgar teen-ager for the dark "demoniacal" nymphet of the novel, with her "elusive, shifty, soul-shattering charm." Humbert is no longer an obsessed erudite madman driven by a fierce passion, but a bumbling professor looking for teen sex. Still others lamented the loss of Nabokov's devilish satire of roadside America.

These 1960 comments seem irrelevant now. Kubrick's use of visual metaphors and *double-entendre* to handle the film's eroticism can now be appreciated, especially as a witty alternate to today's obligatory tumblings, lubricities, and assorted inarticulate cries. Frances Russell's comment was probably accurate as well as prophetic: "I expect it would take 16mm stag films imported from Mexico to satisfy the expectant queues. Maybe we'll get them in another ten years. . . ."

Lolita's change from dark child-woman to sullen, perverse, high-school girl does make *Lolita* the film different, less upsettingly bizarre, than *Lolita* the novel, but this is a weak complaint. Realistically, who'd have paid for a film that couldn't be shown, and aesthetically, why not have allowed Nabokov to treat another, more social if less shockingly pathological theme: the American preadolescent vamp who means it. Pauline Kael points out that Kubrick has been accurate: "Have the reviewers looked at the schoolgirls of America lately? The classmates of my fourteen-year-old daughter are not merely nubile: some of them look badly used."5 Likewise, the loss of the highway grotesques is made up for by new material. One could also work out an argument about the fragmented, impressionistic descriptions being more suitable to a novelist's swift word play than the avid, prying, remorseless Kubrick camera.

The more astute critics had mixed feelings about *Lolita*. Arlene Croce in *Sight and Sound* found Kubrick's directorial style "dry, calculated, and neutrally sinister," like a Carol Reed thriller. "It ripples along cleverly unloading mannerisms: the dead pan (in both senses) objectivity, the deliberate diversion, the swallowed punchlines, the laugh that comes after the fade. It commands two passages of great atmospheric proficiency: the death of Charlotte, and the hospital sequence."3 But Croce feels that what could have been the sharpest scenes—the girls' camp and the night at the first hotel—are somehow wrong, tentative, and enfeebled. Andrew Sarris felt Kubrick's direction lacked Nabokov's delirious approach: "We are never shown the inspired gestures and movements, which transform the most emotionally impoverished nymphet into a creature of fantasy and desire."10

Croce believes the most grotesque aspects of Humbert's passion come off the best: "A cut-in from a Frankenstein movie produces a momentary blazing effect, and the best shot in the film: Humbert in a sweat of panic, while Lolita, wearing a greasepaint getup that makes her look like Jean Harlow as imaged by Audrey Beardsley, sits surreptitiously blowing bubblegum under his very nose."[3] Croce finds this scene terribly right because, as in a Carol Reed thriller, the blank moment takes on an enigmatic ambiance—is she teasing him? Ridiculing him? Testing him somehow? But in a moment the tension fades out of a trivial detail.

Croce goes on to spot a great many well-modulated subtleties: "the exhilarating burlesque of suburban other-directedness is never so broad. Charlotte's exquisitely couched letter of dismissal ["Go! Scram! *Departez!*"] seems incongruous . . . [Humbert's] grim levity, sense of imposture, callousness and howling pain . . . an affective life which the other characters in the film never see."

Interestingly, Croce, discounts what Pauline Kael, in her penetrating review, calls the brilliant heart of the film—Quilty as Humbert's walking paranoia. "Peter Sellers domineers in a series of Guest Star turns without pith or purpose," she comments. Kael would disagree.

Pauline Kael's review of *Lolita* is one of her best—inspired, incisive, exuberant. To her, Quilty is the film's dynamo: "Excitement is sustained by a brilliant idea, a new variant on the classic chase—Quilty as Humbert's walking paranoia, the madness that chased Humbert and is chased by him . . . Quilty, the genius, the man whom Lolita loves, Humbert's brother and tormentor and parodist. . . . 'Are you with someone?' Humbert asks the policeman, and Quilty the policeman replies: 'I'm not with someone, I'm with you!' "[5]

For Kael, Quilty is a character with a merciless talent for impersonations, and the terrors he perpetrates Humbert has coming —not for sleeping with a minor, but for his own obsequious, mealy-minded mask. "Humbert is a worm and Quilty knows it." His thought-police phone call, his intimidating impersonations, his ominous just-out-of-reach pursuit, and his final escape with Lolita are black slapstick, carrying the action forward and commenting on it: "A crazy quilt of psychological, sociological commentary so 'hip' it's surrealistic."[5]

Kael sees Peter Sellers using his lumbering, wide-hipped body to portray perfectly the soft, smug, sly, self-effacing middle-aged man: "His facial muscles are kept flaccid, so he always looks weary, too tired for much physical response. The rather frightening strength of his Quilty (who has enormous—almost sinister reserves of energy) is peculiarly effective just because of his ordinary 'normal' look—he makes unattractiveness magnetic."

For Kael, Humbert is Quilty's foil, making attractiveness tired, exhausted, impotent—his absurd suffering turns him into the perfect comic loser: "His handsome face gloats in a rotting smile." The distant, too tasteful cinematography is wrong for the phantasmagorical chase, and she brilliantly suggests the use of stylized sets to intensify the madness. The faults she finds are all sound: slackness of pace, a false, humiliating attempt to "explain" the plot, clumsy editing, clumsy structuring—after the first hour, all the scenes seem to go on too long, others seem left out, others stuck in pointlessly.

Kael's critique is full of conviction and a pleasure to read, but like some of James Agee's work, it is really a rewriting of the picture on the screen into a more delightful, sharper, more unified film whose elements mostly aren't there.

Her starting point is good. Quilty's first harassment, as the wildly ambiguous, menacing policeman, is truly upsetting—like listening to a panel of psychiatrists nervously explaining how your casual behavior and thoughts prove you should be committed. One can't believe how much they know, what danger they represent—the world splinters into horror and helplessness. But even here, Humbert is not visibly frightened; he gets away from Quilty and finally sleeps with Lolita.

After that, Quilty's effectiveness is spotty. The interview with the transplanted Dr. Zemsh (*Ve Amerikans* indeed!) is much milder—the German psychologist is a familiar caricature, amusing because of his accent and his jumbled-in-translation description of the pubescent female. His threat of an investigation doesn't really come across. Tension is built again with the trailing car, upsetting the sick, distraught, deranged Humbert. But despite Lolita's jabs, he remains calm; Quilty cannot follow up, the threat fades out. The "sex police" phone call to a feverish Humbert sounds off-key, but it sends him running for Lolita.

In the grim corridors of the hospital Humbert's worst nightmares come true in the powerful, terrifying shots of him hysterical and pinned to the floor by doctors and attendants, while someone is sent for a straitjacket. A nurse announces with furious pleasure "This man must be a psychotic!" climaxing Quilty's final, cruelest joke. After a few moments more of writhing, followed by the guile of desperation, Humbert is allowed to limp away . . . alone.

But this sequence doesn't show either "Humbert's walking paranoia" or that Humbert had it coming. There are no scenes at all of Humbert's hypocrisy, timidity, cowardice. Humbert is not afraid, but obsessed—society, Quilty, Charlotte, everybody— they're all just *in the way*. Before going off, Humbert tells Lolita he wants only for things to be as they were at first, when the two lovers were (supposedly) in a world of their own. He doesn't care what anybody thinks, except that they'll put him in jail. He's duplicitous to Charlotte, but not to hurt her, only to stay close to Lolita. Humbert is bizarre, disturbed, and romantic, but not contemptible. He doesn't have anything "coming" to him, and his humiliation is not funny, even as black slapstick. Few viewers laugh at him, even today. Perhaps a case could be made against him for the insecure, overbearing way he handles Lolita, but she gets worse from Quilty, and on her own.

The notion of Quilty as "Humbert's walking paranoia," a comic embodiment of his neurotic fears, also does not stand up. Again, the key is the character. Quilty is introduced in the shabby mansion as a drunk, dissolute, smug, silly, glib weakling, and there's nothing in the movie to change this impression. He patronizes Charlotte, kids meaninglessly with Mr. Swine, is speechless with his zombie girlfriend. The totality of his relationship with Lolita that we see is one wink during the play performance, and the exploitative and sordid story she relates at the end of the film. Lolita, Charlotte, Humbert were all played for suckers by the sneaky hack TV writer—is this the "crazy quilt of psychological, sociological commentary so 'hip' it's surrealistic"? As for his "almost sinister reserves of energy," the most energetic thing Quilty does is to hit a few ping-pong balls. Despite being a wicked mime and manic schemer, Quilty is far from an unstoppable laughable Fury of Retribution . . . the impression is more a slightly shabby, glib, weak seducer and casual sadist, with grubby motives of his own.

As it stands, *Lolita* is probably the biggest creative watershed in Kubrick's career. The light, long, complex social satire was his first real film outside the thriller and combat genres. For the first time he had to maintain dramatic tension in a less than life-or-death crisis, handle touchy tricky subjects (sex, madness), collaborate with a prestigious novelist, work against a topical, controversial subject. The skills assimilated are later displayed in *Dr. Strangelove,* and, to lesser extent, *2001: A Space Odyssey.*

As Kael suggests, the *Lolita* script suffers from several structural problems. The slow pacing discourages the impatient or demanding viewer throughout. The murder scene, while setting up a puzzle, fails to make either Quilty or Humbert sympathetic or exciting. The first hour of suburban satire, with no connections to the shooting, further blunts the hook. Humbert's failure even to seduce Lolita also diminishes interest. The film, though sprightly, seems to be going nowhere. Some hints about Quilty are dropped, but they are too diffuse to mean much.

Suddenly, with little preparation, Humbert marries Charlotte, she's killed, and Humbert gets Lolita without showing any flesh, ending the sex interest. The movie jumps into a whole new story, the sly, unsympathetic Quilty's persecution of Humbert, vaguely motivating the murder. After Dr. Zemsh's interview, we can figure out he and Lolita are in cahoots, specifically motivating the murder. Anyone who stays this long probably won't leave.

There are two more sorts of structural problems. First, motivations are nearly always hidden—probably because of censorship problems. It's never shown how Humbert keeps Lolita under control after she hates him—in the book, with the threat of a public home. Lolita's feelings for Humbert are always vague, and nothing is revealed of Quilty's motives, until Lolita's all-embracing revelations. This makes it difficult to get excited about the characters, who are always doing things from hidden motives, or no motives at all.

The last structural problem has to do with Lolita's final revelation to Humbert. This does a number of good things: It makes clear a lot of the action, even parts not explained directly, like the desperate phone call and mood reversal after the play. It further clarifies Quilty's character (confirming the shabby last moments of the murder). Last, it illuminates, far too late, Lolita's own character, and so makes her sympathetic, an impassioned lover-monster like Humbert, who gets treated just as badly, but survives and manages to make a life. It's a fault of *Lolita* that the last two ideas aren't even hinted at earlier.

Kael feels this revelation is "humiliating," since it destroys the exciting surrealistic slow-motion explosion of Humbert's psychosis. Again, with major revisions, it could be dropped, but except for Charlotte's role, it is one of the few parts of the film that makes anyone sympathetic or even comprehensible. Except for it, *Lolita* would tend toward a sort of cheap "erotic espionage" thriller, with a dopey 007-Humbert tediously, endlessly, and ever more monstrously tortured.

The Humbert character is in many ways a likely source of dissatisfaction with *Lolita*. The book is written from his point of view, a 300-page cascading fireworks of prose. The reader is literally *inside* Humbert's burning, on-the-edge-of-madness mind, delighting in his wicked masquerade. In contrast, James Mason underplays his role, making Humbert always desperate and often pathetic, despite his urbane voice and unshakable smile. Humbert becomes an aloof weakling with whom identification is difficult. He is no longer the protean deceiver: "I'm no good at games or guessing," he keeps repeating. Without major revisions in the role, a delirious directorial style, as Sarris suggests, or Kael's stylized sets, would probably have made him even more a cypher.

The symmetric characters—like right- and left-hand gloves—Quilty and Humbert are a new level of sophistication for Kubrick. Both are part-time criminals and part-time artists (see opening quote in Chapter 7); Quilty is an ambitious hack TV writer, Humbert an amateur poet. Both sleep with Mrs. Haze without any affection as a fast way to get to her daughter. Both reject the social world, the world of appearances. Both are driven, impassioned men. Their differences are equally great. Basically, Humbert is always thoughtful and considerate beyond his obsession, while Quilty is such a master of fantasy, masks, and deceptions that nothing matters to him. This is most obvious in the very first scene in the old mansion. Humbert wants Quilty to know why he is dying, what is happening to him—a very romantic gesture.

But Quilty is so muddled in his jokes and games and tricks he can barely keep his mind on the pistol pointed at him. Even under stress, as when Quilty ominously follows him, Humbert, desperate, sick, and frightened, bumbles through with grace. The two brief glimpses of Quilty's real life, however, are a dark welter of drunkenness, insults, spite, and petty Bohemian degeneracy (e.g., the "art" movie crowd, attendance at executions for kicks). Even Quilty's magnificent intimidating policeman monologue, while having frightening power, can be seen as a simple, cynical, two-level construct: nervous skippings and sly hoppings of exaggerated timidity around the bush, interspaced with vicious, jabbing sarcasms (e.g., "I'm not with anybody, I'm with you!").

Sue Lyon's Lolita is less fascinating, pathologically anyway, than the novel's daemonic child-woman, but the real problems with the role are elsewhere. First, the film does not create its own appropriate erotic atmosphere—the giggling, humid, covert flavor of high-school sexiness. Bubblegum and talk of dates are not enough. Second, if the revelation at the end is accepted, Lolita seems too languid and simpleminded for the already accomplished lover of, and conspirator with, Quilty. For nearly the whole film she's childish and opaque, so that that last speech makes her too devious and impassioned to be consistent. She's never right. It's too bad in a way that Kubrick didn't explore the full implications of Lolita's constant duplicity—he might have come up with a funny, much more insightful version of *Breathless,* with its romantic hero and hollow, semi-psychopathic seductress.

The greatest advance for Kubrick in *Lolita* is his mastery of comedy beyond the humor of the gallows (or firing squad). *Lolita* uses three main comic techniques: inappropriate (and often ironic) responses, light social satire, and the comedy of sexual obsession and confusion.

The inappropriate response, a special form of grotesque irony, is the basis of the film: Humbert does not want adult sex, he wants to go to bed with little girls. The whole film is punctuated with such disquieting, but often exuberant wrong answers. At the beginning, of course, Quilty responds to the threat of death with an invitation to play ping-pong, jokes, absurd bravado ("I want to die like a champion!"), a piano recital, and finally childlike disbelief.

These response errors become smaller but wittier in the first, satirical half, but beginning around Charlotte's terrible discovery ("Harold, look what happened!"), they become more and more monstrous. After Charlotte's death, for example, Humbert reclines delightedly in his bath, while his friends surround and desperately console him. Quilty's policeman monologue is a special case, a nervous, apparently normal man whose apologetic small talk is full of unconscious threats and ironies. The next morning, the innocent young Lolita is the one to seduce urbane Humbert Humbert. A little later, learning of the death of her mother, she bursts out laughing. Much, much later, when a car seems to be following them, the guilty Humbert thinks it's the sex police. Most ironically, when Humbert shows hysterical (but justified) concern for his vanished daughter at the hospital, they almost put him into a straitjacket for it! Near the end, Humbert cries as he counts out the money to Lolita, though of course he's crying over losing her. Finally, he kills Quilty partly for running off and abandoning Lolita, something that in a gentler guise, he would have done eventually himself. (He also kills him for "taking advantage of my disadvantage.")

The second form of humor is light social satire, embodied in the avid, suburban widow Charlotte Haze. She is a satire on nearly every aspect of middle-class pomposity and absurdity: blind culture worship ("Mr. Quilty lectured my club on Dr. Schweitzer and Dr. Zhivago."); parent-child competition ("Is it my fault if I feel young? Why should my child resent it?"); sexual hypocrisy ("I swore I'd never marry again! Take me in your arms!"); elegant homemaking ("Excuse the soiled sock!"); materialism and possessiveness ("Those are Harold's ashes! . . . I have an ambitious fantasy—a French servant girl"). Most critics applauded Kubrick's new skill: Charlotte is funny but her misery and sincerity are genuine; she is never a figure of scorn. In addition, there's the smug Farlow couple ("Before marrying, John and I were both—broadminded"—a joke on what they'd think of Humbert if they knew); and the ridiculous child psychologist Dr. Zemsh ("It's important to prepare for the majority successful mating of the satisfactory children!").

Third, there are the jokes about sex. These are often witty

metaphors and *double-entendres:* Humbert's reason for staying ("Your cherry pie!"); Charlotte's provocative cha-cha ("Let me teach you the newest steps!"); Lolita's hints of her own readiness ("I learned a new game with Charlie, the only boy at the camp!"); a raving Frankenstein symbolizing Humbert's lust. Sometimes they hint at the perverse: Quilty on vacation ("She throws me around all night—I lie there but I love it!"); Lolita at the dude ranch ("a bunch of weird friends . . . he wanted me to cooperate in making some kind of art movie"). Humbert's secret writing in the bathroom, Charlotte's exaggerated widow's itch for a mate, and Humbert's endless frustration are also sexy-funny.

There are, of course, many other sources of laughter throughout the film, among them the funny names (Camp Climax, Dr. Zemsh, Dr. Keygee, the puns on Humbert), the Peter Sellers' caricatures, the absurdly sentimental music.

Finally, Kubrick's characteristic themes appear in full force. It is interesting to trace how they become strengthened and transformed from book to film, and I leave it as an exercise for the reader.

Imaginary worlds. Humbert wants a dream world which he can never have, in which he and Lolita will live and love (making the film a tragedy by Kubrick's definition). Quilty is a creator and juggler of imaginary worlds, but seems to hate and shun the real one. Charlotte has chosen a rigid little world, accommodates everything to it, and cannot see beyond it.

Errors of emotions, futility of intelligence. Humbert's own emotional obsession is always frustrating and degrading, eventually condemning him to emptiness and death. The sly, scheming Lolita is emotionally enslaved as well. Finally, all Quilty's quick intelligence and game-playing skill fails to save him in the end.

Journey to freedom. Sitting around the Haze house, Humbert gets nowhere. The first two car journeys are flights toward some impossible blissful life with his nymphet. Again, at the end, he travels toward her, hoping to reclaim his old bliss. But he only learns the truth, and, his eyes clear, he does the only thing he can, settles his accounts with Quilty.

Triumph of the obsessional, dedicated hero. Since he will always love Lolita and can never have her, the always considerate Humbert gives her the money she needs and leaves her forever. He goes off alone to destroy Quilty "for taking advantage of his disadvantage." His eyes open and his private tormentor known at last, Humbert is a true obsessional Kubrick hero.

Homicide-suicides. Quilty, who jabs and scares and tricks Humbert, perhaps hoping to really drive him insane, then leaves his tracks to be spotted, is a destructive-self-destructive figure. It's clear that with his endless provocative teasing, he's bound to get "what's coming to *him*" sooner or later. Humbert's obsession makes him vulnerable, but with Lolita gone, he too now has nothing to lose, and his retribution isn't tentative or sadistic, but direct and final.

With Humbert and Quilty, Kubrick's suicide-homicide pairings begin an interesting metamorphosis. First, they have less and less to do with any ordinary rules of justice, morality, or social living. Second, they grow more and more transcendent. Colonel Dax and General Mireau fought over the executions of three men merely to soothe the General's vanity, an injustice. The struggle between Humbert and Quilty is purer, one between contrasting instinctive drives. Their corruption takes the form of pointless destructive social games. In the resolutions of *Dr. Strangelove* and *2001: A Space Odyssey,* the metaphysical stakes grow even higher. . . .

The results of Kubrick's satisfaction and success with *Lolita* are apparent in many aspects of these later works—a return to the prominent use of madmen and insanity; a new confidence about the use of sexuality—not so much directly, but by *double-entendre,* visual metaphor, implication, and often of a bizarre or perverse nature; the use of fleshed-out social, ethnic, and political types and caricatures; and finally, the use of an actor in multiple roles for comic or thematic effects.

8

Dr. Strangelove, or
How I Learned to Stop
Worrying and Love the Bomb

The real image doesn't cut the mustard, doesn't transcend. I'm now interested in taking a story, fantastic and improbable, and trying to get to the bottom of it, to make it seem not only real, but inevitable.
—*Stanley Kubrick, 1964*[9]

KUBRICK HAD BEEN interested in the problems of the nuclear arms race for six years before starting *Dr. Strangelove,* including reading over seventy books on the subject of nuclear combat and control, and subscribing to *Aviation Week* and the *Bulletin of the Atomic Scientists.* When he read Peter Bryant's novel *Red Alert (Tho Hours to Doom* in England), he thought he'd found the basis for a serious film about accidental war, and purchased the screen rights. But working on the treatment, the director discovered the best ideas which occurred to him too ludicrous and amusing: "How the hell could the President ever tell the Russian Premier to shoot down American planes?" he later asked, with a broad wave. "Good Lord, it sounds ridiculous."[9] In spite of this, his absurd, silly ideas seemed to be the most truthful, in view of the real problem: "After all, what could be more absurd than the very idea of two megapowers willing to wipe out all human life because of an accident, spiced up by political differences that will seem as meaningless to people a hundred years from now as the theological conflicts of the Middle Ages appear to us today?"[5]

In the end, Kubrick wrote the story as a nightmare comedy, using the lethal paradoxes of accidental war as the big jokes. He saw most of the humor in grotesques, people trying to behave normally in the middle of a nightmare: the Russian premier who forgets the telephone number of his general staff headquarters and suggests the American President try Omsk information, or the reluctance of a U.S. officer to smash open a Coca-Cola machine for change to phone the President about a crisis because of his conditioning about the sanctity of private property.

Kubrick both produced and directed (total control at last!) *Dr. Strangelove* in Shepperton Studios outside London, because Peter Sellers was getting a divorce and couldn't leave the country for an extended period. He cast the film by sketching in the details of each character, listing the actors he knew who might fit, then investigating their availability and how they'd work together. He wound up giving three parts to Peter Sellers.

The director asked no help from the U.S. Department of Defense. The entire simulated B-52 flight deck, which cost one hundred thousand dollars, was based on a single official still carelessly published in a British flying magazine. Most of the shots of the intrepid B-52 were simulated with a ten-foot model, and a moving matte, for $600 each.

Lyn Tournabene visited the *Dr. Strangelove* set, where Kubrick was at work at seven each morning, working as though possessed, seemingly making his film singlehanded:

"This overwhelming omnipresence of the director had a strange effect on his crew. Awestruck and respectful, they appeared to feel that there was no need for their own perfection; the director had more than enough for everyone. They would frequently stand off and watch him rechecking details of their work, not with hostility but with incredulity. There was good humor and loyalty on the set, but there were no loving pranks. When 'Mr. K.' smiled, it was . . . at the completion of some seemingly impossible scene. For instance, interior shots of his killer plane . . . were done in an area about the size of a packed linen closet. When he had finished a take of the plane being struck by a defensive missile, had accomplished rocking that linen closet and filling it with smoke and debris, he laughed in delight and so did the crew. It was the same as applause."[8]

Kubrick allowed Peter Sellers to improvise whole scenes, embellishing or changing his characters, possibly written with him in mind; the level-headed RAF officer, the ex-Nazi scientist, the Stevensonian president. Sellers tended to be very good on one take, never equaled, while George C. Scott was able to do his scenes well take after take.

Scott said of Kubrick: "He is most certainly in command, and he's so self-effacing and apologetic it's impossible to be offended by him."[8]

Kubrick's control of *Strangelove* extended to the final version of the film to be released. He took several weeks to run the film alone and with audiences, trying always to see it afresh. In the end he deleted a final scene in which the Russians and Americans in the great dark plastic-and-silicon War Room have a free-for-all custard pie fight beneath the glowing charts and maps: The scene seemed too farcical, too out of tone with the rest.

Summing up his feelings about filmmaking on the *Dr. Strangelove* set, Kubrick commented: "You really have to care about a project—love it, even—to stay with it and sustain interest during the endless hours it bogs down into routine."[8]

We float in twilight above a sea of clouds, the winds of the stratosphere wailing faintly. In the distance, an island of craggy mountain tops pokes out of the trackless whiteness, half-lit. There is no sign of man.

A commentator begins: "For more than a year, ominous rumors had been privately circulating among high level leaders that the Soviet Union had been at work on what was darkly hinted to be the ultimate weapon, a doomsday device. Intelligence sources placed the site of the top secret Russian project at the perpetually fog-shrouded wasteland below the Arctic peaks of the Zhukov Mountains. What they were building, or why it should be located in such a remote and desolate place, no one could say."

The instrumental "Try a Little Tenderness" follows, with shots of the great silvery SAC bombers refuelling, credits over. First compositions show both planes, then the tanker machine nosing up to the tumescent hose, vibrating delicately, sunlight flashing off highlights in its skin. This aerial mating, or suckling, tender and grotesque, progresses, the planes linked and trembling, flying to the sentimental strings, finally breaking off.

A rapidly rotating radar antenna, an enormous B-52 under floodlights, soldiers on guard. In a bright, clacking computer room, a phone buzzes. Chunky RAF captain Mandrake, all mournful walrus mustache and gentle reserve, answers.

Buck Turgidson slaps his belly: "Bump everything up to condition Red!" The pat on the old middle-aged spread both reassures and suggests comic awareness of mortality. (© Columbia Pictures Industries, 1970)

Ambassador De Sadesky describes the Doomsday Machine. The nightmare War Room decor works against the corpulent comic Russian, with his echoing, fear-ridden voice. (© Columbia Pictures Industries, 1970)

Ripper: "I first became aware of it during the physical act of love. . ." The masculine, beautiful, bewildered face of madness, a disconcerting parallel to the SAC paradox-slogan. (© *Columbia Pictures Industries, 1970*)

Above: Major Kong exhorts his bomber crew. The obsessed, skillful, delighted face of a mass-murder "hero." (© *Columbia Pictures Industries, 1970) Below:* Dr. Strangelove has a plan. His regained ability to walk was a last-minute improvisation during Kubrick's "intensive rehearsal periods." (© *Columbia Pictures Industries, 1970*)

"This is General Ripper. Do you recognize my voice?" Ripper rumbles, a strong-faced man smoking a cigar in a dimly lit office.

Mandrake, dubious, self-possessed: "No sir."

"All right . . . now listen to me carefully. The base is being put on condition Red . . . I'm afraid this is not an exercise," Ripper says slowly. "It looks like we're in a shooting war."

"Oh, hell, sir."

"My orders are to seal this base tight. Now. I want you to transmit Plan R, R for Robert, to the Wing. . . . I want all privately owned radios to be immediately impounded. They might be used to issue instructions to saboteurs. . . . After you've done that, report back to me."

Jets roaring faintly, the B-52s on patrol coast across the sky throttled down, waiting. Contrails and exhaust curve and lance above them, behind them. Shots of the lead plane are cut against footage of squadrons.

Narrator: "In order to guard against the danger of surprise nuclear attack, America's Strategic Air Command maintains a force airborne twenty-four hours a day, deployed from the Persian Gulf to the Arctic Ocean. But they all have one geographic factor in common. They are all two hours from their targets inside Russia. . . ."

We see one plane's flight deck, long as a school bus but jammed with dials, consoles, hatches, screens, buttons, toggles, a thousand controls. Major "King" Kong and his co-pilot stare forward, two more flyers nurse instruments facing back. The plane vibrates, sways slowly. All crewmen wear clumsy flight suits, helmets, boots. One technician leafs through *Playboy,* the other practices card tricks. The co-pilot tries to nap. Kong takes control, a big-faced earnest man with a voice that rasps like Andy Devine, and a thick Texas accent.

The radio blasts, and the wall-eyed Jewish radioman announces dubiously: "Major Kong, I really think this is crazy, but I just got a message from base over the CRM-114 which decodes: 'Wing Attack, Plan R. R for Romeo.' "

Irritated, Kong responds: "Goldy, how many times have I told you guys I don't want no horsing around on the airplane!"

The cold wind of the stratosphere gets a little louder.

Goldberg, under Kong's eye, points out the settings on his instruments, the codebook page. Kubrick zooms in on the machine: CRM-114. Two more flyers pop up from a hatch in the deck. It's a test? No, not likely.

Goldberg: "Major Kong, message from base confirmed."

On snare drum and bugles, faintly, begins: "When Johnny Comes Marching Home."

Slowly, Major Kong opens the plane's safe: "Well boys, I reckon this is it. Nuclear combat, toe to toe with the Russkies."

He stows away his helmet, puts on a Stetson, and returns solemnly to his seat to address his men. Through his speech we keep seeing his big, earnest Texas face, rasping incentives but sincerely torn, totally American, the half-ultimate half-parody celluloid commander. Kubrick cuts to the agonized faces of the all-American crew, their nation probably blasted, as they hover on the brink of battle, the drums and bugles sounding.

"Well, look boys, I ain't much of a hand at makin' speeches. I got a pretty fair idea that something doggone important's goin' on back there, and I got a fair idea of the kind of personal emotions you fellas may be thinkin'! I figure you wouldn't even be human bein's if you didn't really have some strong personal feelings about nuclear combat!

"I want you to remember one thing! The folks back home are countin' on ya, and by golly, we ain't about to let 'em down! Tell ya something else! If this thing turns out to be half as important as it just might be, I'd say you're all in line for some promotions and personal citations when that's over with. And that goes for every one of you, regardless of your race, your color, or your creed. Now let's get this thing on the hoof, we've got some flyin' to do. . . !"

In a luxurious hotel suite, one wall mirrored, a tall and shapely brunette in a bikini is stretched languorously under a sunlamp. The phone rings, and in a throaty voice she calls: "Buck, should I get it?"

A hoarse male voice, silly-cheerful, satiated: "You have to . . ."

What follows is a small masterpiece, the Executive Secretary Running Interference in the Ultimate Emergency.

Miss Scott (officially cool): "Oh yes, General Turgidson is here.

(huskily) Freddy, how are you? Oh, we were just catching up on some of the General's paperwork . . . (to General) General Turgidson, a Colonel Butridge calling!"

Turgidson (annoyed): "Tell him to call back!"

Miss Scott (huskily): "Freddy, the General says to call back in a minute or two. (to General) He says it can't wait!"

Turgidson (sourly): "Find out what he wants!"

Miss Scott (passionate): "Freddy, the General's in the powder room. Could you possibly tell me what it's about? (to Turgidson) They monitored a transmission about eight minutes ago from Burpleson . . . It decoded as wing attack, Plan R."

Turgidson (grumpily): "Wha', tell 'em to call, uh, what's his name, Base Commander Ripper. Do I have to think of everything around here?"

Miss Scott: "The General suggests you call General Ripper, the Base Commander. (to the boss) All communications are dead!"

Eventually, Turgidson, stocky, with a satisfied look and boyish crewcut takes the phone: "Fred? Buck! What's it look like? Yeah . . . You sure it's Plan R? What's cookin' on the threat board? Nothin'? Nothin' at all? . . . I don't like the look of this. Tell you what you'd better do, old buddy." (He slaps his own pot— POW!) "You give Elmo and Charley a blast, and bump everything up to condition Red . . . I'll get back to you."

Turgidson begins getting dressed. "Thought I'd mosey down to the War Room . . . Ha-ha, the Air Force never sleeps!"

General Ripper addresses his men. Artful shots of grim-faced soldiers on sentry beside guard houses, along cyclone fences, outside hangars. Two mechanics stare upward, posed beneath an enormous bomber's engine. A jeepful of tagged portable radios pulls smartly up. MPs peer into the night.

"Your Commie has no regard for human life. Not even his own. The enemy may come individually, or he may come in strength. He may even come in the uniform of our own troops. But however he comes, we must stop him. . . ."

Mandrake, last man in the computer room, discovers a transistor radio yammering popular music. He picks it up.

Echoing Major Kong, to Mandrake's cheap bop, Ripper concludes: "Today, the nation is counting on us. We're not going to let them down."

High in the Polar sky, the B-52 cruises to "When Johnny Comes Marching Home."

From the safe, Major Kong distributes the attack profiles, part of which he reads aloud in his twanging, singsong of command, like W. C. Fields imitating a Texas telephone operator: "This attack profile insures the enemy cannot monitor false transmission or plant false transmission. The CRM-114 is to be switched into all receiver circuits. Emergency code prefix is to be set up at O.P.E. This will block any transmission other than those preceded by such a code prefix." It is done.

At Burpleson Air Force Base, Mandrake strides into Ripper's office. "Excuse me, sir, something's come up . . ." He twirls the dial, talk, slow piano music. Agitatedly: "Our fellows will be inside Russian radar cover in about twenty minutes . . . We don't want to start a nuclear war unless we really have to, do we?"

General Ripper stares at him: "The orders stand."

Mandrake is face to face with it: "That's rather an odd way of looking at it. If a Russian attack was not in progress, then your use of Plan R, in fact, your orders to the entire Wing . . . well, uh . . ."

Mandrake formally asks for the code.

General Ripper, an edge of menace and mania in his voice: "I told you to take it easy. There's nothing anybody can do about this thing now." He uncovers a pistol with a pearl handle.

Ripper settles back and smiles plausibly: "Mandrake, I suppose it never occurred to you," he begins, his voice echoing slightly, "but while we're chatting here so enjoyably, a decision is being made by the President and the Joint Chiefs in the War Room of the Pentagon. And when they realize that there's no possibility of recalling the Wing, there will be only one course of action open. Total commitment."

Kubrick moves into a splendid close-up of General Ripper's strong, masculine, almost beautiful face puffing on his cigar, surrounded by darkness. "Clemenceau once said war was too important to be left to the generals. But today, war is too important to be left to the politicians. They have neither the time, the training, or the inclination for strategic thought. I can no longer allow Communist infiltration, Communist indoctrination, Communist subversion, and the international Communist Conspiracy . . . to sap and impurify all of our precious bodily fluids. . . ."

The Pentagon at night. Cut to the War Room, a brilliant cinematic invention, an immense tent-shaped chamber with concrete walls, glassy silicon floors, immense illuminated strategic maps on the walls. At an enormous round table sit fifty or so military men and civilians below a great ring of illumination that hangs oppressively close, so most of the room is dark. The seated include General Turgidson, President Merkin Muffley, a bald, Stevenson-like Chief Executive, and his aides. Crisply Muffley asks: "Now, General Turgidson, what's going on here?"

Turgidson replies in a calm, disinterested, yet vaguely approving voice: "Mr. President: About twenty-five minutes ago, General Ripper issued an order to his B-52 bombers which were airborne . . . for the planes to attack their targets inside Russia . . . the aircraft will begin penetrating Russian radar cover in twenty-five minutes." Turgidson efficiently points out the flight paths, the primary, and secondary targets on the display (dots, squares, triangles).

For the third time, the crisis is outlined. Plan R allowed General Ripper to start the planes from fail safe, so they won't stop. To call the planes, the CRM-114 must be unlocked by radioing the code prefix, which only Ripper knows. Finally, Ripper has the base sealed off and defended.

Chief of Staff Turgidson enthusiastically reads Ripper's last message to SAC, yet another rallying cry:

"Yes, gentlemen, they are on their way, and no one can bring them back. For the sake of our country and our way of life, I suggest you get the rest of SAC in after them. Otherwise we will be totally destroyed by Red retaliation. My boys will give you the best kind of start, fourteen hundred megatons worth, and you sure as hell won't stop them now." Turgidson cackles. "So let's get going; there's no other choice. God willing, we will prevail, in peace and freedom from fear, and in true health . . ." Slowly, quizzically: ". . . the purity and essence of our natural fluids. God bless you all!" Turgidson knots his brows. "And then he hung up. . . ."

"There's nothing to try to figure out," President Muffley says coldly. "This man is obviously a psychotic." He asks about the human reliability tests.

Turgidson looks pained: "I don't think it's quite fair to condemn a whole program because of a single slip-up."

Turgidson's phone buzzes; he crouches over it, smiling and whispering: "I told you never to call me here! . . . Look baby, I can't talk to you now—my President needs me! . . . Of course it isn't purely physical, I deeply respect you as a human being. Don't forget to say your prayers!" He cradles the phone, smiling, his hands folded on his desk, like a ten-year-old trying not to be called on.

Army General Faceman orders his troops to enter Burpleson, locate General Ripper, and put him in touch with the President.

Turgidson asks to speak, his words echoing in the depths of the great dark chamber (as they echo Ripper's): The hope of recall is low; in minutes the planes will make radar contact, initiating retaliation; this will virtually annihilate the United States. His voice grows conspiratorial: but a coordinated attack launched at once would destroy almost all the enemy's weapons.

Muffley tells him proudly: "It is the avowed policy of our country never to strike first with nuclear weapons."

Turgidson shrugs: "Mr. President, I would say that General Ripper has already invalidated that policy!"

"That was not an act of national policy!"

Turgidson smiles sincerely: "Mr. President, we are rapidly approaching a moment of truth . . . . Truth is not always a pleasant thing, but it is necessary now to make a choice. To choose between two admittedly *regrettable,* but nevertheless *distinguishable* post-war environments—one where you got twenty million people killed, and the other where you got one hundred fifty million people killed."

Muffley, stiffly: "I will not go down in history as the greatest mass murderer since Adolf Hitler."

Turgidson stares at him: "Perhaps it might be better, Mr. President, if you concerned yourself more about the American people than your image in the history books."

Muffley turns angrily away. Upstairs, the Russian ambassador is about to be let in.

Turgidson argues that this would break security. He clutches his strategic charts and manuals to his chest, gestures at the Big Board: "I mean, he'd see *everything!*"

Muffley regards him affectionlessly: "That is precisely the point." To an aide: "Staines, get Premier Kissoff on the hot line!"

On the crammed B-52 flight deck, engines howling, chorus moaning "When Johnny Comes Marching Home," "King" Kong begins to read:

"Survival kit contents check," he rasps happily. "One forty-five automatic, two boxes ammunition; four days concentrated rations; one drug issue containing antibiotics, morphine, vitamin pills, pep pills, sleepin' pills, tranquilizer pills; one miniature combination Russian phrase book and Bible; one hundred dollars in rubles; one hundred dollars in gold; nine packs of chewin' gum, one issue prophylactics, three lipsticks, three pair nylon stockings. Shoot," he yelps, "a fella could have a pretty good weekend in Vegas with all that stuff. . . ."

In the War Room, the Russian Ambassador, a large, haughty, pockfaced man in a frock coat, samples a luxurious buffet, the spotlights behind him flaring. He orders food, Havana cigars.

Turgidson crouches, sneering and petulant, beside the President. "You're gonna let that lousy Commie punk vomit all over us?" He clutches the secret stuff.

"We can't reach him in the Kremlin," an aide calls.

Ambassador De Sodesky smiles: "Our leader is a man of the people, but he is also a *man*."

President Muffley mumbles approval, as Turgidson hisses in his ear. De Sodesky's face burns: "What!"

"I said Premier Kissoff," Turgidson mocks, "is a degenerate, atheistic Commie!" In a moment the two are grappling. Turgidson waves a miniature camera. "Look at this, Mr. President, this lousy Commie rat was taking pictures with this thing of the big board!"

In the Texas dawn, Ripper's defense teams wait. One spots an army convoy rolling toward Burpleson. Their Middle-American voices murmur back and forth:

"Gee, those trucks sure look real."

"Probably bought them from the Army as war surplus. Open up at two hundred yards."

In jiggly battle footage the convoy is ambushed; men duck behind or beneath trucks, a jeep swerves across a field, catches fire. Men fall, machine guns stutter, rifles bang, mortars crash. Faintly begin the cries of the mutilated. . . .

The War Room—President Muffley gets the Ambassador to vouch for him on the hot line, but: "Be careful, Mr. President. I think he is drunk."

Muffley takes over, frantic: "Hello Dimitri . . . do you suppose you can turn the music down . . . Uh-huh, much better. I can hear you fine! Well, then, as you say, we're both coming in fine. . . . Yes, it's great to be fine, ha-ha-ha."

Now gently, jollying along: "Now, Dimitri, you know how we've always talked about the possibility of something going wrong with the bomb . . . the *bomb,* Dimitri, the *hydrogen bomb.* . . . Well, now, what happened is one of our base commanders, he had a sort of—well, he went a little funny in the head. You know, just a little *funny.* And, uh, he went and did a silly thing. Well," tearfully, "I'll tell you what he did . . . he ordered his planes . . . to attack your country—

"—well, let me *finish,* Dimitri . . . listen, how do you think *I* feel about it, Dimitri? Why do you think I'm calling you . . . just to say hello? *Of course* I like to speak to you, *of course* I like to say hello . . . I'm just calling up to tell you something terrible has happened. . . . It's a friendly call, of course it's a friendly call. . . . Listen, if it wasn't friendly"—with a nod to Turgidson—"you probably wouldn't have even got it.

"They will not reach their targets for another hour . . . we'd like to give your air staff a complete rundown of the targets, the flight plans, the defensive systems. . . . We're just going to . . . have to help you destroy them. . . . I know they're our boys. . . ."

The Russian Ambassador takes back the phone. His voice goes from cheerful to grim to horrified. "The fools . . . the Doomsday Machine . . . a device which will destroy all human and animal life for one hundred years."

The dim sounds of gunfire penetrate General Ripper's office.

Ripper: "Mandrake, ever seen a Commie drink a glass of water?"

"Can't say I have," the RAF man answers weakly from the edge of despair.

"Yes." Mandrake almost sobs. "Yes, Jack," he giggles.

"Ever wonder why I drink only distilled water. . . ? Do you realize fluoridation is the most monstrously conceived and dangerous plot we've ever had to face. . . ?"

Directly before them, the window is smashed to flying slivers by a roaring machine gun. The bullets tear pictures from the wall, rip a fluorescent unit half out of the ceiling, explode papers from the desk. The din is terrific!

Ripper strides to the window. "Nice shooting, soldier!"

Pleased, Ripper grabs his golf bag and with Alice-in-Wonderland logic dumps out a machine gun. The ball compartment holds the bullet belt. "Mandrake, in the name of His Majesty and the Continental Congress, c'mere and feed me this belt, boy!"

Mandrake is on the couch. He gasps: "Jack, I'd love to come. But the string in my leg's gone. I've got a gammy leg, oh dear, leg shot off."

Ripper, with lunatic wit: "C'mere, Mandrake, the Red Coats are coming. . . !"

The War Room. The Russian Ambassador stands on the black silicon floor describing the Doomsday Machine: a device that can wrap the earth in radioactivity for ninety-three years built as a cheap alternative to bombers, ICBMs, War Rooms . . .

President Muffley asks his research and development boss, Dr. Strangelove, if the U.S. is working on one.

We hear a high cracked German whine, lingering over words with the taste of power or blood: "A moment, *please,* Mr. President!" A dark shape in a glittering wheelchair, with a black synthetic arm and thick glasses, rolls into view. "My conclusion was that the idea was not a *practical* deterrent for reasons that are now all too obvious."

Turgidson, dreamily: "Gee, I sure wish we had one of them. . . ."

Suddenly Strangelove barks: "Yes, but the whole point of the Doomsday Machine is lost *if you keep it a secret! Why didn't you tell the world, eh?*"

With dignity, the Ambassador replies: "It was to be announced at the Party Congress on Monday. The Premier loves surprises. . . ."

Burpleson Air Force Base: Thump of mortars, crash of machine-gun fire. Hazy vibrating images of a skirmish line weaving past a "Keep Off the Grass" sign toward the glass-and-concrete administration buildings. Rifle shots richochet. A big sign: "Peace is Our Profession." A burst of fire smashes the glass of Ripper's office.

"Ha ha, Jack," the RAF man kids. "Don't you think we'd better get away from all this flying glass?"

"Mandrake," Ripper rumbles earnestly, "do you realize, there were studies under way to fluoridate salt, flour, milk, ice cream—*children's ice cream,* Mandrake!"

Bemused, Mandrake peers at him: "When did you first develop this theory, Jack?"

Ripper looks thoughtful. "Well, Mandrake, I first became aware of it during the physical act of love. A profound sense of fatigue, a great feeling of emptiness, followed. Luckily, I was able to interpret these feelings correctly: loss of essence."

"I can assure you," Ripper tells him challengingly, "it has not recurred. . . . Women sense my power, and they seek the life essence. I do not avoid women, Mandrake, but I do deny them my essence."

Another explosion of rifle and machine-gun fire, but weaker. Cries for mercy, faintly. More shots. In jittery footage, the defense teams, hands up, show themselves, are taken.

"When they get me outside, they're going to give me a pretty good going over . . . for the code. . . ." We see his face in close-up again, his eyes bewildered, features pale and strong. "I don't know how I'd stand up under torture. . . ."

Mandrake sees an approach. Ruthlessly: "Well, the answer to *that one* is that *no one ever does,* and so my advice to you is *to give me* the code." Joyously: "And if those devils come back and try any rough stuff, *why we'll fight 'em together.* You there with the gun, and me with the belt and ammo—*feeding you, Jack, feeding you!*"

"You know, Mandrake," Ripper muses, stumbling to his feet,

"I happen to believe in a life after this one. And I know I'll have to answer for what I've done . . . and I think I can!"

Ripper stands, dangling the machine gun, big pistol jammed in his waistband. He goes into the bathroom.

A dull explosion. Mandrake throws his shoulder against the door. . . .

Roaring of the jets, chorus of "When Johnny . . ." with mournfull trumpet blast. On the B-52's flight deck, a cool voice: "Defense Systems Operator—I have an unidentified radar blip, distance sixty miles. Approximate speed Mach Three. Looks like a missile!"

Trumpets, and a bit of light crawling into a spider-web grid.

"Confirm. Missile track. Commence evasive action!"

Eyes frightened, Kong pulls back his wheel. The B-52 rises violently up from the icy peaks. Calmly: "Still closing range."

Kong dives, plunging. The missile keeps coming. Frightened faces, roaring engines. "Forty miles, still tracking!"

Swiftly the crew adds electronic defenses, the plane dropping, then throwing itself upward, the blip pulsing onward, a frightened-faced Kong, the blip closing, Kubrick's cuts always faster . . .

The blip closer, closer, curves away. . . . The D.S.O., excitedly, triumphant: "Ten miles, missile deflecting! It's—" The blip expands, flaring!—BUZZZWuzzapzziza-PAZZZIZ!!! An electronic blat. WHAM!

With a roar the roof explodes in dust, smoke, flames! An electrical fire spits sparks, buzzing, Goldberg's face terrified, eyes bulging, lips back from teeth, white and black as circuits blink out and flare, fire extinguisher gushing, motors screaming, the B-52 plunging over white peaks, swaying, trailing smoke, going down, Kong doggedly fighting his controls, smoke hazing the deck, Kong pulling her out, the trumpet weakly triumphant, the B-52 soaring between icy crags . . .

General Ripper's office, in ruins, silent. Mandrake studying a doodle pad illustrated with faces, birds, "Purity of Essence" and "P.O.E." written again and again. . . .

CRASH! A bullet shatters the lock.

Rifle at the hip, face creased with a combat man's cunning and wariness, Colonel "Bat" Guano raps out: "Okay, soldier, what the hell is going on here!"

Guano was told to take Burpleson and Ripper. Mandrake guesses the code is some permutation of P.O.E., but the phones are dead.

"All right, Charlie!" cries the tough, excited Guano. "I been wasting too much time on you! Start walking. . . !"

The B-52 careens on, snare drums drilling, engines wailing.

Inside, the flight deck is still smoky, blistered, and broken where the fire ravaged it. Kubrick zooms in on the CRM-114, now fused junk, demolished by its self-destruct system. The plane careens on, a few feet above the broken icefields. . . .

In the cool singsong of combat, "Sir, our radius of action is now sufficient to take out the primary and secondary targets, but we will *not*, repeat, *not*, be able to make it back to any base or neutral country. However, we will have enough fuel to ditch at Weather Ship Tango Delta. . . ."

The B-52 hurtles at delirious speed just above the polar wastes.

Major Kong, still jubilant after outfoxing the missile, his voice twanging happily, crows, "Well, boys, we got three engines out, we got more holes in us than a horse trader's mule, the radio's gone and we're leakin' fuel, and if we were flyin' in any lower, why, we'd need sleighbells on this thing. But we got one little bulge on them Russkies! At this height, they might harpoon us, but they dang well ain't gonna spot us on no radar screen!"

The B-52 plunges on at zero altitude, faster and faster, almost brushing the ice, swinging around a hulking white mountain thrust out of the rubbled plane, rocketing toward target.

In the echoing Base corridors, Colonel Guano marches Mandrake toward the main gate.

Guano barks sourly: ". . . I think you're some kind of deviated prevert . . . you were organizing a mutiny of preverts."

Mandrake browbeats him into calling. "Okay, try and get the President," Guano mutters, gesturing at a booth. "But if you try any preversions in there, I'll blow your head off!"

Mandrake doesn't have change, even station to station. He tells Guano to shoot the lock off a coke machine.

"That's private property!" reproves the Colonel, as if to a child.

"Shoot it off! Shoot! With a gun! That's what the bullets are for, you twit!"

"Okay," Guano says haughtily. "But if you don't get the President, you're gonna have to answer to the Coca-Cola Company!"

He shoots, money flies out, soda gushes into his face. . . .

In the War Room the standing councilmen are silhouetted, cheering, against the Big Board, where the bomber paths are blinking out.

A mechanical voice: "The recall code O.P.E. is being acknowledged by elements of the Eight Forty-Third Bomber Wing. Missions twelve, twenty-two, thirty, thirty-eight destroyed."

General Turgidson whistles, climbs onto the table. "Lord!" he wheezes. "We have heard the wings of the Angel of Death" (shot of Strangelove) "fluttering over the Valley of Fear. You have seen fit to deliver us . . ."

The President's aide calls loudly: "Excuse me, sir, Premier Kissoff's calling again, and he's hopping mad. . . !"

Trumpets triumphant, Major Kong's B-52 rushes on and on, snare drums rattling.

Prissily, the navigator singsongs: "Excuse me, sir, leakage has increased."

"Roger, confirm rate!"

The plane races on, just above the ice. . . .

A nervous, worried President Muffley on the phone: "No, Dimitri, there must be some mistake . . . I'm definitely certain." Hysterically to the room: "He says that one of the planes hasn't turned back! Oh, oh . . . Now he claims only three; the fourth may only be damaged."

Turgidson, sneeringly: "Mr. President, I'm beginning to smell a great big Commie rat. Suppose he's looking for an excuse to clobber us—"

Muffley, ignoring him, anxiously, gasping: "Dimitri, if the plane manages to get through to bomb the target, is this—is this gonna—is this gonna set off the Doomsday Machine? Are you sure?" Audaciously: "I guess you're just gonna have to get that plane! . . . Listen, put everything you've got into those two sectors, and you can't miss. . . !"

Trumpets triumphant! Kong's B-52, in vertiginous flight. "When Johnny . . ." burps away on the tuba.

Navigator, reproving: "If we continue to lose fuel at the present rate, I estimate we have only thirty-eight minutes, which will not even get us as far as the primary."

Kong, sweating, excited: "I don't give a hoot in hell how you do it, you just get me to the primary, y'hear?"

Sweetly: "I'm sorry, sir, but those *are* the figures."

Kong, scornfully: "Well, *Shoot!* We ain't come this far just to dump this thang in the drink! What's the nearest target of opportunity?"

The arrowheadlike plane bullets along, rollercoasting over the snow and ice.

"Sir . . . we *have* a chance to reach *Target Three Eight Four* and make it to the Tango Delta Weather Ship."

Kong mollified: "All right. Designate new target three eight four; give me a new heading!"

The plane begins to turn on a new course.

Exhausted, jacket and vest unbuttoned, the balding, mild-faced President leans on the table. To Turgidson: "Is there a chance for that plane?"

Turgidson becomes excited, gesturing, chuckling: "If the pilot's good—I mean *really sharp*—well, he can barrel that baby in so *low,* you just got to see it sometimes! A real big plane like a B-52, its jet exhaust frying chickens in the barnyard—ha-ha-ha!"

"Has he got a chance, Turgidson?"

Exultant: "Has he got a chance!" Upset, trailing off: "Has he got a chance. . . ?"

The B-52 rollercoasters above hills covered with evergreens, down a river valley.

Inside, the navigator murmurs: "Distance one zero miles. Switch from green grid to target orange."

The big, gravel-voiced Texas pilot and the cool black bombardier singsong their check lists, the Negro hitting buttons and moving toggles in a pit jammed with parallels of switches and lights. . . .

"Bomb fusing master safeties on: electronic, barometric, time, impact!"

"Detonator set for zero altitude!"

The great silvery plane races south over trees and tundra.

Something's wrong! Bombardier, querulous: "Bomb door circuit negative function!"

"Switch in back-up circuit!"

"Engage emergency power!"

"Operate manual override!"

"Fire explosive bolts!"

"Still negative function, sir. Operating circuits dead, sir!"

"Stay on the bomb run, Ace!" Kong yells, waddling aft in his clumsy flight suit. "I'll see what I can do!"

In the bomb bay, Kong works his way between the weapons, "When Johnny . . ." burping along. The bombs are named *Hi There!* and *Dear John!* Above one, a smashed panel dangles wires, spits sparks and smoke.

On the flight deck, Ace: "Target distance: seven miles!"

Kong is on *Hi There!,* absurdly beating out the fire with his hat. His flashlight, slung from his belt, is a shimmering blob of luminescence.

With screwdriver and wire clips, Kong works away at the wiring, his face intent. The music and drums are louder.

"Target distance: three miles!"

On the flight deck, the B-52 noses over a last ridge: "Target in sight!" A flat white valley with a pattern of tiny black spindles in it. Ace, angrily: "Where the hell is Major Kong?"

Kong makes a last adjustment. With a loud and ominous ZZZZZ the bomb bay doors spread wide. Kong stares down, his face desperate. The wind roars in. He starts to reach for the clamps overhead which secure the bomb.

With a great buzz the bomb is released and drops, Kong riding it. In a fantastic, totally impossible image we see him and his "mount" falling toward the missile site at 600 m.p.h. Kong's face is split in a hysterical grin, he waves his Stetson and screams a rebel yell: "Ahhh-YEEOOOW! ahhh-YEEOOOOOOOW!"

A crewman's voice, insanely calm and reasonable: "Hey, what about Major Kong?"

Down, down, stubby missiles, access roads, mountain slopes at the edge. Kong falls, waving his hat, riding it, screaming in triumph/terror: "Ahhh-YEEOOOW! Ahhhh-YEEOOOOOOW! Ahhh-YEEOOOOOOW!" He's faster, closer, down . . .

The screen whites out.

The sound wave follows: BBRRROOOOOOOOOOOOOOOOO-OOOMMMMMMM!!!!!!!....

In the silent War Room, Strangelove spins his shiny wheelchair to face us. "Mr. President?" He mocks shrilly. "I would not rule out a chance to preserve a small nucleus of human *specimens.*

"It would be quite easy . . . at the bottom of some of our deeper mine shafts. . . ."

Strangelove jerks his circular slide rule up to his face, puts it between his teeth. In close-up, the machine-arm, false teeth, great pale eyes swimming behind enormous lenses, high crackling voice, are thrust at us: "Let's see . . . cobalt thorium G . . ." (click) ". . . Mmmm! . . . half-life . . . one hundred years." Shrilly: "*It would not be difficult, Mein Führer!*" Giggling, he goes on: "Nuclear reactors could provide power. Greenhouses could produce plant life. Animals could be *fed,* and *slaughtered!*"

As for Muffley's guilt over the choice of survivors, breathlessly: "It could be easily done with a *computah,* programmed for youth, health, *sexual fertility* . . . our top government and military men must be included!"

Behind him, the shadowy top councilors nod agreement. "*Heil Hitler!*" Strangelove cries, his arm shooting up.

"With a ratio of ten women to every man, I estimate we would re-attain the present G.N.P. in twenty years," the scientist says.

But what about the grief?

Glibly, clipped: "Certainly not . . . When they go down, everyone will be *alive.* The prevailing emotion should be one of *nostalgia* for those left behind, *combined* with a spirit of *bold curiosity* for the *adventure ahead.*"

Grotesquely, the machine-arm shoots up and punches him, then strangles him as he fights it.

Turgidson lounges back and remarks casually: "Doctor, wouldn't this necessitate the end of the so-called *monogamous* sexual relationship?"

"Regrettably, yes." The scientist smiles, his arm, out of sight, twitching rhythmically. "The women will be selected for their sexual characteristics, which will have to be of a highly stimulating order!"

The Soviet Ambassador compliments Strangelove. "Thank you, sir!"

Walking out, the Russian does take pictures of the War Room with a concealed camera.

Turgidson, rattling his saber endlessly: "Supposing the Soviets stashed away some big bombs. When we come out, they could take over . . . they might even try an immediate sneak attack to take over our mineshaft space . . .! Mr. President, we must not allow a mineshaft gap!"

"Sir," Strangelove squeaks. "I have a plan!"

With a cry, his own arm throws him from the wheelchair, and on twisted limbs he stumbles toward the President.

"Mein Führer—I can walk!"

Against Vera Lynn's sentimental "We'll Meet Again" (Don't Know Where, Don't Know When), shots of nuclear explosions, whose own eerie beauty becomes apparent as they go on and on . . .

The critical reaction to *Dr. Strangelove* was extreme praise, combined with varieties of virulent remonstrance. Past the comic characters and excessive incidents, true in their own way, most critics recognized *Strangelove* as a brilliant, stylized, unsparing treatment of the nuclear crisis. Lewis Mumford, in a letter to *The New York Times* dated March 1, 1964, commented succinctly:

What the wacky characters in *Dr. Strangelove* are saying is precisely what needs to be said; this nightmare eventuality that we have concocted for our children is nothing but a crazy fantasy, by nature as horribly crippled and dehumanized as Dr. Strangelove himself. It is not this film that is sick; what is sick is our supposedly moral, democratic country, which allowed this policy to be formulated and implemented without even the pretense of open public debate.

The film is the first break in the catatonic cold war trance that has so long held our country in its rigid grip.[6]

Stanley Kauffmann, whose review quoted the letter, commended *Dr. Strangelove* as "first and foremost absolutely unflinching; relentlessly perceptive of human beings to the point of inhumanity."[6] Kauffmann went on to argue down the easiest objections: simplified ideas ("pop nihilism"), easy targets, and stereotyped characters. Kauffmann replied that satire need not have subtle social ideas, real international politics often resembles a Herblock cartoon, and Kubrick's "King" Kong and Dr. Strangelove are necessary, not impossible artistic choices. The agreeable, subservient bomber crew might be Kubrick's own reply to criticisms of simplification— a cross section of the U.S.A. (the vicarious audience) carrying out total murder like good children, even to the American black who pushes the last button.

Frenzied praise came from Robert Brustein, who saw *Dr. Strangelove* as "the most courageous film ever made." He saw it constantly deferring its audience's expectations to pursue Kubrick's heady artistic course. Brustein summed up Kubrick's *modus operandi* as follows:

This style is Juvenalian satire; this purpose, the evacuation of fear and anger through the acting out of frightful fantasies. Kubrick has flushed a monster from its psychic lair—the universal fear of nuclear accident—and then proceeded to feed and nourish it, letting it perform its worst before your eyes. The consequence of spectacle is . . . a temporary purgation; to witness the end of the world as a comic event is, indeed, to stop worrying and to love the bomb.[2]

Brustein work through the plot, showing how the ironies and excesses prove how inappropriate heroic postures and patriotic reflexes have become in the nuclear age, then points up Kubrick's American caricatures: The General Walkerlike Ripper and Turgidson, along with Peter Sellers' satiric sketches of Mandrake, Muffley, and Strangelove. Brustein concludes: ". . . Although Dr. Strangelove is about a political subject, its only politics is outrage against the malevolence of officialdom . . . it releases, through comic poetry, those feelings of impotence and frustration that are consuming us all and I can't think of anything more important for an imaginative work to do." Kubrick has stated that he would like to see the most prominence given to this review.

An approving but controlled review by John Simon, called "The Struggle for Hope,"[11] said of *Dr. Strangelove:* "thoroughly irreverent about everything the establishment takes seriously," and found the film a *catalogue raisonné* of the ways man dehumanizes himself (e.g., the General whose lust for power is based on puritanism and stifled sexuality). Simon's interpretation of the Dr. Strangelove character is particularly subtle: "the human body so full of artificial or artificially reinforced parts that little of it remains but a machine; and the rallying of these mechanical parts till it is they who come to a dominant and catastrophic life." A final very perceptive point of Simon's is that the film contains no "rebel" character who might be explained away: ". . . there are no rebels, only heroes; heroes of politics, warfare, science, all of them so repellent or, at best, nondescript, that the only rebels must be in the audience—amused, revolted, and ready to revolt." *Dr. Strangelove* perhaps proved there was an audience ready for satire, irreverence, and witty but ultimately serious criticism.

Pauline Kael's attack tried to use *Strangelove*'s virtues to condemn it: "*Dr. Strangelove* opened a new movie era. It ridiculed everything and everybody it showed, but concealed its own liberal pieties . . . it was experienced not as satire, but as a confirmation of fears."[7] Consequently, Kael sees *Dr. Strangelove* as encouraging young people to give up on sanity as always impossible in the real world, because the characters in the movie couldn't keep the bomb from going off. The threat of extinction can only devalue life, making it all a joke. Kael sees the film not producing Brustein's purgation in young people, but hysterical paralysis: encouraging feelings of hopelessnesss, powerlessness, "innocence." "It's not war that has been laughed to death, but the possibility of sane action."

It's pointless to argue with a critic who condemns a movie because kids tell her it justifies their own childish pessimism. As for the hidden liberal pieties, they don't seem that pious: the President wouldn't be browbeaten into a nuclear attack; Russia and the U.S. could cooperate to stop a common threat; most people are well-intentioned, if stupid and bigoted. It's funny for Kael to condemn a film for irresponsibility *and* pieties, anyway.

Six years later, the sympathetic reviews all seem valid and

cogent. All agree that *Dr. Strangelove* works as a purgation of
fears and desires; that Kubrick uses a totally detached, outsider's
viewpoint; that the characters are sharply observed American
stereotypes who form a dehumanized spectrum leading to the
mechanized Strangelove and to the distinctive mechanical personalities beyond: the gaily copulating or madly hurtling death-
dealing plane, the eerie automated War Room, the crashing assault
weapons, the remorseless brooding Doomsday Machine.

The "setting up" of the purgation is subtly handled. The factors
and situations are so complex and interwoven that any movie
moralizing or blame-fixing (e.g., "Commies did it!" or "Ripper did
it!") becomes impossible. General Ripper, who initiates the attack,
is psychotic, so social conventions can't apply. The Attack Plan R
he abuses was approved by the President, Turgidson, and the
whole government, distributing the guilt. The Doomsday Machine
was built because the Soviets couldn't keep up with the arms race
("Our people grumbled for nylons, and sewing machines . . ."),
decided to be "efficient" (the Doomsday Machine is cheap), and
saw a hint we were building one in *The New York Times*. Everybody is to blame, so there's no point smugly thinking about
"blame." The gray-liberal-told-ya-so! gloom of *Fail Safe* or *On
the Beach* is missing. All that matters is the growing, terrifying
probability of destruction, as Mandrake and Muffley shout and
argue and plead into the telephones, and "King" Kong plunges
onward, unstoppable. . . .

Kubrick's detachment is critically noted. Simon incisively
points out that Kubrick has no rebels in his film, unless you count
the filmmakers, or the audience. Kauffmann, in a nice augury of
2001, comments more radically: "*Dr. Strangelove* has been made
from the viewpoint of another race in another universe observing
how mankind, its reflexes scored in its nervous system and its
mind entangled in orthodoxies, insisted on destroying itself."[6] It's
interesting to contrast Kauffmann's summing up of transcendental fatalism with Brustein's analysis: "its only viewpoint is outrage against the malevolence of officialdom."[2] Both attitudes are
present, as they were in *Paths of Glory,* only the agonized fury
seems ready somehow to break out of its fatalistic container. I will
return to this point in my conclusion, but I note here that it is this

tension between hopelessness and hysterical outrage that makes *Strangelove* and, to a lesser extent, *Paths of Glory* and *Lolita,* so exciting. Finally, all the critics see various characters as intense caricatures of American types, attitudes, and obsessions. Comparison indeed reveals new layers of tension and irony: Generals Ripper and Turgidson, for example, are both eager hawks—tough, aggressive, pious, distrustful of the "Russkies." But Ripper is psychotic, apparently impotent and a latent homosexual, gentle, obsessed, concerned for children, the men on the base, Mandrake's opinion of him. Chief of Staff General "Buck" Turgidson, alternately, has a sexy mistress, is brash, chews gum, can't concentrate, is maniacally well-adjusted, and can only rant about tricky Russkies or (as one critic put it), "salivate at destroying every human being east of the Danube."

John Simon's dehumanization typology for the film can be included in an ingenious interpretation offered by F. Anthony Macklin. In his study "Sex and Dr. Strangelove,"[9] Macklin points out how *Dr. Strangelove* is a sex allegory. "From foreplay to explosion in a mechanized world," I have added more supporting information to an expanded outline of Macklin's idea:

The film opens with two enormous silvery SAC planes in titanic coitus, to the music of "Try a Little Tenderness," on station outside Russia—the "foreplay."

A little later, General Jack D. Ripper (pun: Jack the Ripper) initiates the attack. Ripper cannot or will not ejaculate during sex, and he is obsessed by "bodily fluids." At last he has found a release, and what a release! The planes are radioed to use Plan R—R for Romeo.

Captain Mandrake (the only character whose name suggests normal sexuality) is the voice of sanity. Given the opportunity, Ripper pulls out an enormous machine gun and joyously fires it "at his enemies." Mandrake humors him, argues too, but the General keeps a big pistol inside his waistband, finally locks himself in the bathroom with it, and suicides with this phallic symbol.

In the War Room, General "Buck" Turgidson (meaning "male" and "swollen") cheers the assault on Russia, of which he is contemptuous and distrustful (male chauvinsm). Turgidson mixes up weapons and sex: He tells his girl friend to "start her countdown" so when he gets back she'll be ready to "blast off." Later, when she calls about sex, he's too busy with bombs.

President Merkin Muffley (both of whose names refer to the female pudendum) can't stop the attack, so he calls Premier Kissoff (meaning: start of disaster). The two collaborate on the phone like fathers trying to stop a neighborhood rape. ("You'll just have to shoot them . . . I know they're our boys.")

The B-52 is phallic, particularly in its indefatigable race to coitus. ("What's the nearest target of opportunity?" King shouts.) "King" Kong himself is a movie symbol of primitive, civilization-destroying lust. "His" bombs are labeled with two notorious sexual salutations: *Hi There!* (a homosexual advance) and *Dear John* (salutation of letter breaking off an affair). Kong plunges toward the target on the phallic bomb with a yowl of ecstasy. The detonation is the film's own climax.

In the War Room we see a sort of *post coitum tryst,* Strangelove dominating. With a leer, he suggests survival for a few, underground—ten women to every man. The advisers, De Sodesky, Turgidson, even Muffley like this new "strange love." As John Simon points out, the machinery finally takes command. In the deep shafts, life and love will be even more machinelike. Strangelove's new plan will surely be even more dehumanizing.

Dr. Strangelove ends with endless atomic explosions, endless orgasms. Perhaps we are seeing the last desperate fight for "mineshaft space"—breeding space. The repressions of civilization (controlling bombs and sex) are no more. The mechanical and the orgiastic have met, for the first and last time.

This interpretation, while very exciting itself, is only one interesting way of looking at the film. As Kubrick himself wrote Macklin: "I think that you have found a rather engaging way of viewing the film. I would not think of quarreling with your interpretation nor offering any other, as I have found it always the best policy to let the film speak for itself." Despite this silence, it's clear Kubrick has found brilliantly dramatized correlatives for many of the most important psychoanalytical insights about the nature and cost of civilized life, extending them to their limits.

In addition to purging Juvenalian satire or a sexual allegory,

Dr. Strangelove may also be considered as the logical extension of Kubrick's other two war films: *Fear and Desire* and *Paths of Glory*. The parallels between the Kirk Douglas film and *Dr. Strangelove* are striking: a castastrophic attack and the subsequent debacle; levels of command fighting and destroying each other; a comedy of irony and contradictory responses; the basic problem—the survival of anonymous individuals; a never-seen enemy.

In other ways, *Dr. Strangelove* resembles *Paths of Glory* driven to the ultimate limits, jet-propelled as it were: The emotional commander is now not just vain and spiteful but psychotic; the battlefield is again sundered—bomber, base, and War Room —without access or even communications among them until it's too late; the top command is divided into weak fragments— decent, powerless Mandrake, reasonable President Muffley, computerlike Dr. Strangelove (all played by a plastic Sellers); the prize in the balance is not three drab Everymen, but all humanity.

The difficulty in comparison is in the role of the socially obsessed Colonel Dax—who plays this part? Surprisingly, Major "King" Kong does, going bravely on, dodging missiles and radar detection, heading for his target in the grand tradition because "The folks back home is a'countin' on us, and, by golly, we ain't about to let 'em down." The obsessed hero has become an ignorant instrument of race suicide. Nevertheless, he remains a hero.

The similarities with *Fear and Desire,* beyond the themes stated, again lie fundamentally in the characters. The Mandrake-Muffley-Strangelove intellectual corresponds to Lieutenant Corby, the socially driven Kong to Mac, the emotionally unstable Ripper to Sidney, the stoical submissive Fletcher to Guano, Turgidson, and the bomber crew.

Beyond interpretations, there are many more critical points to be made about *Dr. Strangelove*. Visually, it is always fascinating. Each of the three parallel stories is shot in its own camera style: the hazy, vibrating, incoherent battle footage of the assault on Burpleson Air Force Base; the quickly cut, intense close-ups of the bomber flight deck, straining crew, endless instruments— especially the fragmented hysterically tense duel with the missile; the weird immense black steeple of the War Room shot with carefully composed static shots of eerie beauty, the voices now of human quality, now reverberating, as if Turgidson, Muffley, or Strangelove, crouched low under the ring of lights, had momentarily seen it as a halo of the angel of death or vengeance.

There are very memorable images as well. One is the grim, cigar-puffing face of Ripper. Another is a repeated two-shot with General Turgidson ranting in the foreground, and another dignified, self-possessed-looking general behind to the right. You keep thinking: *That's* what a general should be like, and meanwhile Turgidson raves away. The third, laboriously built-up to with all the intense realistic shots of intricate controls, terrified flyers, the B-52 racing over ice and tundra and evergreens, is that one utterly fantastic image, as impossible as the diabolically narrowing streets of *Caligari,* of Major "King" Kong straddling his bomb, and screaming a rebel yell as he plunges down toward the passive target spread out below.

Finally, the visual element adds ambiguity to the prolonged series of bomb explosions at the end. The shots are clearly old newsreel footage of the Hiroshima and Christmas Island blasts. After so much expense, why use cheap footage that everyone has seen many times? Rather than the presumed Doomsday, isn't it a sort of visual cynical shrug—this film won't stop you, nothing has, but bombing's inevitable—We'll Meet Again. . . .

The humor of *Dr. Strangelove* deserves a few words. Critics disagree whether the film is technically black comedy (Kauffman), satire (Simon, MacDonald), or comic nihilism (Brustein). But the comic devices of the film are clear: collision between very extreme and more normal comic caricatures, unsuitable responses to Doomsday, and massive doses of irony.

Thus, the psychotic Ripper explains his fluoridation theories to the worried, humoring British Mandrake; then the distrustful Guano irritates him; intellectual President Muffley has to handle in turn the bumptious, better-dead-than-Red Turgidson, the haughty Russian Ambassador, the drunken, hysterical Premier Kissoff, and the soulless, mechanistic Strangelove; and Major Kong alternately exhorts, teases, cooperates with, or argues with his dead-pan crew. Most of the really funny stuff in the film is mixed up in these grotesque and pathetic exchanges: President

Muffley trying to pry the situation out of Turgidson; the General proudly reading Ripper's crackpot manifesto to SAC; Guano sneering: "Try any preversions in there, I'll blow your head off!"; Muffley in an idiotic argument with Kissoff over who is sorrier; Dr. Strangelove spitting out "*human* error" like rotten food.

A second type of humor, mixed in very much with the first, consists of various unsuitable responses to Doomsday, or made in the context of Doomsday.

The most memorable of these is Kong's ride down on the bomb, whooping and yelling and waving his Stetson like a rodeo performer. Others include President Muffley breaking up a scuffle by shouting: "Gentlemen, you can't fight here! This is the War Room!"; Guano's refusal to shoot up a Coke machine for change: "That's private property!" There are also people who seem to operate all too easily in the Doomsday context: Turgidson's "I don't say we wouldn't get our hair mussed, Mr. President, but only ten to twenty million casualties—depending on the breaks!" Though Kubrick's comments suggest he made the film a comedy because such lines struck him funny, most audiences don't laugh much at them. Rather, it is Kubrick's murderous American stereotypes that the audiences find amusing.

Lastly, *Dr. Strangelove* is filled with ironies, from the soldier's line, "Gee, those trucks sure look real!"; to the SAC motto, "Peace is our Profession," bullet-ridden in the assault; to Muffley's hint to Kissoff that inadvertently helps Kong get through; to Kong's defiant battle cry that dooms them all: "Shoot! We ain't come this far just to dump this thing in the drink!"; to the Russian Ambassador really waving a secret camera after all. From *Paths of Glory,* if not before, Kubrick's work is as full of irony and ambiguity as one cares to interpret it.

In addition to these three broad forms of humor, there are samples of a dozen other forms: the visual grotesque of copulating planes; General Ripper's justification speech, which is completely familiar and sound until the last line reveals him to be totally insane; Strangelove's confusion of past and present employers as he describes the fascist state below; the Nichols and May scene between General Turgidson and his Playboy secretary/mistress;

"King" Kong's funny business with his Stetson and the survival kits, and many more.

The script of *Dr. Strangelove* shows the tightness of *Paths of Glory* and the careful exposition of *The Killing*. The logic of Ripper's scheme and the subtleties of Plan R are explained no less than three times—by the demented General who conceives them, the dubious bomber crew who execute them, and the fast-thinking President who foils them. Naturally, once the order to attack is given (almost at once), suspense, tension, terror, and Kubrick's own peculiar inevitability build faster and faster, particularly after the code is found and Muffley and Kong are waging a desperate battle of wits with life on earth as the stakes.

It is necessary to correct two common critical errors about *Dr. Strangelove*. First, President Muffley is far from the ineffectual, mediocre liberal he is often described as. In fact, he is a shrewd, tough, and protean-decisionmaker. He sorts through the fragmentary and unlikely data he's given, pries more from a bumbling Turgidson, stares down the sly scheme for an unprovoked attack, wheedles the Russian Ambassador into helping him, sweet-talks the drunken Premier into effective full cooperation, almost stymies the Doomsday Machine, and, even then, is open to plans that will preserve something of his nation. A second error is to blame the machines, especially the Doomsday Machine, for the apocalypse. While the Doomsday Machine causes it, so does the mad human being Ripper, the product-hungry Soviets, and their leader who "loves surprises." Machines like radios, telephones, and perhaps automated mine shafts likewise try to avert and cushion the disaster. To put the onus on machines is as incorrect as to put the blame on rationality.

A curiously subtle and effective technique in the script, which might be called "reverberation," is Kubrick's way of repeating ideas in so many ironic contexts that after a while any meaning they have tends to disappear. Consider patriotism. The idea first appears in "King" Kong's moving but misplaced dedication to the bombing mission. ("The folks at home are counting on ya!") Next, Ripper uses almost the same phrases to encourage his defense forces. He, too, in a stranger sense, believes what he is saying. A little later, General Turgidson tells President Muffley that patriotism demands he strike first. ("It might be better if you concerned yourself more about the American people!") And all the time Kubrick keeps cutting back to the indomitable plane, as the All-American, masterful, deluded Kong fights his way gallantly to the target. Patriotism is misinterpreted and misapplied so many times in so many ways that it seems a sort of logical mistake, like a round square or four-corner triangle, or, even more, a short circuit of the nervous system, an intellectual epilepsy, meaningless and lethal. The notions of heroism, piety, and anti-Communism also are mocked to death. By the end, there are no "isms" or rationalizations left. We all die naked.

Finally, Kubrick's constant themes are apparent once more:

Imaginary worlds. In this film, they are the most fragmented and unreal. Many characters live in their private universes: Ripper in a psychotic dream of Communist fluoridation; Turgidson in a slightly saner but hysterical wish for Communist annihilation; Strangelove in a place where humans are clumsy, contemptuous accessories to computers. The three physical worlds of the B-52, Burpleson Base, and the War Room are totally isolated, furiously defended, obsessively driven. Most important, each one comes to be motivated by a perverse dream theory that leads to ruin: The B-52—*we are at war;* Burpleson—*Communist fluorides are poisoning our precious bodily fluids;* the War Room—*we can survive a hundred years in mine shafts.*

Futility of intelligence, errors of emotions. General Ripper, who cannot understand, let alone control his emotions, is driven into insanity, genocidal scheming, suicide. The intelligent Mandrake can't dig the code out of him, nor can bright President Muffley outfox the indomitable Kong. The Doomsday Machine and Plan R, logical end-products of "survival thinking," kill us all. The emotional Premier, keeping his Doomsday Machine a secret, is an accomplice to the slaughter. Though Turgidson, Strangelove, and Muffley may barely survive, one is a fool, one a machine, one an agonized, defeated man (a random selection of mankind!) in an inhuman (breeding pen) environment, bossed by an amoral, inhuman intelligence.

Murder-suicide pair. The two who fit best are General Ripper and Major Kong, or perhaps the whole society and Major Kong. Ripper, emotionally obsessed, orders Kong to his doom. Then he is hounded to death by Kong's comrades, suiciding to avoid them. Kong, socially-personally obsessed, completes his mission, dying to do so, and thus insuring Ripper's death in any case, along with the whole social structure which destroyed him.

Odyssey and obsessed hero. The Odyssey is the terrible journey of Major Kong's B-52. The scenes in the War Room or at Burpleson Air Force Base are all responses to this, explaining why he's flying, why he should be stopped or not stopped, and how they'll try to stop him. By comparison with the epic flight, the goings on at the other two locales are by turns pathetic, ineffectual, silly, hysterical, maniacal, and dumb. When Kong wins through, they might never have been (and shortly won't be). During those last seconds, he surely learns more than anyone else in the film. The movie could even have ended with his winning through, though the last War Room scene is nice because it suggests the farce will just go on and on. . . .

Recently, Kubrick was asked if he felt there had been any change at all in the chances of nuclear war in the five years since *Dr. Strangelove.*[1] He replied that he felt the chances were greater than ever. He dwelt on the possibility of a wily, self-disciplined Jack D. Ripper-type still outwitting the psychological fitness tests and rising to a position of command, or even of a psychopathic, alcoholic, or emotionally unstable President who starts a war during an insane fugue, stupifying binge, or over-the-edge crack-up. Or a deranged underling might dump LSD in a normal (we should be so lucky!) president's coffee. Finally, Kubrick dwelt on the easy acceptance by most ordinary people of the nuclear balance of terror.

Kubrick feels most people know they will die, yet cannot come to grips with all the implications of this, producing emotional anxieties, tensions, and unresolved conflicts expressed as frustration and bitterness, and increasing conflicts "as they grow older and see the grave yawning before them. . . . I actually believe that they unconsciously derive a kind of perverse solace from the idea that in the event of nuclear war, the world dies with them."

Kubrick's own concern with the awesomeness and agonizing loneliness of death seems prominent in his next film, *2001: A Space Odyssey.*

9
2001: A Space Odyssey

I tried to create a *visual* experience, one that bypasses verbalized pigeonholing and directly penetrates the subconscious with an emotional and philosophical content . . . I intended the film to be an intensely subjective experience that reaches the viewer at an inner level of consciousness, just as music does. . . . You're free to speculate as you wish about the philosophical and allegorical meaning of the film. . . .
—*Stanley Kubrick, 1968*[12]

KUBRICK CANNOT REMEMBER when he got the idea to do a film about the idea of intelligent life outside the earth.[1] He became interested in the subject, read omnivorously, and eventually was convinced that the universe was full of intelligent life. It seemed time to make a film about it.

The film took three years. During the six months of preparation, Kubrick and Arthur C. Clarke, a well-known science-fiction writer, worked together to write a 130-page prose treatment, consulting with dozens of scientific authorities and agencies along the way. The treatment was reworked and rewritten into a screenplay, and reworked again as Kubrick made the film. Thus Clarke's novel *2001: A Space Odyssey*[3] is his own version of the film based on the co-authored script, rather than a "primary interpretation" or verbal guide. For example, Clarke makes the monolith a transparent, hypnotic super-testing and teaching machine. Kubrick sought a more powerful and mystical effect with his simple black obelisk. I will discuss only Kubrick's creation, and discount the book except as an heuristic device.

Kubrick has stated his views on extraterrestrial intelligence several times.[7,12] Very roughly, he believes astronomical theory and the laws of statistics make it inevitable that life and intelligence have evolved independently on billions of different planets in the universe, and on some of these billions, far beyond life on earth now. Kubrick speculates: "They may have progressed from biological species . . . which are fragile shells for the mind at best, into immortal machine entities . . . and then transformed into beings of pure energy and spirit. Their potentialities would be limitless and their intelligence ungraspable by humans . . . they would ultimately possess the twin attributes of all deities—omniscience and omnipotence."[12]

On the level of simple plotting, Kubrick has explained *A Space Odyssey* deals with man's contact with such superior extraterrestrial intelligences, though perhaps not quite deities. A first artifact is left on earth four million years ago, to influence the behavior of the man-apes' evolutionary progress. A second artifact signals the intelligences shortly after man reaches the moon, a sort of "cosmic burglar alarm." A third artifact near Jupiter sweeps an explorer into a "star gate," in which he is hurled "on a journey through inner and outer space and finally . . . to where he's placed in a human zoo approximating a hospital terrestrial environment drawn out of his own dreams and imagination. In a timeless state, his life passes from middle age to senescence to death. He is reborn, an enhanced being, a 'star child,' an angel, a superman, if you like, and returns to earth prepared for the next leap forward of man's evolutionary destiny."[7]

Kubrick feels that an actual encounter with such an advanced intelligence would be "incomprehensible within our earthbound frames of reference." Thus his depiction of it in eerie and bizarre images, with the help of the visually orchestrated, ambiguous but comprehensible story would stimulate viewer reactions, including spontaneous metaphysical and philosophical speculations. Kubrick wanted to reach "a wide spectrum of people who would not often give a thought to man's destiny, his role in the cosmos, and his relationship to higher forms of life."[12] A sample of his responses is included in *The Making of Kubrick's 2001.*[1]

When the script was ready, Kubrick spent four months directing the live action sequences of the film, although planning and preparations had been long under way. As in *Dr. Strangelove,* he supervised every aspect of production, from the construction of an enormous spinning centrifuge to simulate the spaceship's interior, to create extraordinarily realistic man-ape costumes, to selecting all his music arrangements, often working all day seven days a week. Gary Lockwood commented that working for Kubrick was like working with a great military commander: "He had this huge labor force working for him and he was always in control of every detail."[1] Finally, Kubrick spent a year and a half shooting 205 special-effect shots, many of them possible only because of technical processes Kubrick himself created. The views of the space vehicles, for example, use models with tiny inserted shots of live action projected from within, a totally new approach. Again, much of this is detailed in *The Making of Kubrick's 2001.*

Kubrick's own interpretation of directing may have been changed by his contact with the scientific concepts. In a recent interview he commented: "A director is a kind of idea and taste machine; a movie is a series of creative and technical decisions, and it's the director's job to make the right decisions as frequently as possible."[7] In another interview, he suggested his creative strategy: "I usually take about a year to get interested in something, get it written, and start working on it, and in a year, if you keep thinking about it, you can pretty well exhaust the major lines of play, if you want to put it in chess terminology. Then, as you're making the film, you can respond to the spontaneity of what's happening with the resources of all the analysis that you've done. That way, you can most fully utilize each moment while you're making the picture."[10]

As with *Dr. Strangelove,* Kubrick tried just before opening to "see the film anew," screening it many times alone and with sample audiences during the single week between completion and release. In the end, he trimmed nineteen minutes which he felt weren't crucial, including parts of "The Dawn of Man," the Orion earth-to-docking flight, Poole exercising, and Poole's pod leaving *Discovery.* Only the last cut elicited any comments: One critic missed the shocking contrast between the endings of Poole's first and second trips outside. Always the auteur, Kubrick showed his film to the New York critics on April 1, 1968.

Writing an abbreviated treatment of *2001: A Space Odyssey* presents special problems. The dialogue, which often does the most to make clear a film's action, is minimal, and often clearly used as a sound effects Odyssey. Verbal descriptions of shots, sounds, and action tend to be less exact, carry a vaguer ambiance. Kubrick constantly admonishes that the film is essentially non-verbal, that "those who won't believe their eyes won't believe this film." To this end I have made the treatment as visual as possible, as well as borrowing from the keen observational power of others, particularly Penelope Gilliatt[6] and F. A. Macklin.[13] Finally, before beginning, I would quote Max Kozloff, whose outstanding critique skillfully suggests the visual force of the film:

Every moment of the lens has a surprising yet slow lift and lilt to it. With their tangibly buoyant, decelerated grace, Kubrick's boom and pan shots wield the glance through circumferences mimed already by the curvature of the screen itself . . . equilibrium seems always to be winding itself through the panorama, and finally tracked across the adjusting tangents of orbiting objects . . . the visual and somatic discriminations that have so long unquestionably been linked to form an order of physical existence are dislodged in this film . . . big as it is, the screen is but a slit through which to comprehend immensities that always escape the frame. The film is haunted by imminences always outside, left and right, above and beneath, its depth of field—imminences which make even the most complete local information look arbitrary in face of the scope now opened up . . .[10]

Title: "The Dawn of Man," over a great quiet cinerama landscape of desert: muted earth colors, yellows, lots of rocks, little vegetation, long lines of hills in horizontal stasis. Tapirs snuffle over the savannahland. We see the life cycle of the australopithicine, the squat, hairy, frisky man-ape: eating grass, scratching and chattering in groups, cowering from howling carnivores. In the dark a leopard with strangely glowing violet broken-glass eyes guards the carcass of a zebra in the moonlight; the vegetarian man-apes huddle in fear.

Gilliatt sees the horrible man-ape overlap: "Their stalking movements are already exactly like ours: an old tramp's, drunk, at the end of his tether and fighting mad." Brute fear has been refined into human dread. In the length of the legs, the glitter in the eyes, man is waiting, trapped in the paradise and prison of the instincts.

In the first dawn light, a tall black rectangular monolith appears among the man-apes, who scatter from it alarmed and chattering

Left: View of astronaut through the eye of HAL. The viewer, intellectual man, is identified with an ultimate intelligence, watching the emergence of a different form of life. *(Metro-Goldwyn-Mayer, 1968) Below:* Scientists view the moon monolith from the lip of the pit, while a three-quarters Earth hangs on the horizon. Even as the killer apes, technologist Heywood Floyd is stirred by his first view of the alien artifact. *(Metro-Goldwyn-Mayer, 1968)*

In one pod, the astronauts discuss HAL while the computer reads their lips from a TV monitor outside. In this composition, men are surrounded, dwarfed, walled in by technology, which hears even their whispered secrets. *(Metro-Goldwyn-Mayer, 1968)*

reprovingly. We hear Ligeti's churchly, wordless "Requiem" and "Lux Aeterna," purposeless, goalless music.

The man-apes finally approach the black monolith cautiously, perhaps drawn on by appreciation of its absolute color and form, its smooth faces and keen edges, its threat of newness, something more—finally touching it and then herding round in awe, a wordless, primitive, poetic moment. The music is Ligeti's "Concrete," sounding like a frantic collage of all the religious themes in the world.

The monolith dominates the shallow depression in the rocks where the man-apes gather, squatting around a water hole. Overhead, unseen, glowing sun and dead moon move toward the zenith together along a vertical plane which includes the monolith: an eclipse configuration. One man-ape reaches out slowly (fearfully? yearningly?) for the great black shape while the music throbs ominously, preparing. The three worlds align, darkness falls, the man-ape touches it, and the great ecstatic "World Riddle" theme from Strauss's *Thus Spoke Zarathustra* bursts forth, a cry of triumph. . . .

Now the same man-ape squats playing with a narrow bone from an antelope skeleton, plunking it experimentally from side to side, the rhythm humorous, sensing how it adds somehow to him. In violent slow motion the man-ape smashes at the skeleton with bizarre delight, the shattering punctuated with visions of a falling tapir.

Another pack of chattering, loping man-apes comes over the rocky crest of the depression, seeking water. In an elaborate, slow-motion charade, with screaming, darting, pathetic attempts at panicking the residents, they war for the waterhole. The new man-apes leap and lunge and chatter about. At last the man-ape with his bone advances dubiously—then attacks, swinging and swinging, brutally killing the leaping, screaming leader of the new pack while his own chatter and cry. The man-ape keeps thumping and thumping away even after the other one is still. . . .

The man-ape practices on the antelope skeleton, demolishing it in slow motion. The smashed bones bounce and fly into the air, the dark hairy arm flowing up passionately out of the sky-blue frame, then crashing down to make spinning, arching white fragments again and again: the tool, the weapon, objective split from subjective, killing, reason . . . The man-ape lets the bone fly upward, spinning, turning—becoming, in the instant of a straight cut, an orbiting satellite, a subtle sophisticated tool of four million years later, by-passing history and culture and civilization, to another subservient instrument whirling on its appointed tasks.

A manta-shaped spaceship coasts upward away from the earth, to the lyrical "Blue Danube Waltz." Within the cabin, like a superjet's but with a glowing sign: *Weightless Condition,* is a single passenger, a dozing, safety-belted, fiftyish bureaucrat, his ballpoint pen floating above his lax arm. Gilliat sees a hidden parallel: "The ape's arm swinging up and into the empty frame, enthralled by the liberation of something new to do." This arm is elaborately sheathed and decorated but slack, passive, flabby.

The Pan American space stewardess, her tight professional grin still familiar, fussily retrives the pen, then continues down the aisle, the lack of gravity letting her continue up the wall and across the ceiling, an astonishing sight. The passenger dozes through all this.

In four-four time to the music, the dagger of the Pan Am spaceship gracefully approaches the central dock of the circular space station, a great copulation celebration against the stars, from which the camera discreetly turns at the climactic moment.

The passenger, Dr. Heywood Floyd, enters the station to polite nothings, social smiles. Inside, a Bell Picturephone, the Pan Am desk, and Howard Johnson's Earthlight Room gets ohs and ahs from the audience, the instinctive affection for one's own culture. A loudspeaker murmurs: "A lady's cashmere sweater has just been found in the lounge." Floyd calls home on the Picturephone. His wife is out, and he briskly interrogates his daughter, ignoring the exciting sight of the spinning earth.

In the lounge, Floyd waits blankfaced with some colorless Soviet scientists, half-squatting on some "modern" magenta armchairs (still man's favorite position). In the dead-white, oddly bright curved-floor lounge, he begins a pathetically banal conversation with the Russians. For a moment it seems to pick up, a probing scientist asking about trouble at Floyd's destination, Clavius.

"I'm not at liberty to say," Floyd tells him with bland smugness, preferring trivialities.

Floyd leaves for Clavius on a clumsy round spaceship, a flying jack-o'-lantern with stubby rockets and legs at the base, two big observation windows for eyes, the pilots' cabin at the stem. As it soars toward the moon, he is again the only passenger, and mostly sleeps or uses an unpleasantly suggestive "free fall toilet." Through all these scenes the pace is slow, the acting understated and naturalistic against the enormous vistas of space. At last the ship drops toward the colossal, sharp-shadowed, craggy lunar disk, which gradually expands to fill the cinerama screen with silent, black-tinged, razor-backed broken magnificence. Stubby landing legs extend, rockets fire from between them; eerily silent, the ship slows its plunge toward the stony world to land amid clouds of driven dust in an underground hangar like a great, red-walled cathedral.

Floyd, an important space official, gives a briefing on the newly found moon monolith to the top scientists and supervisors at Clavius. "Hi, everybody, nice to be back with you," he begins ineptly, hands in pockets. None of *these* squatters display interest or enthusiasm in investigating their monolith. "Well . . . now, ah . . ." Floyd goes on. In dreadfully clumsy dead prose he tells them Clavius has been sealed to keep the secret, and a cover-up rumor spread about a possible epidemic. Only one man mildly objects to hiding this transcendent discovery. "Well, I, ah, sympathize with your point of view," says Floyd in his stultifying, bureaucratic way. No one else wants to ask or argue anything.

Floyd and some Clavius personnel fly out to look at the monolith in a "moon bus," a silvery, bus-shaped, airtight vehicle pushed and supported by jets, soaring above the rugged, bluish lunar landscape. An enormous Earth hangs in the sky.

"That was an excellent speech you gave us," one man tells Floyd.

"Sure was," another confirms ironically.

The first man opens his chemical food with the same good cheer: "They look like ham!"

"Well, they're getting better all the time!"

The specialists and Floyd go over the scientific clues which led to the discovery of the second monolith.

In the lunar dawn, we see a great pit which has been excavated, buttressed and lit. In the end is the lunar monolith, looking small and somehow forlorn, an apparent twin to the one that inspired the man-apes. In their spacesuits, the visitors trot down a ramp into the pit and approach the monolith. One slaps it with his thick glove, to no effect. Now another waves his companions over to pose before it, the traditional portrait of bored tourists or pompous hunters. The photographer waits for the rising sun . . . suddenly a piercing electronic screech, a fierce wail of dissatisfaction! As the scientists instinctively (and uselessly) slap their hands to their ears, the monolith screams and screams. . . .

Title "Jupiter Mission, 18 Months Later."

To Katchaturian's "Gayeneh," dragging, vaguely wandering music, the spaceship *Discovery* flies toward Jupiter. The great spaceship is basically a large white passenger sphere with a slit high in front as a window, connected to an enormous segmented boom, with mounted antennae extending back to the atomic motors. It resembles the vertebrae of some extinct reptile, recalling the man-ape's flung bone. Daniels comments: "The *Discovery*, with its technological sophistication, primitive vertebrate superstructure, and super-rational brain, becomes a brilliant metaphor for the quality of modern life."[4] Silent, isolated, closed to the stars, *Discovery* also has a feeling of stasis, saturated sufficiency.

Within, Astronaut Frank Poole trots around the spinning sphere's skin, looping-the-loop, shadowboxing dead pan, another amusing astonishment of space only we appreciate. Mission Commander Bowman eats the chemical slop food. The two astronauts are unemotional, disinterested. In conversation they're always dry and logical, always agree. A TV interviewer asks warmly: "How is everything going?"

Poole: "Marvelously."

Bowman: "We have no complaints."

A taped cheery message from Poole's middle-class parents produces no response, even as they sing "Happy Birthday to You." The seemingly autistic Poole lies under a sunlamp, tinted glasses hiding any feelings. The interviewer goes on about the other three astronauts, who are "hybernating" during the voyage in electronically monitored sarcophagi: "It's just like sleep, except they don't dream." Thus, the rational technological investigation of the universe: sunbaths, workouts, baby food, isolation, emotionlessness, routine—a sleep without dreams for all.

The last member of the crew is HAL-9000, a super-computer who maintains the ship's systems, his glowing red lantern eyes mounted in all compartments, his ripe soft voice, his TV announcer's vocabulary. "I enjoy working with people," he murmurs pleasantly—"everything is under control." HAL plays chess, asks to see Bowman's sketches, and even monitors the psychological behavior of the astronauts. HAL himself seems to have emotions: a fussy concern about the mission and his effectiveness that makes his spirits rise and fall. Mildly patronized and rebuked, he claims a potential fault in the communications system, and Poole goes out to investigate in a pod, a small one-man spaceship like a portholed diorama egg with long double-jointed mechanical arms. The control panel, like those of all the spaceships, contains many little screens which display quickly changing graphics and equations, a fascinating light show, and a fine rendering of the insensible qualities of space, its real shape and nature.

In the magnificence of space, Poole flies the tiny agile pod along the massive segmented boom, collects and returns with alpha echo three five (AE-35) unit prior to failure.

The astronauts monitor it with their automatic testers, but it seems perfectly in order. The simulated mission with its own HAL-9000 radios that nothing has shown up in Houston. Another computer has coolly corrected HAL.

"Mission control is in error . . . it can only be attributed to human error," HAL replies with face-saving defensiveness.

Poole and Bowman, aware there is major trouble, retire to one of the pods for a private discussion. Moments before mankind's proud vanguard, the two astronauts crouch facing each other in the cramped little room, recalling the cowering man-apes. They agree that if HAL is really malfunctioning, there is no choice but disconnection.

"What do you think?" Poole asks.

"I'm not sure. What do you think?"

"I've got a bad feeling about him."

"You do?"

"Yes, definitely. Do you?"

"I can't put my finger on it, but I sense something strange about him."

Outside in the pod bay, HAL's glowing lantern eye flickers and shifts. The pod is positioned so he can look through its viewport, sees the two men's intent faces. A close-up of their quickly moving mouths, a close-up of HAL's pulsing eye, glowing with menace like a leopard's. The discussion is not secret; HAL knows the threat, he's read it from their lips.

Intermission.

Poole, his face carefully expressionless, takes a pod out to replace the AE-35 unit, a final check before turning off HAL. "Parking" beside the boom, then going out in his spacesuit, his breath roaring like a locomotive over the *Discovery*'s loudspeakers, Poole turns as he senses the pod has begun to move behind him, toward him, reaching for his oxygen lines with its slim but powerful machine-arms. We do not see the murder. Abruptly, the flung-away body is tumbling through space. Like the man-apes, HAL has discovered murder. Bowman desperately tries to find out what's happened. "Not enough evidence to know," HAL remarks with police brusqueness.

Not bothering about his spacesuit helmet, Bowman hurriedly takes a pod out after his colleague. His own decision is admirable, his courage or affection for Poole invisible.

On the empty *Discovery,* we see close-ups of the hybernation machines and their electronic life functions charts: respiration, cardiograms, electroencephalograms—all colored rhythmic curves across glowing screens. Suddenly the lines begun to jump wildly, to a flashing message: COMPUTER MALFUNCTION. The lines sag, jiggling, uneven: LIFE FUNCTIONS CRITICAL. The lines record zero levels and stay there: LIFE FUNCTIONS TERMI-

NATED. Gilliat accurately calls this the most chilling death scene imaginable, the poor technologists dying simply as lines on a chart, statistically.

Outside, Bowman hurtles after the spinning Poole, finally seizing him in his own mechanical arms, a pathetic human shape in the grip of a somehow superior creature (only an enormous head with peering great eye, auto headlamps for spacesight, and great slim steely arms with clawlike hands).

Bowman returns to hang outside the *Discovery* with a new problem: "Open the pod bay door, please, Hal. . . . Open the pod bay door, please, Hal." The shot is bizarrely comic, a ping-pong ball talking back to a volleyball.

"This mission is too important for me to allow you to jeopardize it," HAL tells him coolly. "This conversation can serve no useful function anymore—goodbye!"

Bowman is left, preposterously, murderously locked outside *Discovery*.

Now, for the first time, a modern man acts creatively, improvising something new like the heroic man-ape. Bowman carefully sets his pod beside an emergency, double-doored airlock chamber, ignoring HAL's querulous questions. This outside hatch will open, but is too small to admit the pod, and without his helmet Bowman cannot leave the little spaceship. Bowman opens the hatch anyway, positions himself—then blows the emergency bolts on the pod's hatch, the rush of air exploding him soundlessly into the empty airlock chamber, Kubrick letting him fly boldly right at the camera . . . in frenzied desperation, Bowman closes the outside hatch, lets the air rush into the chamber. . . .

Driven and wilful, Bowman makes his way toward HAL's "brain room." Helpless, desperate, HAL pleads for his life with Quiltylike audacity: "Look, Dave, I can see you're really upset . . . you should sit down calmly, take a stress pill, think things over . . . I know everything has not been quite right with me . . . I feel much better now, I really do . . . I admit I've made some very poor decisions lately . . ."

In HAL's red-lit brain room, Bowman's blazing further emphasizes his ruthless intensity. The satanic coloring permeates the whole room. Bowman begins pulling out the cigarette-pack-sized components of HAL's auto-intellect panels, like tiny souvenir monoliths, so they drift across the room. HAL's voice becomes pathetic, evoking empathy for the only time in the film: "Dave. Stop. . . . Stop. Will you. . . . Stop, Dave. . . . Will you stop, Dave. . . . Stop, Dave . . . I'm afraid . . . I'm afraid, Dave . . . Dave . . . My mind is going. . . . I can feel it. . . . I can feel it. . . . My mind is going. . . . There is no question about it. . . . I can feel it. . . . I can feel it. . . . I can feel it. . . . I'm afraid."

Poetically, agonizingly, HAL's lobotomy mimics natural death, grinding down into senility and finally second childhood. Querulously, faltering, singsong: "Good afternoon, gentlemen. I am a HAL-9000 computer. . . . Mr. Langley taught me to sing a song. . . . It's called 'Daisy' . . . Dai–sy, dai–sy, give—" falters HAL, going down to death. Bowman, his eyes haunted, proven a man by mind and murder, hovers over him. . . .

Dr. Floyd's voice, urban, hearty, suddenly replaces HAL's from the speakers of the blood-red room: "Good day, gentlemen. This is a prerecorded briefing made prior to your departure, which for security reasons of the highest importance has been known on board during your mission only by your HAL-9000 computer. Now that you are in Jupiter space, and the entire crew is revived (!), it can be told to you. Eighteen months ago, the first evidence of intelligent life off the Earth was discovered. It was buried forty feet below the lunar surface, near the crater Tycho. Except for a single, very powerful radio emission aimed at Jupiter, the four-million-year-old black monolith has remained completely inert, its origin and purpose still a total mystery . . ."

Title: "Jupiter and Beyond the Infinite."

In space, the *Discovery* crawls toward the enormous banded shape of Jupiter. A fireball, the distant sun, slowly climbs over the rim—illuminating a bright crescent shape. Jupiter's many moons, like fingernail pairings, all bow to it. The moons, planet, sun, all move into alignment along a single plane with a monolith which orbits through space. Bowman, in a pod, abandons *Discovery*. The moons shift toward alignment. The pod purposely moves toward the monolith. . . .

In the pod, Bowman watches as he plunges, faster and faster, seemingly across an infinitely wide, distant floor and ceiling glowing with luminescent schematics in burning dayglo colors as they rush past. The music is the awesome howls of Gyorgy Ligeti's "Atmospheres," louder and louder, shriller and shriller, as the plunge accelerates—

—into a blazing, wheeling carnival of light, motion! The pod skims over flaring yellow, orange, green landscapes full of crags, mesas, precipices, molten rivers, all erupting and flowing, volcanic dreams, canyons, and ranges full of writhing light. Bowman watches in wonderment, highlights shining on his helmet. Now he seems in the midst of awesome star clouds, a cosmic whirlpool. A *Discovery*-shaped flame drives across the screen toward a pulsing gas cloud. There are solarized close-ups of Bowman's face and eyes, so his sense organs seem to be de-differentiating, dissolving into a primal protoplasm . . . he soars across a cosmic whirlpool, through thundering shafts of flaming colors . . .

Bowman's pod stops in a large green and white room, decorated partly in delicate Louis XVI, partly in Modern: wide coverlet bed, fragile slim-lined furniture, period statues and paintings in framed niches around the walls. The floors, walls, and ceiling glow ethereally. Bowman emerges from pod and spacesuit aged twenty years, roams the premises, the lavatory. The *Discovery*'s survivor returns to see an old grandee dining; the figure turns and it is the astronaut himself in old age. The noise of the moving chair grates in the otherwise silent room. The old man's dinner is bread and wine. Vague laughing sounds drift through. The wine glass falls, breaks. The old man turns to see, and becomes a bald, dying ancient on the bed. He raises his hand, reaching. A monolith stands at the foot of the bed, glowing, ominous, enigmatic. . . .

Bowman is transformed: The man, or perhaps just his head, his mind, is a glowing translucent embryo on the coverlet, a birth. . . .

Now the monolith faces us on the screen, a cosmic midwife, glowing. . . .

The glowing green earth hangs mightily in space, alone among the stars. Music we have heard before throbs ominously again, preparing . . .

The camera turns to another glowing ovoid, orbiting it, a white translucent amnion. From within, a bright-eyed, enormous-eyed, shimmering embryo peers down at the planet as at some new plaything, graphically a match for the whole world. . . . Once more the "World Riddle" theme from Strauss's *Thus Spoke Zarathustra* bursts out in triumph. . . .

The critical response to *A Space Odyssey* was almost entirely enthusiastic, as sampled in *The Making of Kubrick's 2001*.[1] Even the hyperacute Andrew Sarris became a sympathizer after a second viewing: "*2001* now works for me as a parable of a future toward which metaphysical dread and mordant amusement tiptoe side by side . . . I have never seen the death of the mind rendered more profoundly or poetically. . . . *2001* is concerned ultimately with the inner fears of Kubrick's mind as it contemplates infinity and eternity . . . there is absolutely nowhere we can go to escape ourselves."[14]

Though the critics liked the film very much, there was little common agreement on its interpretation and over-all meaning. Penelope Gilliatt, whose review seems especially perceptive, hesitated at drawing conclusions: "I think that Stanley Kubrick's *2001: A Space Odyssey* is some sort of great film, and an unforgettable endeavor. . . ."[6] She ended with her persistent memory of Dr. Floyd's lax, floating arm, versus the enthralled, liberated man-ape swinging his first weapon in delight.

After three years of discussion, two interpretations of *2001: A Space Odyssey* are to me still coherent: a scientific-poetic meaning, and a new myth.

The scientific-poetic meaning is a revised concept of evolution, with an extraterrestrial intelligence appearing to give a helping hand whenever man seems to be at a dead end, by making a basic change in his consciousness. To borrow a metaphor from Arthur Koestler's *Darkness At Noon,* Kubrick's evolution of consciousness operates like a canal with locks, linking two bodies of water at different heights. To get from the lower to the higher body, a species moves into the first and lowest lock. The monolith closes the doors to the outside, and the species (by pumping in water) raises itself to the level of the second lock. Then the monolith opens the doors linking the first and second lock, and the species sails into the second lock. The monolith closes the first-lock-second-lock doors, and the species begins raising itself to the third level. Substitute "consciousness" or "intelligence" for water, "instinct" for the lower water body, "rationality" or "toolmaking" for the first lock, "super-rationality" or "transcendence" for the second lock (or possibly the upper body), "refining techniques" for pumping, and you have an essentially complete interpretation of what happens in *A Space Odyssey*.

Looked at this way, the gross and fine structure of *2001: A Space Odyssey* becomes straightforward, an open-ended comparison of the first two steps of the journey. Both versions of man have reached an evolutionary plateau—the man-apes trapped in their instincts; the men, trapped in rationalism and technology, both squatting and gibbering at each other in vague self-satisfaction. Man-apes and men are threatened by a more ruthless evolutionary equal with red glowing eyes—the cunning leopard in the caves, the super-rational but unstable HAL on board *Discovery*. (Kubrick films sometimes from behind the glowing eye, identifying the precocious, unstable HAL with the audience.) Both man-apes and men eat repellent food, cower from their enemies, generate a hero who can take the next step.

One may also look at man from his discovery of tools to his arrival at the Jupiter monolith—the period of rationality and toolmaking. Gilliatt's intuition, the details of Heywood Floyd's journey and the *Discovery* voyage all suggest that man has followed up and finally over-exploited tools and rationality to the point where his life is sapped of vigor, wonder, or even meaning. (The name "Heywood Floyd" seems itself disoriented; backwards, impersonal, with no apparent connotations.) In space, on the moon, flying to Jupiter, everybody is trapped in a joyless, bland straitjacket of logic, barely covered by pathetic rituals and "sophistication" (re: HAL's TV-announcer voice). HAL, as several critics point out, is the ultimate tool, super-rational, taking these ideas as far as possible. He is actually put in charge of psychologically monitoring the humans, essentially because he is closer to this ideal state. When he begins to acquire emotions, an ego, and the beginning of a personality, when he starts to be a man, HAL begins to misbehave because of the precariousness of his self-worth, his own emptiness. He kills to hide his weaknesses. Thus HAL recognizes their problem more clearly than they do. For this reason his death is particularly tragic. Still, the cultivated decadent old must give way to the crude, vital new, even as the leaping, dancing, screaming man-ape, a master of "instinctual warfare," was murdered by the rather taciturn, aloof, tool-using man-ape. HAL, the ultimate tool, shows that tools and rationality can go only so far, are not enough. In the final moments, Bowman abandons them as he abandons the *Discovery* (a last pun?) and goes through a transformation to the next level of consciousness, the "Star Child." While certainly the strangest and most bizarre part of *2001,* as science-poetry this section seems curiously weak. The depiction of the rest of Bowman's life is done in a series of strange transitions: a middle-aged Bowman "seeing and becoming" an elderly Bowman and finally "seeing and becoming" an ancient dying Bowman. My own feeling is one of meaninglessness and futility, as if anything Bowman would have lived was pointless, as if he'd never lived at all. Finally, the Star Child floats in space beside the earth, enormous-eyed, ethereal, but passive, aloof, hesitant, as the "World Riddle" theme roars. Compare this with the shambling, daring, and then masterful joyousness of the tool-using man-ape.

In terms of this interpretation, I suspect Kubrick hoped the strained but subtle repetitions of ideas, images, and themes running through the Dawn of Man and Heywood Floyd-*Discovery* sequences would establish a sort of subconscious "framework" on which the audience would project ideas about life in the transcendental state. Collected responses to the film[1] indicated that this was not the case: Most of the audience apparently either simply luxuriated in the film, tried to "explain" it, or saw it as a critique and celebration of the present and immediate future.

As scientific-poetic art, an elegant vehicle for ideas, there are two criticisms to be made of *A Space Odyssey.* First, despite its beautiful images, *2001* is anti-scientific. The fundamental discovery of tools, implying scientific thought, is instilled by an outside force, not a human accomplishment. Consistently, astronauts and scientists are shown as unenthusiastic, unemotional technicians whose work is joyless. Science is trivialized: The moon monolith simply "turns up" on a survey.

More repellently, *2001*'s science-poetry is authoritarian and preaches submission. All human accomplishments are implied to be automatic responses to the monolith's inspiration: "Make tools!" The monolith is implicitly giving orders to Newton, to Shakespeare, to Einstein, to Wernher Von Braun . . . but even man's follow-up is so poor more interference is needed. Moreover, the motives of the monoliths are not given or questioned—they are too "superior." But the only real superiority of the monolith is overwhelming power to manipulate and control. The monolith knows best, man is nothing. The terrifying emptyness of the last decade—moments of Bowman's life are all too consistent with this; for contrast, one can look at how Welles builds the dazzling mandala of *Citizen Kane* out of the very same few moments. . . .

A final scientific-poetic criticism of the film involves the Star Child. It is audacious and enigmatic to end with the orbiting space baby, but it also represents a failure of nerve. It's as if an old-fashioned science-fiction movie, like *War of the Worlds* or *The Day the Earth Stood Still,* with its bright schoolmarm, farmers with shotguns, dubious businessmen, and fast-thinking young scientist, had its prologue of "Mysterious sightings, nonsense!" and "This computer must be crazy!" pulled out to two hours, making it a sort of shabby satire. Then when the saucer swoops in, the airlock opens and the Martian emerges, a title flashes: THE END! After all his irony and elegant cinematography, Kubrick has in a sense never really astonished us. He is unable to suggest what a transcendent being would do.

The second systematic interpretation of *A Space Odyssey* has been as a new myth. Daniels[4] has considered this at length. Briefly, a myth is a story which tries deliberately to relate basic truths about life; the characters and events are intended personifications of universal principles and processes. A myth also suggests how people regard the universe.

"The Dawn of Man" theme is clearly, then, the growth of intelligence. Stackhouse[15] sees the monolith as perfection in form, a source of infinite intelligence and knowledge. Daniels[4] initially would see man as a bright, passionate animal, full of awe for the universe, yet capable of murder.

To him, the direct cut to the spacemen implies all of human history is patterned on the prologue, and the remainder of the film is an indictment of the goalless, soulless rationalists who are the descendants of that same toolmaker. They are the children of Dale Carnegie and Tom Swift. On Satellite V, the man-ape descendant fills his time with drab ritualistic conversation. Heywood Floyd's only pleasure comes from refusing to give a straight answer to a Russian's question. Daniels comments that such exhausted remnants, such "last men," have lost the ability to despise themselves. In their certitude, they are themselves despicable.

On the moon, the second monolith is treated without awe or wonder. The scientists and bureaucrats pose smugly before it, like tourists. Daniels finds the terrible *inadequacy* of this gesture, its contempt for the strange and the beautiful, an appalling obscenity.

On board the Jupiter Mission, the nonfrozen astronauts live in pointless cycles, like Poole's circling shadow boxer, opposing no one, preparing for nothing. Daniels: "The *Discovery,* with its technological sophistication, primitive vertebrate superstructure, and super-rational brain, becomes a brilliant metaphor for the quality of modern life." HAL, a transistorized matriarch, tends to everything, the ultimate welfare state, her boys hiding and plotting for "Astronaut Power." HAL is the intellect personified, and the intellect goes wrong, becomes human by the act of murder. Daniels thinks Kubrick is implying that since machines are becoming human, men must become something else, something more. . . .

David Bowman tries to become something more. He proves his legacy of humanity by innovating out of the death trap HAL has set for him, then murders the machine-man. His title of Mission Commander and his sketching suggests a hero and creator. ("Bowman" suggests "Boy-man," and "shooting the arrow of desire beyond man.")

At Jupiter, Bowman abandons the lobotomized, civilized shell of *Discovery* to plunge on a whirling, blazing tour of the cosmos, the whole universe spread before him. He comes to rest in the comforting, attractive Louis XVI chamber; is divested of pod, spacesuit, material body; and becomes a higher being of some sort, no longer enclosed, able to contemplate the whole earth with enormous eyes. . . .

A Space Odyssey, examined as a myth of today, seems to suggest several principles and processes: destiny (the monoliths' masters?) acting within an indifferent cosmos; a hierarchy of consciousness with "super powers" on top, rationality rated low, and instinctual and social behavior at the bottom; technological man as a self-congratulatory, half-dead spiritual pigmy who must transcend himself; human history and social existence as repetitive and empty of meaning.

Are these true mythic principles? By comparison, Edith Hamilton has written of ancient Greek mythology: ". . . the Greeks too had their roots in the primeval slime . . . lived a savage life, ugly and brutal. . . . But what the myths show is how high they had risen above the ancient filth and fierceness by the time we had any knowledge of them."[8] *2001: A Space Odyssey* would then demonstrate modern man's self-awareness and growth from technological savagery.

Looked at this way, the mythmaking of *2001* is quite successful. Kubrick proposes an ordering of the universe, the monoliths' masters as mysterious mentors, like the gods the Greeks invented to replace the terrifying omnipotent Unknown. Unlike the Greeks, Kubrick cannot create attractive, companionable gods in man's image, but he can suggest a relationship of man to gods, and even how men may become gods. Thus he achieves his own version of "the Greek Miracle," showing men what mankind is and can be, making man at least potentially the center of the Universe.

His principles dealing with society are equally sweeping. The old Greek captains and heroes worshipped power and rapine, making life an endless round of violence. Kubrick sees our own captains and heroes as blindly worshipping technology and human efficiency, making life an endless round of check-list spectacles and empty smiles. Zeus was not exactly Justice Brandeis, but in the *Odyssey* he scourges the wicked and helps the canny Ulysses transcend his passion-driven enemies. Likewise, Kubrick's superior beings help Bowman break out of his stultified society into something new.

Besides considering *2001: A Space Odyssey* as a scientific-poetic work of art or a new myth, there have been several other interpretations. Of course, the film is first of all simply a voluptuous, stunning visual and audio environment. *2001: A Space Odyssey* also may be looked at as a comic work, and F. A. Macklin has done this in detail.[13]

Unlike *Dr. Strangelove,* most of the film's laughter seems to be Olympian rather than deliberate: the grotesque, chattering, violent man-apes; the space station concessions; the somnambulent, self-congratulatory astronaut-administrators; the bright-eyed space child. Finally, *2001* has been lightheartedly discussed as a sexual allegory: Arthur C. Clarke's ultimate liberated science-fiction story, in which two precocious boys go off in their space ship looking for adventure, and wind up having a baby. The fact that instead of Adam and Eve, a single creature returns to earth, is also provocative. How will it reproduce?

In terms of Kubrick's previous work, *A Space Odyssey* occasionally seems a "cannibalization" of earlier images and ideas. HAL, for example, has the dedication to duty of a General Ripper, the glib ability to rationalize of a Claire Quilty, the fierce pride and arrogance of a General Mireau. The final plunge through the star gate to the green and white room includes the rushing walls of the nightmare in *Killer's Kiss,* the hurtling at tree-top height over blazing wild terrain of the final moments of *Dr. Strangelove,* and finally, the ethereal echoing death chambers of *Paths of Glory* and *Lolita.* The notion of a "cover story" also appears in the plot, after being used in at least three previous films.

The strongest resemblances, however, are between *2001* and Kubrick's other poetic, philosophical work, *Fear and Desire.* The themes remain very close, the characters even more so: the over-educated, flippant, empty Dr. Floyd and Lieutenant Corby; the precocious, unstable, ultimately murderous HAL and Sidney; the stolid, submissive Poole and Fletcher; and finally, the heroic, obsessed, transfigured Bowman and Mac. This archetype occurs throughout Kubrick's work, and will be discussed in detail in the last chapter.

Finally, Kubrick's themes appear again:

The imaginary worlds. The idea is implicit in the levels of consciousness: to the man-apes the world is a mechanical, fatalistic place over which they have no control; to the spacemen it is a world of cause and effect without purpose, feeling, or meaning; to the ultimate form of life, the monoliths' masters, it is a whizzing, blinding chaos man is not meant to understand.

Futility of intelligence, errors of emotion. HAL, a "pure" intelligence, implicitly includes the seeds of corruption and destruction—dangerous emotions. He is a paradigm of the limits of thought and feeling. Again, Bowman, a human hero with superior intelligence and emotions, must be sheltered and transformed into something else before he can meet his destiny.

Homicide-suicides. HAL kills Poole and the three other astronauts, leaving clues that will lead to his own death. Bowman trustingly leaves himself vulnerable to HAL, then outwits and kills him.

Triumph of obsessive hero. Bowman seems to become re-humanized by saving his own life and killing HAL, his enemy, just as the tool-using man-ape did. His obsession is clear in his drive to reach HAL, and his headless plunge into the "star gate."

Journey to freedom. The space odyssey of Mission Commander Bowman is a journey to freedom, to the truth about himself and life in the universe. It is significant that Bowman becomes neither a monolith himself, nor one of their wraithlike masters, but something else, the Star Child. Bowman, like all of Kubrick's obsessive heroes, must find "another way."

10
A Clockwork Orange

Alex's adventures are a kind of psychological myth. Our subconscious finds release in Alex, just as it finds release in dreams. It resents Alex being stifled and repressed by authority, however much our conscious mind recognizes the necessity of doing this.

—Stanley Kubrick, 1971[6]

KUBRICK READ *A Clockwork Orange* for the first time in the summer of 1969, a gift from Terry Southern. Finishing it at one sitting, he reread it in whole and in parts, and for the next few days thought mostly about its great filmic possibilities: "The narrative invention was magical, the characters were bizarre and exciting, the ideas were brilliantly developed, and, equally important, the story was of a size and density that could be adapted to film without simplifying it or stripping it to the bone."[6]

For the next six months, Kubrick apparently was busy with his project to do a film on Napoleon, but the crisis of confidence Hollywood was undergoing gave him pause. In January, 1970, he got in touch with Malcolm McDowell, whom he had had in mind for the narrator-protagonist from his first reading. The way McDowell tells it,[9] Kubrick simply asked him to read the book, which both agreed was brilliant, then discussed it with him, eventually offering the chief role. McDowell accepted immediately.

From January, 1970, to the shooting which began in September, Kubrick worked on costumes and make-up with McDowell, getting to know his star. The actor has commented that: "It's a different kind of film for Stanley to do, in that it relies totally on the central character. This is why I think he was very concerned with the actor-director relationship."[9]

At the same time, Kubrick was supervising all the other pre-production details. Starting with a finished story allowed him to skip developing a narrative, and the technical background research was limited as well, mostly to behavioral psychology and conditioned reflex therapy. But to keep production costs down, research also included finding locations typified by interesting modern architecture. Kubrick's solution was to buy ten years' back issues of three architectural journals, then to go through them with his art director, organizing his selections with the new German Definitiv display filing system, which allowed almost infinite cross-referencing with color-coded, alphabetic, and numerical signals.

Kubrick has become deeply involved in such production administration because he feels it is where many creative and artistic battles are lost: "You have got to use your resources (money and people) in the most effective way possible, because they are limited and when they are seriously stretched it always shows on the screen."[11] The basic problem, which makes filmmaking such a difficult organizational and administrative business, is that there are almost no regular routines—nearly everything is a "one of" problem. Thus any "staff" that could handle all difficulties would have ten times as many people as anyone could afford.

Kubrick's response is to keep devising new information-handling systems—ways of organizing, remembering, reminding, following up. He also keeps telling his department heads that "merely giving an order to somebody is only a fraction of their job, that their principal responsibility is to see that the order is carried out accurately, on time, and within the budget."[11]

Kubrick's systematic planning seems to have led to several large economies. The Definitiv cataloguing yielded so many locations that he needed but a few days of studio shooting—only the Korova Milkbar and one or two other interiors were constructed sets. He also found the latest developments in cinema technology to be time- and money-savers: mikes as small as a paperclip which almost guaranteed synched-dialogue and eliminated background noise; photofloods and quartz lamps which gave sufficient illumination when placed in a scene's light fixtures; lightweight fiber-glass camera blimps which allowed hand-held sound takes; ultra-fast lenses (fo.95) which permitted low light level takes, and extremely wide-angle lenses (9.8mm) which got long shots in very confined rooms. (Some of this technology may have confused the aesthetics a bit, e.g., Vincent Canby's comment that: "Mr. Kubrick constantly uses what I assume to be a wide-angle lens to distort space relationships within scenes, so that the disconnection between lives, and between people and the environment, becomes an actual, literal fact."[4])

When it comes down to the planning of specific scenes, Kubrick has commented that he "works out very clearly what the objectives of a scene are from the viewpoint of narrative and character,"[11] as well as tries to "anticipate everything that is humanly possible to imagine. The problem . . . is to make sure that something happens worth putting on film."[6] He speaks elsewhere of a critical rehearsal period, in which he will listen to suggestions from anyone in the vicinity—weighing, modifying, or expanding them, then making the final choice. "In a scene that might take three days to shoot, I would probably spend till four o'clock the first day rehearsing and working things out. This period is one of maximum tension and anxiety; angles and coverage is, by comparison, a relatively simple matter."[5] Dr. Strangelove's wheelchair resurrection, and the "Singin' in the Rain" sequence in *A Clockwork Orange,* both came out of these sessions.

A Clockwork Orange took perhaps six months to shoot, being completed in March, 1971. The director has commented that he set out to stylize the narrative's violence by organizing it around the Overture to Rossini's *Thieving Magpie:* "In a very broad sense, you can say the violence is turned into dance." Not formal dance, but orchestrated movements and music: "From the rape on the stage of the derelict casino, to the super-frenzied fight, through the Christ figures cut, to Beethoven's Ninth, the slow-motion fight on the water's edge, and the encounter with the cat lady where the giant phallus is pitted against the bust of Beethoven, movement, cutting, and music are the principal considerations—dance?"[6]

Kubrick, in his interview with Alexander Walker,[16] restates his belief in the importance of editing. His working method in this film was to begin with two Steenbeck editing tables which allowed him to screen continuously, then shift to a movieola for the actual cutting. Working seven days a week, he started out at ten hours a day and worked up to fourteen or sixteen as his deadline approached.

A Clockwork Orange was released in New York City on Monday, December 20, 1971.

Alex and two of his droogs. Sinister ambiance is built up by single false eyelashes, pathological expressions, extrapolated "skin-head" working-class costumes, boots, arrogant postures. *(From the motion picture* A Clockwork Orange *copyright © 1972 by Warner Brothers Inc.)*

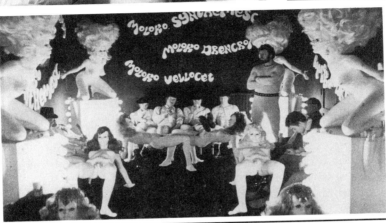

Above: The Korova Milkbar establishes mood of futuristic nihilism with harsh overlighting, hygienic fiber-glass statues of girls used as furniture, gothic organ music, absence of color except for bright, orlon wigs on "girls." *(From the motion picture* A Clockwork Orange *copyright © 1972 by Warner Brothers Inc.) Below:* Alex and his droogs applaud the speech of the old drunkie. Harsh backlighting effect was also used in *Space Odyssey. (From the motion picture* A Clockwork Orange *copyright © 1972 by Warner Brothers Inc.)*

Alex plunges the phallic sculpture at the fallen cat woman. Note ripped-out eyeball ornamentation on his cuff. *(From the motion picture* A Clockwork Orange *copyright © 1972 by Warner Brothers Inc.)*

Kubrick shoots a version of attack on writer's wife. Alex's codpiece offers protection in a rumble, as well as flaunts his sexuality. *(From the motion picture* A Clockwork Orange *copyright © 1972 by Warner Brothers Inc.)*

On blood-red frames, to a gothic playing of Purcell's "Music for the Funeral of Queen Mary," opening titles appear. The first shot is a pair of dark blue eyes, sinister yet humorous, one ringed with false eyelashes, in a dandyish young face. We retreat, revealing the young man who sits between two others, all eerie-eyed, in white shirts and trousers, black boots and bowlers. A young voice, cheeky-cruel yet innocent, begins: "There was me—that is, Alex—and my three droogs—that is, Pete, Georgie, and Dim—and we sat in the Korova Milkbar, trying to make up our rassodocks what to do with the evening . . ." His entire narration will be in this futurish onomatopoetic Cockney.

The camera retreats to show the Korova Milkbar, a bizarre black room decorated with white fiber-glass nudes doing backbends as tables or chained on platforms, phosphorescently lit. Youths in white sit along the walls, zonked out on milk-plus-drugs. "This would sharpen you up and make you ready for a bit of the old ultra-violence . . ."

An old drunk, singing. One thing Alex can't stand, he says happily, is a filthy old drunkie. The bum sprawls below the four, backlit, so the white figures, with exaggerated gestures, black boots, bowlers and canes, fling narrow shadows toward us. The old man, half-contemptuously, asks to be done in, it's no world for an old man, no law and order—and they brutally beat him . . .

To a balletic overture, violins and woodwinds, the camera tilts from a gilded prosceneum. Operatic screams. On the abandoned stage, four mad-faced delinquents are tearing the clothes off a screaming girl. Alex: "We came across Billyboy and his three droogs. . . . They were getting ready to perform a little of the old in-out-in-out . . ."

To elegant waltztime the girl grunts, struggles. A bottle rolls along the littered floor. Alex: "Come and get one in the yerbles, if ya got any yerbles!" In quickly cut flashes of violence, the gangs rumble, all switchblades, judo, heads smashed through plate glass.

In an impossibly low sports car, Alex and droogs race through the night, forcing other vehicles off the road. "What we were after now was the old surprise visit . . ."

Light globes and a little panel: "home." The four, crouched

over, sneak toward an ultramodern home of stone wedges. In the white-walled living room, a man taps his IBM in a bookshelved nook. A handsome woman rises from a mutation Eames chair to answer the door: "There's been a terrible accident," pleads Alex in normal speech.

The writer insists she let him in. The four burst through. While Dim slings the woman over a shoulder, Alex, wearing a grotesque phallic face mask, tumbles books and IBM to the floor. Mildly singing "Singin' in the Rain," he does a soft shoe into stomach and face of the intellectual, then snips away the pants suit of the held woman. Pants at halfmast, he mocks the man, then goes to his wife. . . .

Against the black walls of the Milkbar, the four sprawl. A detail: cufflinks and suspender buttons are simulated ripped-out eyeballs. Some "sophistos" catch Alex's attention when one sings Beethoven. Dim razzberries it, and Alex slams the subnormal with his cane. Dim whines he's no longer Alex's "brother. . . ."

Alex lives with Dad and Mum in Municipal Flat Block A, Linear North. Ultramodern without, the lobby is trashed, the elevator doors broken, a mural of noble citizens pornographically defaced . . .

Upstairs, Alex calls it a perfect evening—what he needs is a bit of the old Ludwig van. He checks on a python in one drawer; watches, wallets, and other loot in another. Then, to a tape of the triumphal music, he lies ecstatically on the bed as Kubrick zooms in on a Beethoven drawing, out on a pornographic one. Quick cuts make four plastic bleeding Jesuses do a tap dance. "Oh bliss oh bliss oh it was gorgeousness!" Alex moans, to flashing images of a woman being hung by leering monsters, primitives crushed by a rockslide, a volcano's eruption. Eyes bulging, apparently masturbating to the "Ode to Joy," Alex climaxes with the music.

Next morning, Alex puts off his clucking Mum and balding apologetic Dad, both simple: "Where does he work? He says it's mostly odd things." Working class in accents and attitudes, they wear tomorrow's bargain basement chic: chubby Mum in a stewardess' plastic mini; shambling Dad in sleazy 1960s Mad. Ave.

gear. The flat is grotesquely decorated, full of ugly knicknacks.

Padding about in shorts, Alex meets his middle-aged, pudgy, sarcastic probation officer, Mr. Deltoid: "That was a bit of extreme nastiness last night . . . ! Next time it's going to be the barry place, the stripy hole!" Deltoid paws Alex shamelessly: "We've studied the problem a century, but we get no further with our studies!"

To "Thieving Magpie," in a flashy plastic boutique, Alex picks up two pre-teens sucking phallus-shaped lollies. In his room, at twelve times normal speed, Alex stages a mini-orgy to the "William Tell Overture" . . . .

In the lobby, Alex meets his droogs again: "Well-well-well-well!" It's a confrontation: Georgie wants them to go after the big-big-big money. Alex: "But you have all you need. . . ."

"Brother, sometimes you talk like a little child!"

In graceful slow motion, the droogs and Alex stride along the marina. Beethoven drifts from a high window, and Alex "vidies" at once what to do—he spins the dissidents into the water, thrusts with his knife: "Now they knew who was master and leader . . ."

But a leader knows when to give and show generousness; Alex accepts Georgie's scheme to visit an almost-deserted health farm. . . .

In a pastel room decorated with mod porn, carpeted with wandering kittens, a wiry Englishwoman exercises, cursing fluently. She rejects Alex's accident story, so he second-stories in, to the strings and woodwinds. Suddenly she sees him: "Hi-hi-hi-hi there!" Alex grins.

Crowing fiercely: "Who are you? How the hell did you get in here?"

Alex fingers a fireplug-sized phallic sculpture, which begins rocking and ticking: "Naughty, naughty, you filthy old sooker!"

"Cut the shit, sonny!"

Enraged, she attacks him with a bust of Beethoven, but Alex holds her off with the sculpture, mocking, the camera spinning and circling them. The woman goes down, and Alex plunges the sculpture at her head! A scream, a pop painting of a mouth within a mouth, both crying out. To approaching sirens, Alex races outside to his droogs, who clobber him. . . .

At the station house, bobbies in uniforms like airliner pilots, but still wearing Elizabeth II's monogram, interrogate a bloody-nosed Alex. Alex: "I know the law, you bastards!"

"We know the law, but knowing the law isn't anything . . ."

A cruel, narrow-faced man hits Alex, who grabs at his attacker's genitals.

Mr. Deltoid arrives fussily: "You're now a murderer! Your victim has died!" The police offer Deltoid a swing at Alex, but he only spits. "I hope to God they torture you to madness," he exclaims.

"He must be a great disappointment to you, sir. . . ."

Helicopter view of an enormous prison, surrounded by green fields. In Alex's always cheeky-cheery tones: "This is the real weepy and tragic part of the story beginning now, oh my friends." Handcuffed to a bobby, Alex is brought in, stripped, examined by a comic ramrod prison guard. . . .

Alex cranks the AV projector for hymns at chapel. When the padre assures them Hell exists, someone belches. When he warns of endless agony, another blows a razzberry. The prisoners wail and groan through "I Was A Wandering Sheep," a homosexual courting Alex by blowing kisses.

In the prison library, a studious Alex reads the Bible. He likes the scourging and crowning with thorns, and "could imagine myself helpin' in, or even takin' charge!" We see an agonized Christ carrying the cross, pan to Roman officer Alex lashing him. Images of Alex as an Old Testament leader in an orgy with his wives' handmaidens, chopping away at infidels in battle. "That kept me goin'!"

Meeting the bluff chaplain in the library, Alex asks for a new rehabilitation treatment, the Ludovico technique: "I want the rest of my life to be good—one act of goodness."

The father is thoughtful: "The question is whether or not this technique really makes a man good. Goodness comes from within —goodness, is chosen. When a man cannot choose, he ceases to be a man."

To "Pomp and Circumstance," the inmates circle the yard, then line up for inspection. An official glances into Alex's cell, noting pin-ups and a bust of Beethoven. The same man urbanely lectures prisoners and staff: "Soon we may need all prison space for political malefactors—common criminals are best dealt with on a purely curative basis. Punishment means nothing to them!"

"You're absolutely right, sir!" Alex calls out. Attracted, the official asks his crime.

Alex: "The accidental killing of a person, sir!"

Guard: "He brutally murdered a woman in the course of theft."

"Excellent! He's enterprising, aggressive, outgoing, young, bold, vicious—he'll be transformed beyond all recognition!"

Alex is methodically signed out. The warden is not pleased: "An eye for an eye, I say. . . . The new view is that we turn the bad into good!"

The ramrod guard delivers Alex to the Ludovico facility, whose white-coated staff casually accept him. He is given an injection, then strait-jacketed and strapped before a movie screen. His head is wired with electrodes, eyes held open with clamps. A technique lubricates his pupils at intervals. In the rear of the theater, a Dr. Brodsky and his assistants observe his reactions on instruments.

In the first film, a man is assaulted by a teen-age gang, much to Alex's delight: "Soon the red vino began to flow! It was beautiful!" Next a young girl is being given the old in-out-in-out by first one rapist, then another, then another . . . By the seventh malechick Alex feels really sick, but can't close his glozzies. Belching, choking: "Let me up—I wanna be sick!"

Brodsky, a balding, serious fellow, murmurs that the drug will soon cause "intellect paralysis"—deep feelings of terror and helplessness, very like death—when the subject will most associate his catastrophic experience with the violence he sees. In the front, Alex begins crying for help again.

In his room, a woman scientist explains that he's getting better: "You see when we're hateful, and respond to the hateful with fear and nausea. . . ."

On the screen next day, Hitler stomps and seig-heils to classical music. Alex: "Then I noticed in all my pain and sickness what music it was—" Beethoven's Ninth. Alex screams: "Stop it, I beg you, it's a sin!"

Brodsky responds: "Sin? It's the punishment element, perhaps. Sorry, Alex, this is for your own good . . ."

"It's not fair!"

"You must take your chance, boy! The choice has been yours!"

In a lecture hall, the Minister of the Interior, arms crossed, introduces a shyly smiling Alex: "Tomorrow we send him out into the world again, as decent a lad as you will meet . . . our party promised to restore law and order . . . But enough of words— actions speak louder than! Action now! Observe all!"

On the platform, an abusive tough comments on Alex's horrible smell. In moments he has knocked a craven Alex, sick and belching, to the ground. Alex must lick his shoe. Always cheeky-cheerful, the narrator comments: "And would you believe it, your narrator pushed out his red yahsick a mile and a half to lick the grahnzy, onny boot!" The audience applauds enthusiastically.

To the eerie "Music for the Funeral of Queen Mary," a lovely girl wearing only bikini pants walks toward Alex. First thought: "He'd like to have her down on the floor with the old in-out-in-out real savage." On his knees, eyes glazed, he reaches for her—but in an instant he's belching, sick, can't touch her. . . . The Minister lets her trip off, giggling. . . .

The official urbanely gushes that: "The tendency to act violently is accompanied by feelings of distress . . . so the subject switches to a diametrically opposed attitude."

The chaplain objects: "The boy has no choice . . . the fear of physical pain drove him to self-debasement. . . . He ceases to be capable of moral choice. . . ."

The Minister is impatient: "Padre, these are subtleties. We're concerned with cutting down crime." He's applauded, puts his arm around a shy Alex. "He will be your true Christian, ready to be crucified rather than crucify! Reclamation! The point is that it works!"

To a bouncy tune, "I Want to Marry a Lighthouse Keeper!" Alex's Mum and Dad study newspapers headlined: CAT WOMAN KILLER ALEX FREED! Alex embraces them: "I'm completely cured!" On the couch, a young man studies him coolly: "That's Joe, the lodger."

Joe isn't so forgiving: "Breakin' the hearts of your poor grievin' parents!" Stung, Alex strides toward him, then lurches, belching, sick: "It's the Treatment!" Joe: "It's disgustin'!"

To violins, Mum weeps, Dad dithers, Joe righteously says it's just his craftiness, and Alex announces he'll make his own way. "May it lie heavy on your conscience!"

By the Thames he rewards a shabby panhandler (and an old victim), who starts and cries: "It's the poisonous young swine!" In a dark underpass old bums, like piles of rags, rise from the sides to swarm over Alex: "It was old age having a go at youth . . . and I couldn't do a single cowardly thing!"

Two young bobbies rescue Alex—Georgie and Dim! Grinning delightedly: "A job for two who are now of job age—the police!"

Belching and choking, Alex is manhandled into their patroller. "The old days are dead and gone!" he feebly jollies. Dim giggles: "This is to make sure you stay cured!" Down a bright forest lane in a long, long tracking shot from behind, the two drag Alex to the grim "Music for the Funeral of Queen Mary," a Moog synthesizer making the chords hang eerily. They force Alex head-first into a watering trough, Georgie holding him under while Dim slams away with his nightstick to the vibrating chords. . . .

Thunder and lightning. A terrified Alex lurches through the storm. A small sign glows below two light globes: "home." "It was home I came to, not recognizing it was where I had been before. . . ."

Repeating the first pan of the interior, we see the old writer now typing from a wheelchair, the Eames chair occupied by a young weightlifter. Since he had worn a mask, Alex isn't recognized: "The police beat me up!" he gasps.

"*I know you!*" the writer cries. After a heartfreezing instant: "In the papers—the victim of this horrible new treatment—my heart goes out to you!"

Soon a dazed Alex floats in a warm tub, the writer crouched over his phone outside: "Most potent weapon . . . government boasts about the conditioning technique . . . the thin edge of totalitarianism . . . tradition of liberty is over . . . the common people must be led, driven, pushed!"

Alex, dopey and dazed, hears water dripping, softly croons: "Singin' in the rain." Echo-chambered, the lyrics twist the face of the writer . . . he knows who his guest is.

The three sit. *"Food all right?"* The writer grits out angelically. "Great sir," Alex nods.

"Try the wine!" quavers his host, teeth drawn back, eyes bulging.

Alex glances at him, lifts the glass, peering at the stuff anxiously, sniffing it, examining the bottle, finally swallows it down. "Wife away?"

"No, she's dead!!!! She was very badly *raped,* y'see. . . ! the doctor told me it was pneumonia but *I knew* what it was! A victim of the modern age! Now you! Another victim!"

But Alex can be helped; the writer has phoned some friends who want to help, important people interested in Alex. They arrive, an intellectual fat man and an intense blond. Alex confirms he's been conditioned against violence and Ludwig van. "When I hear it I just want to die peaceful—with no pain . . ."

Doped by the wine, Alex collapses face first into his spaghetti and meatballs. . . .

He wakes up belching, sick, locked in a lavender-papered attic room. The Ninth pours up from below. He staggers around, crying out. Downstairs, the writer grins fiendishly, turns up the volume. "Suddenly I vidied what I had to, wanted to do—and that was to do myself in, to snuff it." Alex forces a window, teeters, plunges. The screen goes black. . . .

We pan across a hospital bed, two legs in traction, a gauze-wrapped Alex: "I came back to life after a long, long gap of what might have been a million years . . ."

A sighing, moaning duet is explained by a doctor and nurse who come from a screened bed, adjusting their clothes: "Oh, he's recovered consciousness. . . ."

From a fisheye lens at Alex's point of view, we see his visiting parents mouthing: "It's said how the government drove you to do yourself in . . . our fault too . . . y'home's y'home, when all's said and done . . ."

His next visitor is a psychiatrist. Alex: "I've been having this very nasty dream—doctors' playin' with the inside of me brain." All part of the recovery process, he's told. Showed cartoons to caption, Alex gives childish violent-mocking replies (e.g., a customer tries to return a useless watch. Alex/watchmaker: "Stick it up your ass!"). When do I get out of here? Alex asks. He's told: "I'm sure it won't be long now!"

Alex's next visitor is the brisk, urbane Interior Minister: "Glad to see you on the mend!" An attendant who's been feeding Alex a steak exits.

"I've suffered the tortures of the damned, sir," Alex moans as the Minister feeds him.

The Minister and his government are deeply, sincerely sorry. They followed bad recommendations; an inquiry will fix responsibility. They want to be his friends, are putting him right, never wished him harm. There were some who wanted to use him for political ends, glad to have him dead and blame it on the government. A certain writer of subversive literature who has been howling for Alex's blood has been put away, for his own protection, and Alex's. He believed Alex had done him wrong . . . he was a menace! They shall see to all. A good job at a good salary.

"What job and how much?" Alex demands.

An interesting job, adequate salary for the job, as compensation for what he believes he has suffered, and because (the Minister smiles) you are helping us!

The Minister pauses. "The government has lost a lot of popularity because of you . . . but public opinion has a way of changing . . . you can be instrumental in changing the public's verdict. Of course I make myself clear!"

"You can rely on me!" Alex announces.

Into the room rush a dozen reporters, flashbulbs popping, and attendants with baskets of flowers and hi-fi speakers pouring out the triumphal "Ode to Joy." (A symbol of our new understanding, the Minister adds, "an understanding between two friends!") The Minister poses beside Alex, an arm around him, both smiling. For a moment we see Alex's face alone, eyeballs rolling (in mockery? conditioned fear? private delight?).

Suddenly, a silent dream image blazes on the screen: Between two rows of Victorian Londoners, the men dressed in top hats and the women holding parasols, all applauding mildly, a nude Alex copulates with an ecstatic blond wearing only black silk stockings.

Back in the hospital, Alex's expressive young face shivers with anticipation and he announces triumphantly: "I was cured all right! ! !"

End titles, to "Singin' in the Rain!"

Kubrick himself would interpret *A Clockwork Orange* in a three-fold manner: first, as a social satire on the use of psychological conditioning; second, as a "fairy tale of retribution"; and third, as a "psychological myth," a story constructed around a fundamental truth of human nature.[8]

The satire on conditioning seems fairly clear: we are shown that society is actually based on power and dissembling on both the Left and the Right; it follows that a man conditioned to be "good" in all circumstances is continuously vulnerable. Kubrick comments that this interpretation makes explicit a very contemporary paradox: "We have a highly complex civilization which requires an equally complex social structure and political authority . . . yet against that the goal should be to destroy all authority, so man in his natural goodness may emerge . . . this Utopian view is a dangerous fallacy . . . [All such efforts] eventually fall into the hands of thugs. . . . The weaknesses [don't stem] from an improperly structured society. . . . The fault is in the very imperfect nature of man himself. . . ."[2]

The interpretation of the film as a fairy tale, Kubrick feels, comes from the way the plot is set up: both before and after being conditioned, Alex meets his family, the wino, his droogs, and the writers. This doubling resembles the plot of, for example, "Goldilocks," in which the little girl uses the bears' chairs, porridge, and beds, then the bears track her down through the living room, dining room, and bedroom. The first time around, we're secretly pleased with Goldilocks' cleverness; the second time, increasingly afraid for her. So with Alex; during the first encounters we're titillated by his violence; the second time afraid for his life, and guilty about the first response.

But the most powerful meaning the film has, Kubrick believes, is as a "psychological myth." As Kubrick put its: "Alex represents natural man in the state in which he is born: unlimited, unrepressed. When Alex is given the Ludovico Treatment, you can say that this symbolizes the neurosis created by the conflict between the strictures imposed by our society, and our primal natures. This is why we feel exhilarated when Alex is 'cured' in the final scene."[2]

This statement raises questions, both about the fundamental correctness of this particular "mythic truth" as well as the honesty and effectiveness of Kubrick's exposition of it, which I will deal with in time. . . .

The critical response to *A Clockwork Orange* was violent and illuminating.

Vincent Canby's first *New York Times* review[4] praised the film's technique ("it dazzles even as it turns the old red vino to ice"), while stating without elaboration its satirical meaning ("the value of free will, even if the choice is tearing through the night, robbing, raping, and battering citizens"). Canby also makes a point of questioning the underlying ideas ("Alex the hood is as much a product of conditioning as the denatured Alex").

In a later essay,[5] Canby offered some new thoughts: that *A Clockwork Orange* "describes horror with such elegance and beauty [that] Kubrick has created a very disorienting but human comedy . . . with the only 'hope' for the future in the vicious Alex." This response does make some sense: Alex is in many ways similar to Chaplin's "Little Fellow"—he is witty, graceful, energetic, and straightforward—and when he's aggressive and violent, it's characteristically toward the pompous, the hypocritical, the vindictive—the sophisticated versions of Sennett's bullies, cops, and scoundrels, the stiflers of today. One must note that in many of the old silents, the Chaplin character, like Alex, will assault some ogre on instinct, and often deals out retribution of undeserved ferocity, like the homemade gas chamber he makes from a gas lamp to stop a bully on *Easy Street*. Yet this treatment of the film as a human comedy ("a terrible sum-up of where the world is at") can't include all of Alex's behavior.

An essay by Clayton Riley, run with Canby's, argues that *A Clockwork Orange* not only supplies perverse thrills, but that "in the name of free will, all self-expression becomes highly valued—even the freedom to commit atrocities." Encouraging this dangerous prerogative is "both criminally irresponsible and stupidly naive." Riley isn't conscious of subtleties or ironies or humor, strongly rejecting Alex as simply "a one-dimensional cretin . . . the sort of folk hero Charles Manson may ultimately become in a world raised on the adventures of Bonnie and Clyde."[14]

Riley's essay, while not aimed precisely in Canby's direction, implies that *A Clockwork Orange* isn't adequately described as a comedy. Alex's opponents are too close to comic villians, and Alex is only partly successful as a comic hero. Quick and sharp as Chaplin's "Little Fellow," unlike him Alex seems cold, and neither has nor seeks any human relationships; at best he patronizes his droogs and the prison chaplain, and never seeks affection, a great flaw in a comic hero. Imagine if you can an aloof, skeptical Chaplin, Langdon, Chico Marx, or other comic innocent. They "get away with it" because we know there's some higher purity underneath. Even seemingly aesthetic or negative comics—Keaton, Groucho Marx, W. C. Fields—go their own way or carp against humanity, but they don't really hurt people.

Many critics accepted *A Clockwork Orange* as a cold but effective satire, going along with Kubrick's vision to various extents. Judith Crist noted that in his inevitable-seeming future world, "hoodlums and criminals rule after dark amid the rubble of affluence. . . . The cry is for law and order, and in its name the mind is bent, the law is brutalized, and moral choices are banished."[6] *Time* magazine reviewer Jay Cocks sees Alex as the true child of the near future. "Who would understand and enthusiastically approve of Charles Manson's credo: 'Do the unexpected: No Sense Makes Sense.' "[2] Cocks's review shows the limits of Riley's simplistic approach: what one fears, the other expects. Cocks feels Alex simply comes full circle in the film: "Ready to embark on a life of ultra-violence with the blessings of the Minister of the Interior himself." Paul Zimmerman of *Newsweek* sees the various inadequacies, contradictions, and anomalies in Kubrick's treatment of emotions as simply a directoral inability to move us: "a characteristically frosty piece of filmmaking, shorn completely of sentiment, working through brilliant ironies and dazzling dramatic ideas that please us, provoke our laughter, galvanize our intellects, win our admiration—but never touch our hearts."[20]

Certainly the most passionate and dramatic rejection of *A Clockwork Orange* was written by Pauline Kael. Her critique sees

Kubrick as having "assumed the deformed, self-righteous perspective of a vicious young punk who says 'Everything's rotten. Why shouldn't I do what I want? They're worse than I am'. . . . when his bold aggressive punk's nature is restored to him it seems not a joke on all of us but, rather, a victory in which we share. . . . The look in Alex's eyes at the end tells us that he . . . prefers sadism and knows he can get by with it."[10]

Kael goes on to elaborate and give more evidence. The brutalized writer and art lover are, for her, "cartoon nasties" that nobody will miss. At the same time, Alex is made enormously sympathetic, a lone rebel fighting brutalizing system, which tortures him with straitjacket brainwashing, parental rejection, murderous police, psychopathic Leftists, and treacherous officials. Kael sees Kubrick as appealing to the worst in his audience, but even doing that badly—the depictions of the rapes and beatings "have no ferocity and no sensuality; they're frigid, poetically calculated . . . there is no motivating emotion." Kubrick estranges the victim, Kael states, to let you enjoy the violence, but leaves the viewer coolly repelled.

Kael works by assuming Kubrick's intentions, then looking for justifications in the film. The technique is powerful, but a two edged sword. Surely, for example, if Kubrick wanted to make Alex sympathetic, he would have had the state brutalize the hero before he started hurting people, like the plots of the old gangster films. Moreover, after what is clearly a first-degree murder, how many in the audience, even from the counter-culture, will consider two years of jail and a week of assorted sufferings sufficient restitution?

I feel, rather reluctantly, that while some of Kael's arguments have value, and all are interesting, she is so suspicious of Kubrick's intent that she ignores or rejects aspects of the film that don't fit her thesis. The stylized violence, for example, is written off as a mistake, and the ambiguous ending is ignored.

One of the more interesting essays on the film was by art critic Robert Hughes,[9] who discussed its decor. Hughes pointed out that the film is cultural satire as well as social satire, a chilling prediction of the roles of cultural artifacts: paintings, buildings, sculpture, music. The omnipresent erotic decor, from the fiber-glass nudes dispensing mescaline milk, to the garish erotic health-farm paintings, is to Hughes totally alienating—made up of cultural objects that have no connection with life, no meaning. The cat lady's cry of: "Don't touch it, it's a very important work of art!" is pathetic. How complex can one's feelings be about a giant white plastic sculpture of penis and scrotum that ticks as it rocks? Likewise, when romantic and classical music is used as the background for rape, Hughes feels Kubrick is saying that the old idea that Art is Good for You, Art Gives Moral Uplift, is a lie. Beethoven to Alex means sex and slaughter.

An alternate conclusion, and one I find more significant, was suggested in conversation with Sig Moglen. To him, Alex's musical tastes are one more restatement of the basic paradox of the film. The disciplined ecstasies of Beethoven suggest the moral limits in which man may truly be fulfilled. Both Alex and the society which has produced him are morally undisciplined, yet he can still find delight in Beethoven. Alex's virtue is thus demonstrated while the society around him moves toward empty eroticism and full-scale decadence.

The basic paradox of free will—the importance of man's power to choose, if only violence and destruction—is the fundamental idea behind both Burgess' novel and Kubrick's film. Though it follows the novel closely, Kubrick's *A Clockwork Orange* has changes worth noting.

Kubrick's changes would emphasize the satiric and mythic-psychological interpretations. The final scenes, for example, point up the director's satire of conditioning as a "cure" for social progress.

At the same time, the addition of the classical music and dream images, especially the final enigmatic Victorian scene, give the film the unreal quality Kubrick apparently sought. He states at one point that *A Clockwork Orange* "communicates on a subconscious level, and the audience responds to the basic shape of the story on a subconscious level, as it responds to a dream."[18]

Regardless of this, criticism must take place in the domain of consciousness. As such, the dream image leaves the mythic meaning of the film far from clear. It may suggest that Alex's future violence is simply sanctioned by the state—a bright ecstasy sedately applauded by gloomy elders. Recalling that Alex's other dreams were flashes of pure murder, pain and death, the final sex scene suggests his mind has been somehow gentled and transformed—his future violence will be only that of the "two-backed beast."

The problem of this last image leads to more basic difficulties noted earlier in Kubrick's concept of a "psychological myth."

To start with, unlike the mathematical and astronomical theories that were the basis of *A Space Odyssey,* ideas about the existence and nature of the subconscious today are very tentative and disputed. Kubrick may accept the unconscious, but to give it mythic status seems pretentious. Kubrick reveals that he wanted to show "Alex's guiltless sense of freedom to kill and rape and to be our savage natural selves."[18] But consider Poe's objection to the idea of "natural savagery": "What right have they to suppose this is his natural state? Man's chief idiosyncrasy being reason, it follows that his savage condition . . . is his unnatural state. The more he reasons, the nearer he approaches the position to which his chief idiosyncrasy irresistibly impels him; and not until he attains this position with exactitude . . . not until he has stepped up to the highest pinnacle of civilization—will his natural state be ultimately reached."

Even assuming a natural savagery and an unconscious to contain it, there are further problems. Kubrick seems to want to have the viewer experience this psychological myth "on a subconscious level."[18]

I am not prepared at this time to found a school of subconscious film criticism, but it would seem the way to a man's subconscious is through an appeal to the primal, sensual self—the great baby in each of us that wants what he wants when he wants it. (In some ways Harry Langdon's comedies approach this idea.) Yet this is the very quality that *A Clockwork Orange* lacks—coherent, emotional affect. Instead of playing distinctively on the keyboard of familiar emotions, Kubrick has struck strong discordant chords that disturb the viewer without providing resolution.

Nevertheless, *A Clockwork Orange* remains largely successful as a visual treatment of Burgess' bitter satire on the paradoxes of free will.

Finally, all of Kubrick's characteristic themes are present in full measure:

The imaginary worlds. Alex lives in a perversely innocent world, lashing out at adults, believing childishly that no harm can come to him if he only "steals what he needs"—the innocence of many Kubrick heroes. The Leftist writer lives in a self-contradictory, liberal fantasy—he "must" open his door to anyone in distress. Alex's parents cannot face up to the truth about Alex; they always react passively and irresponsibly.

Futility of intelligence, distrust of emotion. The worldly "cat lady's" caution is insufficient to prevent her murder. Mr. Deltoid admits one hundred years of studying delinquency has led nowhere. The scientific conditioning system makes Alex a social "throw-away." The Leftist writer mocks his own "civilized manners" as he feeds Alex.

Homicidal-suicidal pairings. Alex attacks the writer, then falls into his hands—whereupon he's drugged and pushed toward suicide. With the Minister's help, he has the writer put away. Alex's relationships with his droogs and family also decay into hostility, hatred, and mutual rejection. Alex and the Minister grow closer as they obtain power over each other.

Obsessed hero. Alex is an ultimate version of Kubrick's obsessed hero, his drive to violence so deep he thinks of it as his essence, clear in every cheeky-cruel remark. It suggests a final bleakness, as if candor, wit and intelligence are essentially aspects of the will to seize and abuse or pick apart anything of interest.

Odyssey toward freedom and knowledge. Alex's adventures are a tour of how his society is organized. It functions, at least in terms of social relationships, as a vast network of guile, cant, and naked force. At the end of the film he announces: "I was cured all right!" This is at least a triple irony: The public believes him "good," but he is, even as they, only "wised-up" about life; the actual cure, the conditioning to be "good," was terrifyingly dangerous, but it is that he is cured of! Finally, Alex has been "cured" of his perverse innocence about society—he has made his sly "bargain" with the powers that be to purchase his primal freedom.

11

Barry Lyndon

There is such a total sense of demoralization if you say you don't care. From start to finish on a film, the only limitations I observe are those imposed on me by the amount of money I have to spend, and the amount of sleep I need. You either care or you don't, and I simply don't know where to draw the line between those two points.

—*Stanley Kubrick, 1975*[7]

PERHAPS IT WAS Stanley Kubrick's stately and beautiful eighteenth-century English manor home itself that eventually led to his choosing a novel of that period for his next film—W. M. Thackeray's *Barry Lyndon*. Originally he hoped to shoot the entire picture within a ninety-minute radius of his exquisite home, using portions and locations belonging to similar "great houses" within that circle. After studying photographs of the possible filming sites, however, he concluded that they did not adequately embody the "look" he sought. Perhaps too the area proved to be too built up to be suitable for the special visual style he had chosen—one typified by long slow backwards zooms from tight close-ups of his players to breathtaking natural landscapes, and so much resembling the work of painters of the period.

As always, Kubrick had conducted extensive research before setting to work—not only mastering the literary work and its associated historical context, but also deciding his own film's tone, themes, and attitudes, as well as their visual correlatives. After further investigations, it was decided to begin filming in Ireland. Slowed by bad weather and Kubrick's exceptional artistic standards, however, after ten weeks and the full expenditure of the $2.5 million original budget, less than 10% of *Barry Lyndon* was finished. Finally, telephoned threats to the set caused Kubrick to shift his production to rural Great Britain, where the film was eventually completed.

Throughout the shooting period, the director constantly sought an authentic ambience or "feel" for the work. No sets at all were used—instead Lady Lyndon's Hackton Castle, for example, was the product of cutting together shots of rooms from at least four mansions. Similarly, many of the "costumes" were not costumes at all, but rather authentic antiques. In several sequences, Kubrick used special lenses that permitted him to film night or indoor scenes by candlelight alone—so as one critic pointed out, we see the re-created past as its inhabitants did, and as no living person has ever done. A gambling den lit in this way held players whose faces were covered with the heavy white lead "makeup" of the times—used to hide both dirt and the ravages of disease—a long way from traditional Hollywood studio costume dramas.

For 250 days, Kubrick's cast and crew of 170—joined at times by groups of technical experts as well as hundreds of additional extras—crept from location to location across two adjoining nations. Each morning, the director would arrive on the dressed and lit set to deliberate over the first shot of the day. A single start-to-finish camera operation could take four days or more to set up and rehearse—then the director might decide to delay or cancel. In addition, at some sites Kubrick was very restricted by the need to protect irreplaceable homes, art, or artifacts. For these and other reasons, the total production cost rose to $11 million.

Typically, the visual elements of *Barry Lyndon* consistently showed Kubrick's fascinated but probing attitudes towards the past as both history and art. The slow backwards zoom shots not only link the motion picture with the period's characteristic visual art, but also draw attention to the ordinary viewer's preconceptions about historical fact—suggesting that he temporarily suspend or at least be aware of his way of regarding "the dead past." Shots of several characters are also planned and composed to recall period art—for example, the frames of the choleric Captain Quin and Sir Charles Lyndon suggest the social criticism implicit in the work of William Hogarth and others. Nearly all the actors are also cast and directed for a kind of "psychological opaqueness" (e.g., Ryan O'Neal, Marisa Berenson, Patrick Magee). Conventional Method or motivational acting is replaced by an emphasis on socially driven and determined behavior, as does the fiction and reportage of the period. The openness and liveliness of the child actors (Leon Vitali, Philip Stone) implies the potentials of the species.

The sound elements also show the director's thoughtful attentions. Exquisite period music—Franz Schubert, Johann Sebastian Bach, Antonio Vivaldi, Wolfgang Mozart—suggests the complex controlled moods and rhythms of the age, its rigid measured ritualistic social patterns and attitudes. The choice of the worldly, cynical tones of Michael Hordern to narrate the tale, like the narrations in *Lolita* and *A Clockwork Orange,* tend to confirm Kubrick's characteristically bitter, pessimistic outlook.

In long shot, framed by trees, distant costumed figures face off across a quiet Irish meadow, as dark stormclouds begin to gather far away. Dueling pistols pop faintly—and the narrator's worldly tones tell of the death of young Redmond Barry's father in a duel, even as they suggest his son's cutoff prospects.

In a simple garden, a smitten adolescent youthful Redmond Barry (Ryan O'Neal) dallies with his coy, charming, but more adult cousin (Gay Hamilton). The two's extreme self-consciousness suggests the young man's initial naïveté, but perhaps even more the past's basic strangeness and difference from our times.

The following scenes show the crude run-down rural life of the Irish farm family, and young Barry's rival for the girl—a well-fixed pudgy blowhard of an English officer (Leonard Rossiter). As we discover this second couple, the late afternoon sun sets along with young Redmond's romanticism. Furious, he challenges Captain Quin to a pistol duel, apparently kills him, then flees with the help of his family. After being robbed of money and gifts by a highwayman, he is recruited into the English army. Throughout these early scenes, the camera continues to frame and track the ignoble events so they resemble lyrical period art. The mood is broken only briefly when Redmond Barry takes part in a bare-knuckle boxing match with another dragoon—Kubrick's filming with a handheld camera suggesting raw animal energy and emotions momentarily unchecked.

In the ranks, Redmond Barry encounters an old friend, now a

Slow backwards zoom shots link the film to period visual art, and call attention to preconceptions about historical fact and the "dead past." (Museum of Modern Art Film Stills Archive)

One becomes aware of the inertia, rigidity, and closed-off quality of personal life among the upper classes. (Museum of Modern Art Film Stills Archive)

Conventional or motivational acting is replaced by an emphasis on socially driven and determined behavior. (Museum of Modern Art Film Stills Archive)

Some shots suggest period art, such as the social criticism implicit in the work of Hogarth. (Museum of Modern Art Film Stills Archive)

fellow soldier (Godfrey Quigley), who confides that his rival for Nora, now her husband, was only briefly struck down by a special rubber bullet—the family could hardly afford the loss of the officer's income! Captain Grogan and Redmond Barry are soon thrust into the Seven Years War, in an engagement the narrator gravely describes thusly: "Although the battle was not recorded in any history book, it was memorable enough to those who took part."

Kubrick precisely and horrifyingly re-creates the period's military tactics, with the British line of pink-coated troops marching helplessly into the ravaging enemy musket fire, and falling like toys in the cascades of death. Awkward cutting suggests the mechanical, helpless quality of the experience. Shockingly, Grogan dies covered with blood beside the young protagonist, even as the narrator had fatalistically foretold a few moments before. The crumpled figure gasps hopelessly: "Kiss me, for we'll never meet again," and then he is gone—just one among the other faceless horizontal figures around them. A little later, in the confusion of a counterattack's carnage, the young man drags his superior officer from a blazing building. The promotion that follows provides Redmond an opportunity to desert.

Fleeing on horseback, disguised as a diplomatic courier, the young man stops for a brief "time out of war" with a beautiful young German peasant widow (Diana Koerner). Again, the photography and pacing are used to create a brief sense of dazzling romantic enchantment, not completely undercut by the narrator's words: "A lady who sets her heart upon a lad in uniform must prepare to change lovers pretty quickly, or her life will be a sad one. This heart of Lischen's was like many a town in the neighborhood in which she dwelt, and had been stormed and occupied several times before I came to invest it."

After bidding a fond good-bye, the deserter passes soldiers looting another farm and setting it afire, the mature narrator mocking the notion of chivalry in wartime, even as the images confirm his decision that he cannot escape society's malevolent struggle.

Next the disguised fleeing deserter is forced to dine with a sly, grinning Prussian officer (Hardy Kruger), who toys with him before coldly announcing, "Will you join and take the bounty, or will you be given up?" Rather than die, Redmond travels to Imperial Berlin with its wide lawns and gorgeous salons, where his military superiors set him to spy on a suspicious, half-shabby old chevalier (Patrick Magee). Beneath his cheap finery, eyepatch, and makeup, Redmond discovers an old uncle, and the two escape across the Prussian border, then make their way as a pair of elegant traveling cardsharps, cheating and outwitting the ghoulish upper classes with their curdled faces and gray powdered wigs.

Somewhere in this period the cynical worldview of the mature narrator grows to accommodate the audacious young protagonist, though they never become identical. Living from his small winnings and wits, spending more and more time among the corrupt repulsive rich and their magnificent possessions, Redmond sees himself increasingly as a manipulator and ladies' man, and his only hope to acquire real wealth by marriage. Yet even as the cool, handsome foppish calculating striver sets his sights on the beautiful, vaporous, upper-class Lady Lyndon, the narrator tells us, "Barry will end his life poor, lonely, and childless." In a red-lit hellish drawing room, the bitterly angry Sir Charles Lyndon furiously condemns the young man to his friends. A swift heart attack, however, removes the main obstacle to Barry's upward striving as part 1 of the film ends. . . .

The courtship and wedding of Redmond Barry and Countess Lyndon are filmed as a sequence of elegant, ponderous, romantic portraits—exquisite frozen images that allow the viewer to dwell on the young woman's lovely but remote and haunted face, and the young man's dissembling yet still half-innocent expression. Amid the loveliness, one becomes aware of the colossal inertia, rigidity, and closed-off quality of all personal life among the upper classes. By implication, Countess Lyndon's behavior, even more than Sir Charles's, seems the result of a lifetime at the top. The robed priests dwelling on fornication at the wedding seem thus highly ironic.

The subsequent narrative sequences strongly suggest Hogarth's *The Breakfast Scene* and similar sardonic period treatments of marriage. Locked together but with no common life, the couple are opaque figures in the great home's elegant landscape. The emotional void is at last filled when they have a son (Philip Stone), whom the narrator terms "hope of his family, pride of his manhood." The little boy-child is indeed bright and endearing, though when he fights with Sir Lyndon's sullen son Lord Bullingdon (Leon Vitali), it's not made clear which one is to blame.

Meanwhile the marriage continues its stately, empty minuet; Barry Lyndon briefly enjoying himself with a maid and then two other women, being ritually forgiven by his more and more withdrawn and neurasthenic wife. It is made clear that the family retainers disapprove of the upstart.

The calm is broken by violence at a musicale or music recital, when little Lord Bullingdon, contemptuous of Lyndon for his insults to his mother and perhaps unjustified punishment, insults him and his family. Again, Kubrick shoots the frenzied loss of control in a wild handheld camera style, catching the shocked expressions of the handsomely clad guests, and Barry's furious energy as he nearly strangles the youth. Seen afterwards, the boy is forced to leave.

The familiar rigid rhythms of upper-class life resume, though their tone lightens as Barry Lyndon takes more and more pleasure in his growing son. He also tries to use Lady Lyndon's money and position to win a peerage for himself—and so permanent financial security. In endless strangled scenes, however, his contributions to the Royal Army putting down the American rebellion are mocked, and other lords snub him.

Worse is to come, when his child is fatally injured in a riding accident. In a prolonged deathbed scene, the bright-faced child's limbs, wrapped in white, gradually go numb. As his parents hover over him, he sweetly asks that they fight no more, so they might all be happily reunited in heaven. To cheer the boy, Barry can only tell a made-up tale of his battlefield valor—inevitably recalling the real meaningless deaths he was forced to witness, notably that of his friend Captain Grogan, who of course expressed no hope of heaven. On and on the scene goes, the sweet little boy fading away with the inevitability of death itself. The elaborate, beautiful, and beautifully shot funeral procession is clearly also a cortege for all of Barry's hopes for the future.

The next event is the return of Lord Bullingdon, the young man demanding satisfaction of Barry Lyndon in a pistol duel. In still another elaborate ceremony, the two face off across the transept of a dark abandoned church. Faces and voices conceal all emotion, the manner of the upper classes again sustained even in the face of death as the two confront each other. But when Lord Bullingdon shoots and misses, he sweats, shivers, and vomits drool, betraying himself. Across the aisle, staring at the boy, his own face as in a trance, Barry Lyndon raises his pistol—and fires into the ground.

Lord Bullingdon looks up. His second shot smashes Barry's leg, so his stepfather collapses. Again the boy betrays himself, crying out harshly in joy.

In a bedroom in a nearby inn, Barry Lyndon lies recuperating from the amputation of his leg. He is joined by his own now-aged mother. With him leaning on her arm, the two make their way out to a coach that will carry them back to Ireland.

In the bleak splendor of Hackton Castle, Countess Lyndon, with Lord Bullingdon and a pair of retainers, is signing checks— including a small compensation for her once-husband. The viewer notes the date—December 4, 1789, the date of the French Revolution—portending more violence and the decline of this moribund society. As the ritual of check signing goes on and on in the cold empty spaces of the castle, the narrator concludes by bringing us to the present: "They are all equal now."

The critical response to the release of *Barry Lyndon* was appreciation for a serious artistic work, but one without much chance for popular success. Like most sympathetic journalistic critics, Vincent Canby of the *New York Times* praised the film's aesthetic richness (comparing it to "an environment" rather than a movie), and also commenting on its subtle social satire: "a great deal about the privileges of class."[2]

Pauline Kael saw the film as an "honorable failure" and still another dose of Kubrick pessimism. For her, Kubrick suggests that all mankind is corrupt, and because *Barry Lyndon* is neither entertaining nor involving it is a very vain movie: "Kubrick's message is that people are disgusting, but things are lovely."[6]

Hans Feldman, in a long essay in *Film Quarterly*,[5] suggests that

2001, A Clockwork Orange, and *Barry Lyndon* may all be seen as treating aspects of how western civilization fails to deal with the violent part of man's nature. In *Barry Lyndon,* which takes place while society is still little marked by terminal decadence or excessive technology, the protagonist's violence is transferred into rituals, most often duels that occur long after its spontaneous expression. For Feldman, the film implies that such sublimated social forms result in harmful spiritual corruption and physical deformity. Such might be said of the crippling and loss of status of the protagonist at the end of the film, despite his moment of decency towards his stepson (the spontaneous fight between the two boys, and the later formal [undeserved?] punishment of Lord Bullingdon, is what sets up the disaster). On a much larger scale, the reasons for the Seven Years War's grisly battles, and even the record of the engagements themselves, are implied to be obscure and valueless—but the ritual slaughter is tragically real.

Feldman also suggests that while Thackeray condemns the insensitivity and cruelty of individuals and society, Kubrick's film is more a probing of the imperfect social forms that generate and sustain these attitudes. Unfortunately, neither Feldman nor Kubrick seems to suggest how to set up a social system that could accommodate people's violence without even more petrification and decadence, much less harmful side effects. Probably such a system is impossible to imagine, perhaps especially so for a modern intellect. Freud's *Civilization and Its Discontents* for example implies that individual suffering and unhappiness is the cost, and indeed the definition, of a social system.

The radical Marxist critic Irwin Silber in his *Guardian* essay also sees *Barry Lyndon* as a basically detached, analytic view of the past. Kubrick's closing line "They are all equal now" for him clearly defines the existential attitude current among bourgeois artists—that history is fundamentally meaningless, and all that matters is survival and the moment (as opposed to the Marxist analysis of history, elaborating its dialectic class structure). Silber suggests Kubrick's depiction of society is an elaboration of the existential worldview—money, power, and property are shown to be the only things that really command respect, and human existence is simply a scramble for social position. Except for the two brief interludes—love with the German widow, comradeship with Grogan—Silber sees the adult characters as more or less socially alienated at all times.

Silber's analysis, while having the neatness of all single-determinant systems, can be faulted as far too schematic. For example, family feeling plays a central role in the protagonist's existence: saving him from his first deadly duel, rescuing him from the Prussian spymasters, presumably providing spiritual sustenance when he becomes poor and crippled. In fact, without Barry Lyndon's own hopes for his son, the film's story and characters would become hopelessly unpleasant. Moreover, if director Kubrick did not believe such feelings were justified as well as sustaining, he could just as well have had Barry's son grow up to be a typical, sullen, cruel, upper-class snob. Though the son dies, Barry's self-sacrifice for Bullingdon suggests the possibility of idealism and decency.

Michael Dempsey, in a long review in *Film Quarterly*,[4] implies that the central aspect of the film is not so much its analysis of society as its portrayal of the transience of life itself. "The zoom-away contrasts the majestic, indifferent beauty of nature with scurrying, greedy people . . . putting humanity in a timeless perspective." For Dempsey, the glory of the film is its paradoxical flying portrait of life—endless rituals, pointless striving, unforgettable emotional moments—even as they flash past and are gone to dust. Dempsey's long essay refines and extends this critical approach, elaborating the film's complex devices for the precise, sensitive treatment of experience as memory. Even as Kubrick ponders death's inescapability, he suggests that life does matter— for him, Dempsey insists, Barry's refusal to fire on his stepson is a moment of spiritual transcendence, and a genuine affirmation.

Dempsey's analysis is so personal that it is hard to criticize, though one may clearly cite his tendency to read into the images. Another weakness is that by the last duel, the sense of doom and futility has become so overwhelming for many that *anything* the protagonist might have done would not have affirmed his own existence, let alone existence as portrayed over the previous three hours.

Presaging the previous three essayists, Andrew Sarris's closely reasoned early review summed up *Barry Lyndon* as an "impressive testament of the artist as a majestic mourner for the idle vanities of our capitalist civilization. . . . Kubrick has simplified the novelistic intrigues in order to intensify the cinematic mood of implacable sorrow."[10]

My own first impression was to regard *Barry Lyndon,* like *A Clockwork Orange,* as another footnote to *2001*—a close analysis of an early stage in the petrification and degeneration of Western society. In line with this, the artifacts of the society remain lovely, while its human products become increasingly destructive and self-destructive as one ascends the social ladder (that is, the more they live by its doomed values). The elaboration of that structure—in terms of acquisitiveness and emotional numbness—is totally negative (an interesting paradox follows from this: Why do such people want such pretty things anyway? And who creates them, and how are *they* inspired among such spiritual rot?).

It has been suggested that *Barry Lyndon* can also be seen as a covert American bicentennial commentary, alluding to the American Revolution as faintly parallel to the Vietnam War. More basically, it seems to outline an imperial power's growing internal corruption at the presumed height of its global power.

A striking feature of the film is the extent of its formal structure. For example, like *A Clockwork Orange,* it employs a disembodied narrator presumably expressing the director's point of view—or at least the thoughts of the protagonist reorganized from the director's perspective. Such elements incidentally create resentment in many of the critics (e.g., Corliss,[3] who feels stifled and prodded by the director, complaining that he assumes his case easily and early, rather than proving it). Sympathetic critics (i.e., Dempsey, Sarris, Silber) tend to acknowledge and accept Kubrick's worldview at least temporarily, then comment on how well the artist realizes his arguments and ideas.

Another interesting formal element is Kubrick's organizing of the plot into pairs of similar incidents: Barry's naïve frustrated romance with his cousin and his worldly, consummated yet lyrical affair with the war widow; the duel over his cousin with an older man and the climactic one with his stepson; the death of Captain

Grogan and the passing of his son; the violent boxing match and his near strangling of Bullingdon.

Presumably in the later incidents Barry is somewhat shrewder, more knowledgeable and more powerful. Yet there is no clear case that things work out better the second time around. Rather the viewer is increasingly aware of the precise limits of hope, endurance, and chance—and how an awareness of these pains and shapes an individual's personality and character. Thus Barry, liberated by cynicism and despair, loses his inhibitions and romanticism by the time he meets the young widow (Kubrick's ironic commentary makes the transformation less of a triumph). But the death of Grogan and the death of his son are equally agonizing, and Barry's dissipated naïveté and faith afford him no sources of consolation in the second instance.

For the record, Kubrick's characteristic themes are present once more in *Barry Lyndon:*

Imaginary worlds. For the protagonist, successively romantic fulfillment, economic security, vicarious happiness through his son, and at last spiritual justification through an act of decency. Perhaps the last belief will be maintained, since his family supports this ideal.

Futility of intelligence, distrust of emotion. Barry's two most blissful periods are the products of chance, and cannot be maintained by cleverness—in fact the film suggests both are futile, dangerous fugues. Barry's cleverness wins him only a sterile existence. His love of his son, his strongest emotion, betrays him into twice antagonizing Bullingdon—his ultimate undoing.

Homicidal-suicidal pairings. It has been pointed out that Lord Bullingdon's role in part 2 closely resembles Barry's in part 1: refusing to accept a marriage, humiliation, and being stripped of his fortunes and initiating a duel. Both characters are also strongly attached to their mothers. One critic has suggested that the two are in fact irreconcilable opposites—robbed innocent versus wasteful spender, who must necessarily come into conflict. Dueling, in passing, seems to be a social invention for expression of a homicidal-suicidal personality.

Obsessed hero. In a way, Barry's life's pattern may be traced back to his first romantic object, which he was denied because he was too poor. His marriage is a way to win real money by providing the illusions of love—money that he will give his son to forestall the same obsession. From a psychological point of view, he constantly seeks to deny and reject his own origins and attitudes—making the nature of his selflessness when confronting Bullingdon more problematical. From a Freudian point of view, the shot unmans him—perhaps an unconscious goal.

Odyssey towards freedom and knowledge. Though he constantly strives for apparent self-advancement, Barry Lyndon does in passing come to travel through nearly all levels and aspects of his society (save the unseen intellectual, artistic, and leadership/governmental). In his position of greatest social power and prestige, he chooses to abandon its sterility for a chance at moral self-justification and emotional warmth.

In discussing *Barry Lyndon,* Kubrick has commented that he has fulfilled his basic ideal, to shoot "economically and with as much beauty and gracefulness as possible. [Beyond that,] all you can do is either pose questions or make truthful observations about human behavior. The only morality is not to be dishonest."[7]

12

The Shining

I've never achieved spectacular success with a film. My reputation has grown slowly. I suppose you could say that I'm a successful filmmaker—in that a number of people speak well of me. But none of my films have received unanimously positive reviews, and none have done blockbuster business.

—*Stanley Kubrick, 1980*[8]

PREPRODUCTION ON Kubrick's film *The Shining* began just after release of *Barry Lyndon* (December 1975), when Kubrick acquired rights to the Stephen King novel of the same name, a pulpy but thrilling supermarket gothic about a family threatened and isolated in a snowed-in hotel, progressively menaced and aided by demonic forces and/or mental aberrations that beset the father and son.

Kubrick commented that "what intrigued me about Stephen King's novel . . . was the way in which the author kept the reader guessing about what would happen next."[8] He added that "there's something inherently wrong with the human personality. There's an evil side to it. One of the things that horror stories can do is to show us the archetypes of the unconscious: we can see the dark side without having to confront it directly. Also, ghost stories appeal to our craving for immortality. If you can be afraid of a ghost, then you have to believe that a ghost may exist. And if a ghost exists, then oblivion might not be the end."

Diane Johnson, who worked with Kubrick on the screenplay, suggested in an interview[7] that the director was drawn to the novel because of its "psychological underpinnings. A father threatening his child is compelling. It's an archetypical enactment of unconscious rages. Stephen King isn't Kafka, but the material of this novel is the rage and fear within families." Kubrick reportedly hired Johnson partly with the goal of turning out something different than the contemporaneous flood of *Exorcist* and *Omen* imitations. The novel's wasp attack and hedge animals that come to life were dropped, for example, the latter when special-effects experts could offer no sufficiently realistic way to achieve the transformation.

According to Johnson,[7] almost all the substantive decisions about the screenplay were made before the script was written, over numerous dinners of take-out tandoori chicken in the living room of Kubrick's London house between June 1977 and January 1978. Both Johnson and Kubrick read Freud's essay on "The Uncanny" and Bruno Bettelheim's book about fairy tales, *The Uses of Enchantment*. Each then wrote a short outline, which were then reconciled into a longer one (a typical scene: filled with expectations, Jack and his family arrive at his new job at the hotel). Johnson felt the outlines resembled the "moving kits" that are used to guide moving men, consisting of cardboard furniture in a cardboard dollhouse. "The writing was secondary to knowing who the characters were, what the events were, and the exact function of every scene," Johnson commented, adding that Kubrick told her "when you know what's happening in a scene, the words will follow."

Johnson makes two notable points about the horror genre. For one thing, the nature of any ghosts must be decided—actual real spirits that can act in the material world, or people's imaginative projections that are just an aspect of individual madness. She adds a third possibility: "the psychological states of the characters can create real ghosts who have physical powers—if Henry VIII sees Anne Boleyn walking the bloody tower, she's a real ghost, but she's also caused by his hatred." The decision about which of the three kinds of apparitions would be used was not made at the start, but Johnson said it would be clear in the end. A second point made by Johnson is that endings of horror films are usually disappointing, because the explanation is emotionally unsatisfactory (e.g., improbable, or arbitrary, or gratuitous). Kubrick and Johnson apparently worked very hard to reconcile the supernatural and the reestablished sense of reality, providing, in Johnson's words, "the artistic satisfaction of a fairy tale."

The pair also spent much time screening classic horror films, and those of the major actors. Jack Nicholson, Kroll suggests,[11] was cast as the nice guy from Vermont who becomes a raging fiend chiefly because of his unique face. "The sharp nose, wide mobile mouth, and angled eyebrows that can redeploy themselves in an instant from sunny friendliness to Mephistophelean menace." Shelley Duvall was cast as a figure of wifely banality, while young Danny Lloyd was chosen as a charming child.

The main set, the Overlook Hotel in the Colorado Rockies, was created entirely in the studio, a major triumph of set design—a catacomb of corridors, rooms, lobbies, lounges, giant kitchens, and basements, through which Kubrick's camera would restlessly prowl. The exterior of the hotel was constructed fullscale on the Elstree Studios back lot.

A hedge maze, one hundred yards long in the script, was also built, the setting for a new ending. To capture realistic winter scenes, a second unit shot several sequences in Colorado, including establishing scenes and the race to rescue the family at the Overlook during a snowstorm.

The shooting began on May 1, 1978, at EMI Elstree Studios in Borehamwood, England. As usual with Kubrick's films, the project was filmed in complete secrecy, with no outsiders allowed on the set, nor any interviews with the director or actors until their work was finished.

Probably the most remarkable technical device employed was the extensive use of the Steadicam, a camera that permitted whizzing at child level behind a pedaling youngster, or wheeling and spinning in a terrifying trajectory that follows the final outdoor chase through the snowy maze at midnight. Shiff[18] comments that the camera technique has the result that "most of the film feels like an endless subjective shot: we appear to be watching the hotel and its inhabitants through the eyes of an unearthly prowler, someone who sees very differently from the way we see."

Shiff also commented on the sound track: "Kubrick's now famous method of using existing recordings of music, in this case by Bela Bartok, Gyorgy Ligeti, and mostly the Polish modernist Krzysztof Penderecki. The sound track becomes a dissonant wailing pounding but seductive symphony of human fear as it makes contact with the irrational energies buried deep inside its heart."[11]

Kubrick's perfectionist tendencies regarding performances had

The Jack Torrance family early in the fil[m] a "reasonable" husband and his tro[u]blesome family. (Museum of Modern A[rt] Film Stills Archive)

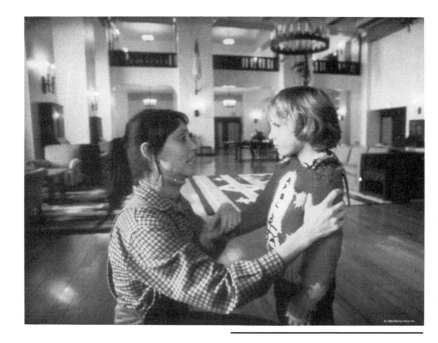

Wife Wendy and son Danny in the elaborate Overlook Lodge. (Museum of Modern Art Film Stills Archive)

Jack Torrance and Danny—the metamorphosis from affectionate father to
murderous demon. (Museum of Modern
Art Film Stills Archive)

not diminished. *Newsweek* quotes Scatman Crothers's comments: "In one scene, I had to get out of a Sno-Cat and walk across the street, no dialogue: forty takes. He had Jack Nicholson walk across the street, no dialogue: fifty takes. He had Shelley, Jack and the kid walk across the street: eighty-seven takes. Man he always wants something new, and he doesn't stop until he gets it."

Jack Nicholson added: "Stanley's demanding. He'll do a scene fifty times and you have to be good to do that. There are so many ways to walk into a room, order breakfast, or be frightened to death in a closet. Stanley's approach is, how can we do it better than it's ever been done before? It's a big challenge. A lot of actors give him what he wants. If you don't, he'll beat it out of you—with a velvet glove, of course."

Perhaps the hardest role was given Shelley Duvall, who had to stay hysterical for nearly four months. Kubrick would tell her fiercely but never raising his voice: "Shelley, that's not it. How long do we have to wait for you to get it right?"

Just before the film's release, Kubrick commented optimistically: "If a story interests me sufficiently to spend two or three years turning it into a film, then I believe it will interest many others as well."[8]

The Shining opens to ominous horn music, together with snake rattles and bird trills, with an extreme helicopter long-shot view of a tiny yellow Volkswagen driving up serpentine roads to the protagonist's job interview for winter caretaker at the enormous ominous Overlook Hotel in the Colorado Rockies.

We watch ex-teacher and struggling writer Jack Torrance (Jack Nicholson) being interviewed for the caretaker job at the luxurious but empty hotel during the brutal winter, while the resort is closed. The corporate executive, Ullman (Barry Nelson), with his blown-dry hair and US flag pin, is ritually deferred to by Torrance, the two both sounding like pompous/glib local TV anchorpersons—a typical grim/funny job interview. The executive tells Torrance about a horrifying incident that occurred at the hotel some years before when a previous caretaker, Grady, possibly affected by the isolation and loneliness, murdered his two little daughters with an axe, shot his wife, and blew out his own brains with a shotgun.

Nicholson smiles: No need to worry about anything like that with him, a nice guy from Vermont. The smile is the first of many.

Directly after Nicholson accepts the job, we see his son Danny (Danny Lloyd), talking to his "imaginary friend" in a mirror, then see images of two little girls, first alive, then butchered. Danny then sees a hotel elevator disgorging a flood of blood, and faints.

A woman doctor visits the Torrances' apartment in Denver to check up on the child, and it soon becomes clear each family member has his or her own version of past events. His wife Wendy (Shelley Duvall) says that five months ago (Torrance says two years ago), Torrance, returning home drunk, saw his latest manuscript spread across the floor (Torrance says they were Danny's papers), and picked up Danny by one arm, dislocating the child's shoulder. Since then, Danny's had episodes of fainting and visions, via his "imaginary friend" Tony, who he says lives in his mouth and tells him to keep the visions secret. The doctor tells Wendy such imaginary friends and even visions are normal in a child, though they strike Wendy as uncanny. In the background copies of the *New York Review of Books* lying around the shabby apartment suggest Torrance's intellectual and literary aspirations.

A title: "Closing Day."

The Torrances—Jack, Wendy, and Danny—are driving up to the Overlook to move in. It's not a pleasant trip; Jack berates his family sarcastically, the woman and child suffering in silence.

Soon they're touring the immense structure, the manager Ullman explaining that the hotel is built on an Indian burial mound, and also decorated with authentic Indian designs, in an apparent combination of Navaho and art deco. Outside the entrance is an enormous hedge maze.

Next the good-natured head chef, Halloran (Scatman Crothers) takes the family on a tour of the enormous kitchen and pantry, showing them the almost incredible bounty of the Overlook. In a moment alone, Danny and Halloran acknowledge that they share the psychic ability the black man calls "shining," visions of danger in the past or future, as well as a kind of telepathy. Halloran explains to the child that past events often leave traces that can be dangerous to those with this gift, and cautions him to avoid room 237.

The Overlook is closed, and only the family is left inhabiting its multitudes of rooms and corridors. While Wendy drudges at family tasks, Jack types away in a large lounge.

Now, in one of the film's most chilling scenes, Wendy looks through a pile of manuscript the writer has been working on and finds it consists of a single sentence, "All work and no play makes Jack a dull boy," typed over and over and over, as dialogue, paragraphs, stanzas of poetry.

Life goes on. Danny, on his little tricycle, endlessly cruises the empty labyrinthine corridors of the Overlook, from vast lobby to monumental halls, so we begin to learn our way through the hotel.

Still later, Danny is shown with his neck bruised. Wendy claims Torrance did it, Torrance says Danny did it to himself, and Danny says a crazy old woman in room 237 did it. By the time we hear the last version, Torrance has visited the old crone, though he tells Wendy he has not.

Danny, fearing violence from his father, starts "asking" for help from the shining cook Halloran, via his imaginary friend Tony. The film now begins to cut back and forth between the deteriorating situation at the Overlook and Halloran as he first tries to call the hotel, then flies to Colorado, borrows a car and then a Sno-Cat which he drives through a snowstorm towards the Overlook.

Accused of mistreating the boy again, Torrance begins to frequent the Gold Room, a large ballroom, filled with Fitzgeraldian ghostly revelers in Jazz Age costume.

Titles now begin to appear at odd intervals, "Tuesday" or "Saturday" or "3:00 P.M.," a parody of thriller chronology. Torrance and his family quarrel more and more often. The writer tells them he loves the hotel, and wishes they could stay there "ever ever ever!"

Torrance is seen again in the Gold Room, conversing with the seemingly real barman Lloyd (Joe Turkel). Torrance, who promised to give up drinking after he hurt his son, tells the empty ballroom: "I'd give my soul for a drink!" and looks up to see the satanically red lit bartender.

Torrance returns to room 237, now holding a slim nude aristocratic young woman who rises from her bath and embraces him, though the mirror reveals only a rotting crone laughing at him.

In the ballroom, now filled with stylish couples in 1920s dress, Torrance bumps a headwaiter who takes him into a bloodred men's room to wipe off a spilled drink. The man, named Grady (Philip Stone) like the previously murdered caretaker, tells Torrance that not he but Torrance has always been the caretaker of the hotel. Grady explains how he "corrected" his wife and daughters when they got out of line, and warns Torrance that his son Danny is trying to contact outside help to use against him.

Soon Wendy, like Torrance, begins to see the same blood pouring from the elevator, and to hear people chanting. Upset by her husband's increasingly hostile and bizarre behavior, she manages to lock him in the Overlook's enormous pantry—yet somehow Torrance is able to enlist "Grady" to unlock the door and set him loose.

Wendy, swinging a baseball bat, backs away from Torrance as he moves toward her—the writer slowing advancing even as she brandishes the bat at him. Wendy backs slowly away across a room and up a staircase, finally swinging it in front of her to keep him at a distance, what Kael calls "a ghoulish parody of a courtship dance, staged with hairbreadth timing." Torrance lunges, and Wendy and Danny take refuge in a tiny bathroom.

Halloran now appears, at apparently just the right moment, when Torrance is just about to burst through the bathroom door. Danny has meanwhile become a kind of "mirror self," repeating "Redrum" (murder) over and over.

Meanwhile, Torrance ambushes and kills Halloran with an axe—coming in and calling and suddenly chopped down. Moments later Torrance is chopping at the door to his family's refuge, a nightmare parody of the good husband braying: "Wendy, I'm home!" and then mocking Johnny Carson's "HE-E-E-E-R-E'S JOHNNY!" as he sticks his head through the smashed door. But Wendy and Danny have escaped through the tiny bathroom window into the winter world outside, sliding down a snowbank and running for the great maze.

Torrance chops through the bathroom door, calling himself the

"Big Bad Wolf," and follows. In the final chase through the maze in the frozen dark night, the hunched-over limping father, axe in hand but animal-like, dogs his son's footprints in the snow, making inarticulate sounds.

Meanwhile the cunning son erases his tracks and retraces his steps, trapping Torrance in the maze. The final picture of Torrance, frozen in the maze in the present, is juxtaposed with a view of a look-alike frozen in the past in a photograph of the ballroom on July 4, 1921.

A majority of the critics, though they found *The Shining* flawed, said they felt Kubrick must be praised for seeking to move beyond the horror genre. Jack Kroll,[11] for example, comments that in *The Shining,* he understands that the point is not all the supernatural machinery, but "its effect on human beings. For all its brilliant effects, the strongest and scariest element in *The Shining* is the face of Jack Nicholson undergoing a metamorphosis from affectionate father to murderous demon." Likewise, David Cook[4] argues that "we're being told that true horror is not extraordinary but surrounds us every day and, as Auden wrote of evil, 'sits with us at the dinner table.'"

Kroll feels that the oedipal theme is successfully realized, adding that "this is that rare horror film in which we sense its intelligence even as it scares us . . . when Torrance turns on his son in a mad rage, *The Shining* becomes a kind of perverse reversal of *Kramer Versus Kramer,* where father and son found mutual flowering in each other. There is a grisly psychological accuracy in this that affects us more than the spooks and haunts in the Overlook." Ultimately, Kroll feels, Kubrick in his films seems to "construct an alternate reality, something more logical and precise than the real world with its sloppy design and dangerous leaps of the unthinking heart."

An interesting review by Myron Meisel[14] calls *The Shining* "our first modernist medieval morality play, an odd amalgam of antique metaphysics, harsh Calvinism, and contemporary absurdism." To Meisel, the Torrance character is in league with literally real demons, while the only true spirituality (God never shows up) comes from the impulse for self-preservation, mother love, and the "shining" (e.g., ESP), which for the critic suggests a tantalizing linkage to the *Star Wars* saga. Meisel concludes that Kubrick may not believe the worldview he propounds, but is interested in "rigorously exploring a vision dictated by a belief in sin and pre-destination," and the resulting insights, while "hard to digest and impossible to accept, have some validity in upsetting intellectual complacency."

A majority of the film critics, however, disliked *The Shining*. Typically, David Denby commented that "without a central idea, Kubrick's *The Shining* is stiff and pompous, an anthology of horror film flourishes. . . . *The Shining* might be more effective if Kubrick weren't so vain of his integrity: you feel he's too proud to descend to such vulgarities as pace or wit or suspense."[5] Like a number of other critics and reviewers, Denby felt a major flaw lay in the characters: Jack Torrance was already wildly smirking and fearfully out of control before the film started, while his wife stayed a simp victim and their child cool and distant—a family unlikable and perverse from the word go.

Pauline Kael[10] is perhaps the most thorough cataloger of the movie's imperfections. On the visual level, she finds the reversal of genre convictions, shooting in broad daylight, fails because the horrors are not integrated with it, but rather appear like flashing slides inserted into the film. Dramatically she finds many flaws: Torrance's long static conversations with demons; characterizations that are static and unsurprising ("Kubrick's 'tools' "); a family theme that consequently doesn't jell.

On the metaphysical level, Kael finds the film confusing. At first Danny's behavior and Jack's activities seem explicable by Jack's madness. But soon, she notes, Wendy also sees and hears the bloody apparitions. Do the family tensions generate real appari-tions, Kael asks, or do the apparitions multiply the family ten-sions, or is it an intertwining process such that both are one—the tortured family both source and victim of monsters that live on? (Diane Johnson, Kubrick's cowriter, also discussed these pos-sibilities.) Kael notes the clues as she sees them, as well as various anachronisms, mirror images, and the deconstruction of time and dating, and sees the conclusion as hinting at reincarnation. She concludes Kubrick's strategy is to draw us in so our view of time is gradually disoriented, and we accept the ugly theme of the timelessness of murder—but feels the various apparitions never really form a pattern, so the film finally seems not to make sense, except on the simplest level: "He seems to have gone back to his view at the beginning of *2001:* man is a murderer throughout eternity."

Perhaps the harshest criticism is that of Stephen Shiff,[18] who complains that *The Shining* begs for a payoff that never comes: "*The Shining* is a sadistically directed movie, not because it tortures us with fear, but because it refuses us pleasure—the cathartic pleasure of a real confrontation with the terrors it promises." In addition, the critic sees the film as filled with empty fetishism—like the forty, fifty, or eighty-seven takes, or the enormous "novel" that uses one sentence thousands of times arranged in paragraphs, sonnets, and blocks: like that "book" *The Shining* has its own habit of falling into meaningless fussiness, endless empty fetishistic symmetries and arrangements.

A couple of interpretations of *The Shining,* based on complex cultural theories, have also been proposed. David A. Cook[4] offers a Marxist view of *The Shining,* seeing the film as a metaphor for a society that is based on exploitation and even murder and genocide, just as the glorious Overlook Hotel is built on an Indian burial mound. He views this idea as signaled by the early hypocritical job interview, in which job hunter Torrance tells how "eager" his family is to be locked up in the snow. Later, isolated, Torrance gradually becomes obsessed with his "work," preferring the company of the cruel ghostly employees of the past as well as the spirits of the snobbish clientele. The futility of his job and impossible writing aspirations is symbolized by the sentence he types again and again, "All work and no play makes Jack a dull boy." For Cook, the Overlook stands for the violence of our economic system, which bursts out amid the abundant emptiness of the resort. Shiff supports this idea,[18] commenting that: "At the heart of [Kubrick's] joke is the notion that inside every loving husband and father is a striver, a careerist who is the enemy of the family—who could ultimately murder them."

A long analysis of *The Shining* by Christopher Hoile[9] is based on the two books that Kubrick and Johnson reportedly read while writing the script—Freud's essay "The Uncanny" and Bruno Bettelheim's *The Uses of Enchantment* (1976). Both books explore the mind in terms of psychoanalysis, and discuss man's relationship to an "animistic" universe—one in which good and bad spirits inhabit all things, and thoughts and wishes can control reality. Bettelheim sees children as inhabiting such a universe, which is reflected in fairy tales (and TV cartoons), while Freud argues that adults surmount it and madmen are trapped in it— their "selves" lost and their actions apparently involuntary.

In *The Shining,* Hoile argues, the animistic universe is shown in interaction with the oedipal world of father, mother, and child. For example, in the dreamlike climax, the animistic world takes command, as in the ghost's freeing of Torrance from the storeroom, and the perfectly timed arrival of the rescuer Halloran. According to Hoile, "Like Wendy, we discover we are trapped between two people living in an animistic universe—a son who has not yet surmounted it, and a father who has sunk back into it." For Hoile, "The horror in *The Shining* does not lie in the ghosts, but in the inseparability of the oedipal tensions in the family, of which they are an expression." Hoile concludes that like all Kubrick's films, *The Shining* is concerned with the illusion that man's will contributes to his progress, in this case his supposed progress beyond animism. "But there is no progress, and [Torrance] becomes a horror movie character to his wife, and to us."

The narrative preoccupations present in Kubrick's previous films can be detected yet again:

Imaginary worlds. Jack Torrance's own view of the world remains always that of a "reasonable" husband and father trying to deal with his troublesome family, as well as his other personal limitations. His son Danny, so far as his own viewpoint is clear, identifies with and accepts his psychic powers, at least as correct intuitions, which he follows in dealing with the world. Wendy Torrance is an unfortunate ordinary person trapped between the psychic and the psychotic.

Futility of intelligence, failure of emotion. In *The Shining,* as has been pointed out, man's supposed progress beyond the irrational and unconscious fails under stress and he regresses to playing out the Oedipus myth. As Hoile puts it: "The father, feeling threatened by his son, tries to kill him, only to be killed at the crossroads as the prophecy is fulfilled and the son runs off with his mother."

Journey to freedom. Danny Torrance is seen to progress through a series of psychological states, sometimes normal, sometimes psychic, to the point where he can both surmount his animistic obedience to his father and use rationality and cunning to escape his murderous rage.

Obsessional hero. Torrance is a tragic obsessional hero, basically decent but unable to escape his obsession with running his family, and doing his job, even as it degenerates into destructive madness.

Homicidal-suicidal pairings. Father and son progress from apparently normal behavior into destructive and self-destructive patterns. Torrence, the clearly murderous, is left frozen in the maze at midnight, mentally if not physically destroyed. Danny, who in desperation lured him into this final dead-end state, presumably survives.

A final note: The video and 16-mm rental versions of *The Shining* currently in distribution run 120 minutes, deleting 23 minutes from the theatrical version here discussed. Cutting or dropping includes several important sequences such as the doctor's visit in Denver, and the tour of the hotel. The result is a more traditional if confusing horror film, but one for which much of the critical material in this chapter does not apply.

13

Full Metal Jacket

The structure making a movie imposes on your life when you're doing it again feels like it felt each time before. So there is a kind of wonderful suggestive timelessness about the structure. I'm doing exactly the same as I was doing when I was eighteen and making my first movie. It frees you from any other sense of time.

—Stanley Kubrick, 1987[3]

READING VIRGINIA KIRKUS reviews seeking fiction that might be material for a film, Kubrick encountered Gustav Hasford's novel *The Short-Timers,* a short first-person novel of a marine's experiences at Parris Island, South Carolina, and on a one-year tour (hence "short-timer") in Vietnam. Kubrick particularly admired the novel's "economy of structural statement," which he sought to transfer to film: "quite literally because the dialogue is almost poetic in its carved out, stark quality."

Kubrick's films have all been based on previously published material, and discussing *Full Metal Jacket* he once again tried to define what he sought as raw material: "The sense of the story. The first time you read it is the absolute critical yardstick. I remember what I felt about the book, I remember what I felt in writing the script, and I try to keep that alive in the very inappropriate circumstances that exist on a film set . . . trying to sustain a subjective sense of what it is emotionally—as well as what it is that pleases you."[3]

A number of major changes as well as rearrangements were made with respect to the novel—these to be discussed later—as well as major additions. Lee Ermey, a technical advisor and former Vietnam marine and Parris Island drill instructor, was eventually made a member of the cast, and many of his insults and repartee were eventually included in the script. Ermey told one interviewer that a drill instructor is an actor anyway: "Nobody can be that nasty." Interestingly, he was never rehearsed with the film's actual actors, so that their first terrified reactions to his harangues might have more of an element of actuality.

Production design received much attention. The details of boot camp were worked out by the former drill instructor, down to the special poodle-hair clippers employed by the marines to shave recruits almost completely bald. Becton, an old 1930s gasworks town in England that lies abandoned by the Thames, was reborn as the destroyed fiery pockmarked Vietnam city of Hue, the site of the film's climax. The final set design was based on thousands of photographs of the original city, copying everything from the 1930s European architecture to the local advertisements, signs, and billboards.

Filming on the seventeen-million-dollar production was carried out from August 1985 to September 1986. After long rehearsals, each scene would be shot three or four times on videotape. Every film take, sometimes as many as seventy-five for a single scene, would also be printed and reviewed. Kubrick told actor Adam Baldwin: "Why not see it all? The film is the cheapest part."

Production of this war movie in fact resembled an armylike routine: the actors were up at dawn for the hour-long ride to the docks, stopping some days for a half hour under the tanning bulbs. Then followed Kubrick's never-ending takes.

The camera work, clean and effective, was most notable for employing long traveling shots that give a feeling of an actual world, rather than a limited set. The film employs a characteristic look of subdued desaturated colors, mostly greens, blues, and grays.

Over the country-and-western "Good-bye My Darling, Hello Vietnam," we see the heads of various marine recruits being shaved clean, a comic effect anticipating the rising comic-grim emotional crescendo to follow.

Classic jut-jawed insult-barking marine drill instructor Sergeant Hartman (Lee Ermey) shouts curses at his young recruits as he passes down the two rows of them by their barracks bunks, the pale shaved figures suggesting helpless mental cases. "From now on you'll speak only when spoken to, the first and last words out of your mouths will be sir!"

"Sir yes sir!"

A thoughtful-faced youth pipes up mockingly: "Are you John Wayne? Is this me?" He is at once renamed Private Joker by the sergeant, even as he's punched so he falls gasping to the floor. A black becomes Private Snowball, a Texan Private Cowboy. A fat helpless-looking private, unable to stop smiling hysterically, is renamed Private Gomer Pyle, and tongue-lashed by the furious sergeant: "Get on your knees and choke yourself!"

The recruits march, run in formation, climb ropes. Pyle, putting his rifle on the wrong shoulder, is made to toddle behind the marching squad, shorts around his ankles, thumb in his mouth.

The shaved recruits, helpless-looking in their underwear, are made to sleep with their rifles, rise at dawn, swing quickly along overhead parallel bars. In pairs they must climb a colossal obstacle, a sort of great vertical ladder with two-by-four rungs. Pyle, frightened, cannot make it over the top rung, and must absorb a hysterical screaming diatribe by his sergeant: "Whatever you do, Private Pyle, don't fall down!"

In the barracks, the DI loudly confronts Joker: "Do you believe in the Virgin Mary? Are you trying to offend me?"

"Negative, sir. The private believes that any answer he gives will be wrong, and the senior drill instructor will beat him harder if he reverses himself, sir."

The sergeant makes Joker squad leader: "Private Joker has jelly in his nature, but he's got guts, and guts is enough." Joker teaches Pyle everything, from tying his shoes to cleaning his rifle. The job of turning the young men into killers proceeds: running, climbing, drill, drill, drill. "Your rifle is only a tool, it is your hard heart that kills!"

Pyle can't learn. When the DI finds a forbidden jelly doughnut in his locker, the other recruits must do push-ups while Pyle eats it. Pyle tells Joker they all hate him, he can't do anything right, he needs help. That night, in eerie blue light, the other recruits hold Pyle down and beat him with bars of soap wrapped in towels, and under their eyes Joker also hits Pyle again and again.

On the rifle range, the DI proudly refers to Charles Whitman and Lee Harvey Oswald, a Texas mass murderer and a presidential assassin, as showing what a motivated marine and his rifle can

Sergeant Hartman confronts Private Pyle during training—the Marine drill instructor as madman. (Museum of Modern Art Film Stills Archive)

Soldiers fall amid slow motion gouts of blood—war as corruption and devastation. (Museum Modern Art Film Stills Archive)

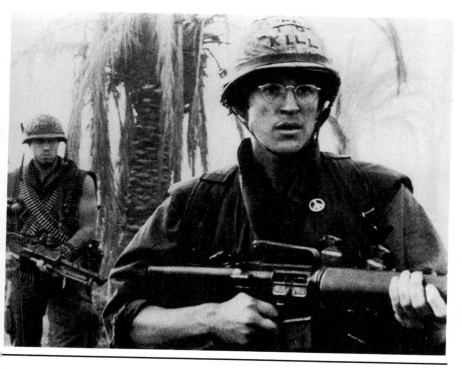

Corporal Joker and Animal Mother advance; "Born to Kill" notice on helmet and peace insignia button suggest the American forces' "split personality." (Museum of Modern Art Film Stills Archive)

do—"and before you leave my island, you'll be able to do the same!" Pyle, his eyes snaky cold, watches silently.

In the washroom, Joker tells Cowboy that Pyle has begun to talk to his rifle, and is Section Eight—seriously disturbed. The next day, though, their DI is congratulating Pyle on his shooting. Joker murmurs over marching scenes: "The Marine Corps does not want robots. The Marine Corps wants killers. The Marine Corps wants to build indestructible men—men without fear."

Graduation follows. The pugnacious DI calls out the recruits' assignments. Most are going to the infantry, including Pyle ("You made it!"). Joker will go to military journalism school.

On the last night, Joker is on firewatch. In the coldly blue-lit washroom, Pyle sits sprawled on a fixture in his underwear, a rifle and cartridge case in his arms, a snaky-eyed expression on his face: "Hi, Joker," he singsongs in an eerie voice, clutching the rifle's magazine: "762-mm, full metal jacket—I am in a world of shit," he says, voice echoing off the tiles as he does his rifle drill.

The DI rushes into the washroom in his own T-shirt and khakis, shouting questions.

Joker: "Sir, it's the private's duty to inform the senior drill instructor Private Pyle has a full magazine. It is locked and loaded sir!"

In the cold blue echoing room, the DI tries to stare Pyle down: I want that rifle and I want it now—

Pyle is making moaning hissing sounds.

"What is your major malfunction, numbnut? Didn't Mommy and Daddy show you enough attention when you were a child—"

Pyle shoots the DI, so he falls sprawled on the tiles. Joker tries talking to him softly, but staring and staring, sitting on the fixture, Pyle jams the muzzle into his own mouth and fires, bloody brains exploding on the white tiles behind his head. . . .

To Nancy Sinatra's scornful-happy "These Boots Are Made for Walkin'" ("You keep sayin' you got somethin' for me. . . . you been messin' where you shouldn't been messin'"), Joker and a new marine friend Rafterman (Kevyn Major Howard) sit at an outdoor café table in a shabby Saigon square. From behind we watch a young Vietnamese whore and her skinny pimp approach, the whore in black leather skirt making loud kissing motions: "Me so horny! Me so horny!" The marines argue over prices, then the skinny pimp grabs Rafter man's camera, makes Bruce Lee moves, and flees on a friend's motorbike.

As their copter settles at Da Nang marine base, the young photographer complains: "We're supposed to be helping them, but they shit all over us every chance they get."

In a Quonset hut, Lieutenant Lockhart briefs his young marine journalists, including Joker, summarizing *Stars and Stripes* journalism: "Ann-Margret will be here next week—I want to see fur and early mornin' dew. . . . In place of search-and-destroy missions, substitute sweep-and-clear. . . . We run two basic stories: grunts who use half their pay to buy gooks toothpaste and deodorants—hearts and minds—and combat activities that report in a kill—winning the war. . . . I've had my ass in the grass. Can't say I liked it much. Lots of bugs and too dangerous. As it is, my present duties keep me where I belong—in the rear with the gear."

That evening the Tet holiday cease-fire is broken, the sky full of fireworks that are artillery barrages and flares. The journalists help defend the base, shooting up a suicide truck full of explosives that bursts into silvery explosions. Lieutenant Lockhart briefs them: "In strategic terms Charlie's cut the country in half, the civilian press are about to wet their pants, and we've heard even Cronkite's gonna say that the war is now unwinnable."

Joker: "Sir, does this mean that Ann-Margret's not coming?"

Joker and Rafterman are assigned to cover combat. The two ride a gunship, the gunner firing bursts at any Vietnamese he sees in the paddies below: "Any one who runs is a VC. Anyone who stands still is a well-disciplined VC."

"How can you shoot women and children?"

"Easy. You just don't lead them so much."

On the ground, they talk with Cowboy's platoon leader, while on one side of a road soldiers slog into combat, and on the other an endless column of refugees goes the other way. The two, mouths and noses covered, look into a large pit holding Vietnamese corpses covered with lime. An officer asks Joker why he wears a peace-symbol button on his body armor, but has "Born to Kill" lettered on his helmet.

"I think I was trying to suggest something about the duality of man, the Jungian thing, sir."

The officer can respond only in clichés: "How about getting with the program? Why don't you jump on the team and come in for the big win? All I've asked is that my marines obey my orders as if they were the word of God." And so on.

Joker and Rafterman find an old temple where an exhausted squad of marines sit around, among them a delighted Cowboy. Another, a gigantic sort of Rambo clone named Animal Mother (Adam Baldwin), carries a large machine gun in his arms and wearing crisscrossed bullet belts, challenges Joker. Both imitate John Wayne: "You can talk the talk, but can you walk the walk?" Animal Mother pulls the hat off a slumped figure to reveal a dead young Viet Cong soldier: "This is his party, he's the guest of honor!"

Joker and Rafter man accompany the squad into combat, the marines walking beside tanks that rumble through the smashed-up urban concrete landscape, several of the buildings burning brightly, perhaps from artillery hits. The platoon leader is shot, but, their faces frightened, the soldiers continue to advance through the grim landscape.

To "Surfin' Bird," a medical copter loaded with casualties pulls itself heavily into the air. Spaced along a low wall, the marines turn to face a combat film crew working its way past them, taping a line from each:

"Are you John Wayne? Is this me?"

"Then start the cameras! This is *Vietnam, the Movie!*"

"If you're John Wayne, then I'll be a horse."

"Where're the Indians?"

"We'll let the gooks play the Indians—"

Inspecting the bodies of two casualties, the survivors are far less articulate:

"Semper fi."

"Better you than me."

"Well at least they died for a good cause—"

"What cause was that—?"

"You think we waste gooks for freedom? This is a slaughter!"

Answers to the question of whether America belongs in Vietnam similarly cannot rise above the most immediate facts, knee-jerk emotional responses, or incoherent cynicism, patriotism, and absurdism:

"Well, it's like a war, what I thought about a war, what a war was supposed to be—there's the enemy—kill 'em!"

"Well I didn't think there's any question—when the shit really hits the fan, we're the ones they call—mother green and her killing machine!"

"*They* don't want to be involved in this war. They think, it's sort of like they took away our freedom and gave it to the gookers, and they don't want it, they'd rather be alive and free, I guess, poor dumb bastards."

"We're gettin' killed for these people and they don't even appreciate it. They think it's a big joke. If you ask me we're shootin' the wrong gooks!"

Joker: "I wanted to see exotic Vietnam, the jewel of Southeast Asia. I wanted to meet interesting, stimulating people of an ancient culture, and kill them."

"I wanted to be the first kid on my block to get a confirmed kill!"

Before a Vietnamese movie house, the plush seats visible, the squad bargains with a prostitute and her pimp: "Suckee, fuckee, she give you anything you want, long time!" The GI repartee goes back to World War II ("We'll trade you some ARVAN rifles never fired and only dropped once!") and forward to street-smart pimpese ("She looks like she could suck the chrome off a trailer hitch").

The squad is sent to check out enemy troop movements, moving slowly through more urban ruins, resembling a smashed-up construction site. The leader is killed by a booby-trapped toy doll, so Cowboy takes over. Now lost, the black soldier ("Nigger behind the trigger") scouts out the terrain ahead. From inside a building we watch him approach, to be shot in a slow-motion gout of blood.

At once the soldiers pour the fire into the building front, windows and ornamentation crashing to the street. Cowboy calls for tank support, and when the medic rushes in, he's also cut down, more blood explosions splashing from both bodies.

Cowboy: "I seen this before. The sniper is trying to suck us in one at a time."

The massive Animal Mother, hugging his machine gun, repeatedly questions the withdrawal order, the two cursing back and forth. At last Animal Mother runs forward ducking around a building out of the line of fire while the casualties are hit again, screaming amid more splashing blood.

In a skirmish line the squad moves forward, taking refuge in a shattered building except for Cowboy, who's killed by the sniper. Throwing obscuring smoke grenades, they advance again ("Let's get some payback!"). Running through a field of concrete pillars as they fire, then forcing their way inside the building ahead, the marines confront a young Vietnamese woman with a rifle, and gun her down: "We got the fucker!"

She gasps for breath on the floor of the building, murmuring prayers amid the wreckage.

"No more boom-boom for this baby-san! There's nothing we can do for her. She's dead meat!"

Joker wants to know what about her. They can't just leave her here. The room is dark, the surviving marines' faces half-black, half-illuminated by the fiery orange pillars outside.

The woman gasps: "Shoot . . . me. . . . shoot . . . me. . . . shoot . . . me."

Joker does it.

"Joker, we're gonna have to put you up for the Congressional Medal!"

It's night, and against the fires of the burning city buildings, the marines move, spread out and guns at the ready. A faint song rises: "M.I.C., K.E.Y., M.O.U.S.E. . . . Forever let us hold our banner high high high high—" it goes on—

Joker's voice tells us: "My thoughts drift back to a red nickel wet dream. About Mary Jane Rottencrotch and the Great Homecoming Fuck Fantasy. I'm so happy that I'm alive, in one piece, and short. I'm in a world of shit, yes, but I'm alive and I am not afraid."

The marines' voices come up: "—and join our family. Who's the leader of the club, that's made for you and me—M.I.C., K.E.Y., M.O.U.S.E. Hey there, hi there ho there . . . ," in the darkness, which covers them all.

Responses to Kubrick's film were, as usual, diverse and heated. *Variety*'s "Cart" perhaps anticipated the critical spectrum best: "Most of what's on view here has been seen before in some way or another . . . and is perhaps lacking that extra philosophical dimension that has marked Kubrick's greatest films. But this graphic portrayal of two levels of hell on earth generates considerable power via many riveting sequences, extraordinary dialogue, and first-rate performances."[2]

Certainly the most favorable review was by Jack Kroll,[9] who saw the film as "scorching you with the absolute chill of his depiction of the war as a plague of corruption and dehumanization." Kroll points out that like the contemporaneous *Platoon,* with its good and bad sergeant/father figures, *Full Metal Jacket* tries to suggest the split personality of the US in Vietnam by the protagonist's wearing of a peace insignia on his jacket while "Born to Kill" is painted on his helmet. The use of language in the film, Kroll notes, is similarly fragmented: the marine DI raves like a madman, while the young soldiers mostly mutter clichés and incoherent fragments of thought.

New York Times critic Vincent Canby[1] compares the film to "a series of exploding boomerangs. Just when you think you can relax in safety, some crazed image or line or event will swing around to lodge in the brain and scramble the emotions." He sees Drill Instructor Hartman as the real heart of the film, whose ecstatic brain-and-body washing of the recruits repeatedly acts as such boomerangs, hilarity suddenly returning as shock and sorrow.

J. Hoberman of the *Village Voice* in a sophisticated review[8] sums up *Full Metal Jacket* as "sometimes unpleasant and often wrongheaded, but it's more than once indelible and hardly ever boring." He notes that the beginning of the film clinically depicts the view that killers are made, not born (reversing *A Clockwork Orange*), while Parris Island resembles Kubrick's outsized images from other films—here a "vast prison of space." Hoberman also notes that unlike *Platoon* and *Apocalypse Now,* which focus on massacres of civilians, symbolizing the loss of US innocence, Kubrick takes US corruption for granted, as in the scene of the potshotting gunship gunner. Rather, Hoberman sees Kubrick seeking some cosmic significance in the war, implied by the Dehumanized Combat Zone, the abstracted rifle squad, and the lack of female characters. Hoberman concludes that this is one distanced film: "Joker must be speaking of his creator when near the end of the film he proclaims, 'I am in a world of shit, but I am alive and I am not afraid.'"

David Sterritt of the *Christian Science Monitor*[11] found *Full Metal Jacket* more concentrated and streamlined than previous films about Vietnam, its emotions on a very tight leash: "For all its battlefield realism, this is also an exercise in motion picture poetics." Sterritt notes that the peace symbol/helmet duality is part of a more general vision: "The contradictory human urge towards destructiveness and healing which is one of Kubrick's chief subjects." The final mercy killing for him further suggests this viewpoint.

A comparison of the source novel *The Short-Timers* and the film *Full Metal Jacket* suggests some of Kubrick's artistic priorities. In terms of organization, while the Parris Island section is followed very closely through the two deaths, the Vietnam part of the novel has two "mercy killing" sequences of increasing moral complexity. The first, like the film's conclusion, has Joker finish off a wounded enemy sniper. While in the second, only in the novel, a squad is pinned down by an extraordinary sniper who seems able to kill them all as they try to aid those already wounded in the open. Joker responds by killing the wounded Cowboy, his last friend, shooting out his brains from a distance, the doomed friend egging him on, so that the squad of marines can withdraw "honorably." Certainly by ending his film with the first sniper incident, Kubrick spares himself the full savage thrust of the dehumanization that has been the theme of the novel: "We try very hard not to think about anything important, try not to think that there's no slack and there's a long walk home."[7] By comparison, Kubrick's ending is almost upbeat.

Kubrick's film also differs from the book in its fastidiousness towards the behavior of US troops. The Americans, except for the murderous gunship gunner, are upright tough fighting men. By contrast the US forces in Hasford's novel are full of sadists and other clear pathological types, from the GI who chops off his victims' feet and hauls them around in a sack, to the casual cutter-off of the sniper's finger to salvage her wedding ring (her head is also removed), to Animal Mother who kills his Jewish squad leader, to the tank commander who likes to run down soldiers who try to leap aside from his roaring vehicle.

A second interesting way to look at *Full Metal Jacket,* alluded to by some critics, is to explore how the two sections relate to each other. In fact there are several hints within the film that these parts are meant to comment on each other. The first begins with a furious four-minute introduction to the corps by Sergeant Hartman, the second with a "public relations" monologue on Marine Corps morale by Lieutenant Lockhart. (The first introduced by the sweet "Good-bye My Darling, Hello Vietnam," the second by the sarcastic "These Boots Are Made for Walkin'.") The first section builds to a crescendo of murder and suicide, the second to scary ambushes followed by a mercy killing.

One does not want to reduce this complex film to a schema of ideas, but looked at in this way does suggest that the first half, the brain-and-body washing of the recruits into fearless but flawed killers, is basically commented on in the second half, in which the resulting personalities, now tools of the high command, are forced to deal with the multifaceted nature of combat, which is not that different from "ordinary life" in its complexities and paradoxes. For example, asked whether America should be in Vietnam, the marines respond only as unthinking killing engines, unable to speak of "freedom" except with inadvertent comic/contemptuous overtones. As is soon clear, these fearless killers have adapted a very esoteric "freedom," whose social aspect is only a precarious tribal camaraderie. The final overruling of marine combat doctrine by Animal Mother suggests they've survived both boot-camp brainwashing and enemy guile, and are reunited as a crude band of brothers ("Who's the leader of the club that's made for you and me?" does not suggest a sophisticated social outlook).

Joker has reached a slightly higher plane; like Pyle, he can kill when he finds himself in an unbearable situation, but unlike Pyle, he can live with himself afterwards: "I'm in a world of shit, but I'm alive and I am not afraid."

Kubrick's characteristic narrative motifs are once again present as well:

Imaginary worlds. The succession of such worlds includes the authoritarian world of the boot camp, the artfully shaped world of military journalism, and the wolf-pack world of combat shared by the rifle squad.

Futility of intelligence, distrust of emotion. The training camp is a world of arbitrary power, where the fact that one is punished regardless of his behavior is made explicit. The world of combat is shown very much the same, in which brains are of marginal utility, and the average individual finds it easiest to respond to events only with clichés and stereotypical brutality.

Homicidal-suicidal pairings. Pyle, who murders his drill instructor and then himself, is in several ways a counterpart of Joker, the mercy-killing protagonist. The cleverest recruit and the clumsiest, they both cannot fully control their spontaneous responses to their environment, and find themselves both living in "a world of shit" they cannot really join. Both kill, but one is in the end happy to be alive, the other tormented unto death.

Obsessed hero. Joker seems in an awkward sly way to continually seek out the truth by taunting his superiors: he questions his drill instructor's sadistic "logic"; his military newspaperman boss's mind control; his rifle-squad mates' brutal responses to combat.

Odyssey towards freedom and knowledge. Joker works his way from the most arbitrary controlled environment, boot camp, to the naked face of combat, while becoming more and more aware of his true feelings, and increasingly responding to them.

14
Eyes Wide Shut

"I think that the enemy of the filmmaker is not the intellectual or the member of the mass public, but the kind of middlebrow who has neither the intellectual apparatus to analyze and clearly define what is meant, nor the honest emotional reaction of the mass film audience member. . . . I think that it is a monumental presumption to summarize what the intention of the film is."

—*Stanley Kubrick Interview, 1968*

KUBRICK HAD BEEN trying to find a way to transfer Arthur Schnitzler's 1926 novella *Traumnovelle* (Dream story) to the screen since the early 1970s. Very briefly, this is the story of a doctor in Vienna in the 1890s, who with his wife attends a masquerade ball. Both propositioned, their attitudes toward fidelity and each other start to change. The two proceed to analyze their feelings and desires, the wife confessing a strong attraction for another man during one of the couple's holidays.

The doctor is called to a counselor's bedside, where his daughter/ nurse confesses her love for him. He encounters a prostitute, but her youth causes him to refrain from sex. He meets a medical-school friend, who now plays the piano at the orgies of the rich. The young doctor learns their password, acquires a costume from a pederast/pimp, and attends, finding a masked and beautiful company who soon disrobe. A woman guest intuits he is an interloper, and warns him to leave. The doctor is threatened, but the woman demands to be the scapegoat. He refuses to let her take his place, but is told "there's no turning back." Sent home, his wife has dreamed of herself in a shameless orgy with the desired man. The doctor investigates and finds that the pianist has been forcibly sent away, the costumer's pederasty continues, the masquerade ball's hosts are now threatening him, the counselor's daughter is off to be married, and the prostitute is diseased. A newspaper report of a countess's poisoning leads him to the morgue, but he cannot be sure if the deceased is the same woman who saved him. He goes home and tells his wife what has happened, to which she replies they should be happy they've survived, dream or reality.

"It's difficult to find any writer who understands the human soul more truly and who had a more profound insight into the way people think, act and are," Kubrick said of Schnitzler in a 1960 interview.[21] Having been moved, Kubrick's vision of his film gradually evolved over the years. In 1980, he saw it as a sex comedy, with a wild and somber streak, perhaps starring Steve Martin.[8] (He was very impressed with Martin's *The Jerk*.) But most writers he discussed it with—Michael Herr, David Cornwell, Diane Johnson—saw the work as more severe and upsetting, basically sinister.

Kubrick contacted Frederick Raphael, writer of such romantic dramas as *Darling* and *Two for the Road*, about working on the project in spring of 1994. Raphael has described the process of collaborating with Kubrick at some length in his book *Eyes Wide Open*,[17] from payment concerns to electronic communications to Kubrick's psychology to Raphael's approaches to story problems. His research, for example, included supposedly highly classified FBI reports on a wealthy, hedonistic pro-JFK group called "the free," who engaged in orgiastic behavior—which Raphael later admitted he totally made up for fun.

Raphael soon realized that he was there to provide script,[2] which Kubrick would then use as "A blueprint for performance and photography." Raphael in the end concluded that Kubrick's films were "about situations, never about people." He described his rewriting as a color-it-yourself book to which Kubrick would add his own characteristic tones. Kubrick wanted the spaces to have seductive outlines, but not to carry any instructions.

In the end, Kubrick revised the final script, which led to neither alarm nor praise by Raphael. In addition, Kubrick's "rehearsing/rewriting" production methods (see below) surely led to major, if not total, additional changes. When Terry Semel, co-chairman of Warners, approved the project, he said: "What I would really love you to consider is a movie star in the lead role; you haven't done that since Jack Nicholson" (in *The Shining*). Kubrick worried that such a star wouldn't share his total commitment, but approached a series of couples.[1]

Both having "flipped over the script and anxious to work with Kubrick" (*Variety,* December 31, 1995), married couple Tom Cruise and Nicole Kidman were cast in the principle roles ("Kubrick, Kidman, Cruise Open *Shut* Deal"). Cruise's acting fee was reportedly $20 million, Kidman's $5 million. They were joined by Harvey Keitel and Jennifer Jason Leigh. By mid-1997, Keitel quit and his scenes were reshot with Sydney Pollack.

Director Pollack sees Kubrick's European productions as a canny filmmaking strategy: "Stanley has figured out a way to work in England for a fraction of what we pay here. While the rest of us poor bastards are able to get sixteen weeks of filming for seventy million with a twenty-million star, Stanley could get forty-five weeks of shooting for sixty-five million. . . . He ensured himself the luxury of trying to work out something that's as complicated emotionally as the film is."[1]

Warner Brothers announced production of *Eyes Wide Shut* in December 1995. Filming began at Pinewood Studios in England on November 4, 1996. Kubrick was credited as producer and director, with Douglas Milsome, Kubrick's director of photography since the making of *2001,* in his usual role.

Because of the special subject matter—and consistent with earlier projects—Kubrick himself usually functioned as camera-person, allowing only a handful of crew on the set. *Boogie Nights* director Paul Thomson Anderson, visiting, asked, " 'Do you always work with so few people?' He gave me this look and said, 'Why? How many do you need?' "[20]

Much of the script was completely reworked on the set through a series of evolving retakes: "We'd rehearse and rehearse a scene," explained Todd Field (the pianist character): "and it would change from hour to hour. We'd keep giving the script supervisor notes all the time, so by the end of the day the script might be completely different. It wasn't really improvisation . . . it was more like writing."[20]

This rehearsing/rewriting process would sometimes take all day. Then, finally, filming would begin. Actress Vinessa Shaw (whose role of prostitute took two months to shoot) commented: "I remember, one time, around three in the morning, I did my sixty-ninth take of a scene . . . and then I ended up doing twenty more takes. . . . It gives you a real sense of freedom . . . doing a scene over and over, all of a sudden you see it as completely different. It gives you a chance to explore."[20]

Like many directors, Kubrick created a special mood on the set. Kidman commented on the nude scenes: "When I was shooting it, I didn't even think. We just entered what we called Kubrick World. You're so lost in the characters at that stage and we'd been working on it for so long that we had lost perspective. It sounds so stupid, but when you're actually making the film, you forget that millions of people are going to see it."[19]

Kubrick always maintained his uncanny camera sense. According to Sidney Pollack, in one take, he told Tom Cruise "You're standing closer to the camera than you were. Cruise said he was on his mark, so Kubrick told the cameraperson 'Then you're closer.' They took out a tape measure, and he was an inch closer!"[21]

Kubrick apparently grew very close to his lead actors during filming. Days were supposedly spent in deep discussions on the subject of sexual obsession between Cruise, Kidman, and Kubrick. Afterward, Kidman told a journalist: "Kubrick knew us and our relationship as no one else does . . . he was like a father. He understood your humanity and reveled in your dedication." For shooting the sex scenes, only Cruise, Kidman, and Kubrick were on the set.

Tom Cruise has pointed out that *Eyes Wide Shut* is an autobiographical film for the director as well, in that the main characters' apartment looks very much like the one that Kubrick and his wife, Christine, occupied in 1960s New York City, and is decorated with her paintings. Kidman chose books, window shades, and personal items such as clothes and makeup. The Pinewood Studios craftsmen had also set about creating a contemporaneous Greenwich Village. Kubrick went so far as to send workmen to Manhattan to measure street widths and note newspaper-vending-machine locations. The director also set camerapersons to shoot real city footage for rear-screen projection, for scenes of Tom Cruise strolling around town.

Kubrick's compulsive perfectionism eventually led to some of the familiar responses. Tom Cruise apparently started off very gung ho, but in fact developed an ulcer during filming. Kidman has stated: "I think Stanley would have been tinkering with it for the next twenty years. He was never finished. It was never perfect enough."

Filming finally ended in June 1998, fifteen months after starting. The average major studio movie today only takes two months. Even *Titanic* only took six. Kubrick's deal with Warner Brothers gave him the right of "final cut" of his film. The company expected an R Rating. However, as Terry Semel, company co-chairman put it: "It was not only our deal, it was what Stanley wanted. He wanted the film to be available to the masses."

Kubrick's elaborate control in some ways simplified the editing of the film. Unlike almost every modern filmmaker, Kubrick did not have to show the studio executives his director's cut, which is often a starting point for further editing and even additional filming. There were also no previews to gauge audience reactions.

Editing ended in fall 1998.

Kubrick died March 7, 1999, just after viewing his final cut.

An NC-17 version, (no one under seventeen admitted) was to be shown in Europe.

To get an R rating—anyone under seventeen must be accompanied by an adult—scenes of an orgy with various sexual couplings were subsequently partially shielded by computer-generated spectator figures. In both versions, this sequence lasts about sixty-five seconds. The stars' publicity agent claimed that not a frame was cut, and Kubrick approved this change to get the R rating. Critic Janet Maslin of the *New York Times,* quoted by Bernard Weinraub, called the changes "a joke . . . the meaning and effects of the acts witnessed remains the same."[22]

Not everyone has accepted the Warner Brothers version of the final preparation. Several critics argue that the film clearly needed additional editing, looping, and other work; whereas some claim the final still highly flawed work was made by other directors.

Jay Hoberman, for example, argues: "The ponderous Temple of Doom orgy, crassly matched location inserts, reliance on cross-cutting, and atrocious mixing (most obvious in the orgy's dreadful dubbing and oscillating hubbub level) all suggest the movie was quite far from completion when its notoriously perfectionist author passed away."[9]

An interview with independent Canadian feature filmmaker David Cronenberg also supports this view: "He died too young, Stanley, and I'm sure he's absolutely pissed off being dead. And I think his movie was not finished because he had the sound mix still to do and the looping with the actors, where you add dialogue and so change performances. It's only people who don't know about filmmaking who think it will be Stanley's movie, because a huge part of it won't be, and I wonder who the hell is finishing it? Are they going to get Spielberg?"[3]

Marketing *Eyes Wide Shut* posed a challenge. It's been twenty-five years since Hollywood's last sexually provocative films, *Midnight Cowboy* and *Last Tango in Paris*. Like these, more recently *The English Patient* and *Boogie Nights* opened in the fourth quarter at a few major-market theaters, before gradually expanding nationally.

For Kubrick's film, a new strategy was chosen for the 2,500 theaters across the United States. The $64 million film opened "wide," its distributors seeking a broad audience, with its themes of sexual relations, marital fidelity, and affluent New York society as if it were a conventional summer blockbuster. The studio counted on advance buzz to bring out audiences—from websites describing the three-hundred-day shoot to dozens of Kubrick retrospectives following up the director's death, to special articles in major magazines. The TV ads and trailers' strategy was to use a few tantalizing brief scenes, focusing on the stars. Posters, billboards, and magazine ads stressed the names CRUISE, KIDMAN, and KUBRICK against an image of the stars kissing; all these concepts and orchestrations supposedly being the late Stanley Kubrick's ideas.

Kubrick's one-line blurb described the film as "a thriller of sexual obsession and jealousy." Kubrick and Warners's Terry Semel saw it as a high-profile-adult film in contrast to the summer teenage glut.

But not all the marketing signs were positive. Cinemascore president Edward Mintz, who tracks opening-night responses, was interviewed in *Newsweek* for August 2, 1999, and stated that *Eyes Wide Shut* got some of the worst grades in his twenty-one years of polling: seventy-three percent of people twenty-five and over gave it an "F." "You start getting 'D's' and 'F's'," says Mintz, "and a movie shouldn't even have been made."

Because Kubrick's films do better overseas, where moviegoing peaks in the fall, the July release was decided by working backwards. Kubrick's films also do better in big cities than small towns, but Tom Cruise may improve this situation, as well as the particular shortage of adult fare. Critical responses might also help.

Briefly viewed, against hot orange wall, beautiful young Alice Harford (Nicole Kidman) models a black-sheath dress, drops it, and we see her nude from behind.

Dr. Bill Harford (Tom Cruise) and Alice stand nude, necking before a mirror while lewd rock music throbs. They dress in their luxurious New York West Side home for a Christmas party, the rich successful happy pair saying good night to their girl child. The party, attended by very attractive socialites, is held in an enormous luxurious home, brilliant lighting making it a rosy fairyland. They meet their host, Victor Ziegler (Sydney Pollack), and an old-medical school classmate.

Tipsy, Alice chats with a European sophisticate, seductively telling her that women marry only so that they might have any man, as she could. Alice charmingly refuses the advances. Dr. Harford is likewise enticed by two lovely models, who want to take him "where the rainbow ends." Host Ziegler interrupts, taking Harford to help save a naked, overdosed young woman.

At home, the couple smoke pot, then fall into an intense discussion of their erotic temptations. Dr. Harford claims that despite temptations he has stayed chaste, and that women avoid such impulses once married. Alice angrily denies this and recalls a man she met on their vacation for whom she would have given up husband, child, and marriage. In a sort of black-and-white porno-film fantasy, Dr. Harford sees them coupling.

Harford is then called to the deathbed of a wealthy patient by the man's daughter. By the deathbed, the daughter suddenly declares her love for the physician. Her own fiancé arrives, a virtual double in looks for Harford.

Overwrought and drifting through Greenwich Village, Harford is picked up by an attractive hooker, but gets a cell-phone call, which forestalls intercourse. Next, he visits a club where the medical-school friend from the party is a pianist. The man reveals that he plays at very private parties filled with stunning, naked women. Entry requires a password, mask, and costume. Harford extracts the details and visits a costume shop, seeing the owner, his daughter, and visitors who have unclear sexual relationships. Harford then grabs a cab to the party, at a Long Island mansion, still imagining his wife and lover in congress. Gaining admission, Harford finds many rooms filled with guests masked and robed, and quasipriests, also totally covered, encircled by a score of tall, beautiful, masked "super modelish" women.

To eerie music and chanting, the silent, tall women drop their robes, revealing near-naked-showgirl figures, and go off with the robed, masked men. Wandering through the mansion, Harford sees a joyless orgy, with couples and groups engaged in various sexual activities, while others look on. He is joined by one of the naked, stunning women, who eerily suggests his wife's appearance with stylized eyeglasses on her mask. She warns him that he is in deadly danger, and must depart.

Masked figures arrive to see Harford to his taxi, but instead take him to the "ceremony room," where the others confront him and tell him to remove his mask, and then clothing. He is told he must pay a terrible penalty for his deception. Abruptly, the woman who warned him appears on an interior balcony. She will take the penalties. Harford is removed from the party.

At home, Harford finds his family asleep.

The next day, the doctor proceeds to recapitulate the encounters of the previous night. He calls the home of the deceased rich man, but when his "double" answers, he hangs up without speaking. He visits the prostitute's apartment, whose roommate tells him she has since gotten a positive HIV diagnosis. He locates the pianist's hotel, but the desk clerk tells him his old friend had checked out— bruised, frightened, and accompanied by two toughs. He returns the costume—the company owner now seen clearly pimping for his young daughter, the two previous visitors being her happy clients.

Harford, perhaps followed, picks up a tabloid with the eerie headline: YOU'RE LUCKY TO BE ALIVE! An article notes that a beauty queen

n Cruise as Dr. William Harford, Nicole Kidman as Alice Harford. Alice: "I was ready to
e up everything. . . at the same time you were dearer to me than ever." (1999 Warner
thers. Courtesy Museum of Modern Art Film Stills Archive)

le Kidman as Alice Harford, in eyeglasses: counterpart of the beautiful feathered mask
ysterious Woman, who tells her husband, "Stop. Let him go. Take me. I am ready to
em him." (1999 Warner Brothers. Courtesy Museum of Modern Art Film Stills Archive)

has drug overdosed and has been admitted to a local hospital. At that hospital, he learns the woman has since died. In the morgue, he studies the tall beauty. Could this be his savior from the orgy? Harford gets a call from Ziegler, the rich party thrower. Visiting him, he is told that Ziegler has had him followed since the orgy, which he also attended. The costume-rental stub gave his identity; the taxi showed that he was an outsider.

The doctor wants explanations: of the missing pianist, the dead beauty, the eerie sinister orgy. Ziegler counters that the pianist was roughed up and shipped home because he gave away secrets, the woman was a hopeless addict sure to die—and was found at home behind locked doors. The orgy could have been a masquerade just to fool him, and in any case, the people there were so powerful he had best do nothing about it. ("If you only knew who was behind the masks, you would lose sleep!") Ziegler shrugs: "Life goes on, it always does, until it doesn't."

Exhausted and apparently weeping from reaction, Harford leaves. When he visits the orgy estate, he's given a grim warning to do no more.

The doctor returns home, and finds his wife sleeping and weeping. She has just had a dream in which she was being made love to by many anonymous men. With him there it was awful; with him away, it was delightful. He tells his experiences of the past days. In her first "unglamorous" image in the film, she says that they should do nothing more. The pair go shopping for Christmas gifts for their child. They also discuss what their experiences mean. She tells him that she is as certain about the last twenty-four hours as about anything: "I think we ought to be grateful that we have come unharmed out of all our adventures, whether they were real or only a dream."

"Are you quite sure of that?"

"Just as sure as I am that the reality of one night, let alone that of a whole lifetime, is not the whole truth."

"And no dream is entirely a dream."

"There's something that we must do as soon as possible—fuck!" Blackout.

Since *Eyes Wide Shut* was Kubrick's final film, many of the critics sought to evaluate it as exemplifying his whole career.

The *New York Times*'s Janet Maslin commented: "This astonishing last film is a spellbinding addition to the Kubrick canon. . . . The man who could create a whole new universe with each undertaking chose the bedroom as the last frontier, to the point where prolonged conjugal conversations are major events in a long winding and surreal story . . . the dreamlike intensity of previous Kubrick visions is in full force here."[13]

A second *New York Times* evaluation by Stephen Holden had a more cynically hip but still approving interpretation. "*Eyes Wide Shut* is that almost unheard-of phenomenon, a serious major studio film that contemplates grown-up sex and its discontents . . . an extended Freudian dream grafted onto another dream: of contemporary New York as Sin City, in which sexual predators from all sides threaten to devour the innocent doctor and his wife. Their only protection from the encircling demons is a frightened, trembling commitment to monogamy. . . . *Eyes Wide Shut* is oddly romantic in its belief in the existence of a secret sexual world, accessible only to an elite cogniscenti of the damned. . . . It certainly doesn't fit today's climate of proliferating telephone sex, escort services, internet pornography and people's obsessions with body fat."[10]

Daily Variety's Todd McCarthy gave the trade paper's usual shrewd appraisal, as well as a very enthusiastic one: "After all the curiosity and attendant hype is washed away, what one is left with is a riveting, thematically probing, richly atmospheric and just occasionally troublesome work, a deeply inquisitive consideration of the extent of trust and mutual knowledge possible between a man and a woman. This meticulous, deliberate and precise picture casts a particular sort of spell, one that will captivate older and thoughtful audiences. . . . Less ascerbic and more optimistic about the human condition than any of the director's previous films, [it] remains remarkably faithful to its source, while also trading in familiar Kubrick concerns such as paranoia, deception, the literal and figurative masks that people wear and the difficulty for even intelligent human beings to transcend the base and self-destructive impulses that drive the species . . . [the] film is unique in the late director's oeuvre in that it is women who far outshine the men. The fact that the conclusion here is at least guardedly hopeful suggests that, at the end, Kubrick believed in some sort of progress after all."[14]

Peter Rainer found the quality of personal obsession fascinating: "It's a powerful movie without always, or often, being a very good one; watching it is a bit like being inside the twistings and conniptions of a control freak who's longing to lose control, only to pull back tighter than ever. . . . In the film's archetypal scene, William on a house call is lured by a patient while a corpse rests in full view . . . the film is a male fantasy of how women's imagined urges can destroy you just as if they were real . . . still, none of the personal destructions on view resonate because the movie seems to be populated by the soulless. . . . Kubrick wasn't able to relinquish his customary iron grip over his material, and move into more perilous and mellifluous realms of desire."[16]

Godfrey Cheshire also approves of the film as a tour de force, part of a great symmetrical design in Kubrick's work: "*Eyes Wide Shut* comes off as a de facto companion piece to *The Shining.* . . . Both treat home as a metaphor for marriage . . . one is a comic nightmare, the other a dark dream. . . . You could say that sex outside marriage is a tempting but icky no-no . . . to give it great elegance, you could say that every marriage requires endless surrenders of self interest . . . and that illicit fantasies are legitimate ways of venting disallowed desires. . . . Kubrick's genius always resided somewhere just beyond the horizon of ideas, words, stories."[2]

Several critics judged *Eyes Wide Shut* a failure. Owen Glieberman saw its dream strategy as just not working: "*Eyes Wide Shut.* A mystery that intertwines lust, fear, and death, wants to show the temptations of the everyday transformed into a whirlpool of fantasy. . . . Yet what we see instead is a vague fragmentary mishmash of ominous and cheap thrills. . . . *Eyes Wide Shut* is structured as an amorphous series of cliff hangers, each of which promises a kinky catharsis which never quite arrives. . . . Kubrick clearly hasn't seen enough straight-to-cable thrillers, which routinely transmute nasty sex into death. The bad babe who ends up a white wax corpse, the pillar of society who's really a paragon of decadence—these characters have little thrust in a world where sexual transgressions long ago saturated pop culture and middle-class life itself."[7]

David Denby sees the film as undeveloped and incoherent: "Kubrick and Raphael haven't developed the relationship between the couple well enough for us to see what's at stake, and they've neutered the emotions that might have pulled the movie together. . . . He's a protagonist without a purpose, wandering through an indistinct Kubrickian worldscape in which everything seems wrong. . . . Kubrick and Raphael should have been ashamed to have been engaged in this kind of pretentious mystification."[4]

Jay Hoberman is not simply dissatisfied with the film, he sees clear evidence of corporate tinkering: "*Eyes Wide Shut* has more than a few problems . . . Cruise is blatantly miscast as his character is incoherent . . . the ridiculous orgy and the botched sense of place would have been difficult to repair . . . notwithstanding the misguided attempt . . . to rationalize Schnitzler's evocative material with a heavy-handed and ultimately nonsensical, plot device, I'm not even convinced that this 'haunting final masterpiece' has the tone that Kubrick intended. . . . Someday some dogged cinearchaeologist will get to the bottom of this corporate restoration."[9]

I myself find the film fascinating and successful on a number of levels, though additional editing and other reworking might have improved it. Most obviously, its structure is more thoroughly dreamlike and multileveled than the original Schnitzler story, proceeding in alternate waves of irresponsible fantasy and disturbing nightmare that intensify as the film proceeds. The key is to see everything outside the physician's home as progressively more unreal. Even the first "real" Christmas party is held in a fantasy world, filled with only the most handsome and beautiful, and lit and decorated like a Shangri-la. The almost comically vampirish old-world seducer and stunning models who stalk the couple are hip precursors who foreshadow the patriarchal nightmare and feminine masochism of the orgy. Ziegler's open, lordly authority, and Alice Harford in her charming spectacles, foreshadow the dictatorial priest and head-dressed, defiant beauty who sacrifices herself for the physician's survival. The orgy mansion is the upper-class Christmas party stripped of its own masks and conceits, reduced to its naked sexual assertions of power and submission.

Likewise, the dreamlike repeated series of encounters (Recall Goldilocks entering the bears' home, room by room, then the bears following), is similarly used to pull away the illusionary veils of sexual opportunities surrounding each incident: a woman made willing by circumstance; an apparently risk-free professional; a panderer with a promiscuous child; orgiasts both vengeful and unforgiving. This seems to be the meaning and lesson of the never-explained film title—with regard to sexual impulses, we must be aware that we live with our eyes "wide shut," that is, seeing the world as both objective situations and as moments richly colored by our sexual impulses: both desires and fears. Both sides of life must be acknowledged and dealt with.

Another absorbing aspect of the film is the perhaps climatic confrontation between Ziegler and Dr. Harford. The scene has been criticized as clumsily done, an awkward tying up of plot details. But it can also be viewed another way, as the furthest most hellish extension of the fantasy landscape. Ziegler could *be* the orgy priest, but he is something worse. He is the master and enforcer of those fiends, and also their apologist. He explains how each abuse and execution can be carried out and smoothed over, since "If you only knew who has behind the masks, you would loose sleep." Behind the masks are not just Washington powerbrokers and corporate masterminds, miscellaneous spin doctors and influence peddlers: behind them are impulses and obsessions that inevitably twist those who achieve leadership and control, as they twist us all—a human predicament for which Kubrick acknowledges there is no answer. (In passing,, how *else* can the scene be taken? As critics note, and most alert citizens are aware, real modern power players do not engage in such risky anonymous mass orgies, but simply dial up their local Heidi Fleiss or other moguls' madam.) The physician's collapse and retreat are thus entirely appropriate.

The terribly bleak, pitiless tone of this scene has yet another simple if unwelcome interpretation. It is a view of a world without the possibilities of fantasy or true affection, a world of self-righteous power games and total control—a world in many ways toward which we are moving.

Finally, the themes that I have proposed, which govern Kubrick's work are once again present, and shall be recorded.

* * *

Imaginary worlds. The theme is most highly elaborated in this last film. Outside the physician's home, the world is a dreamscape, beginning with the glorious Christmas party and erotic opportunities, which are revised into trials as the film goes on.

Futility of intelligence, distrust of emotion. Faced with an intimate challenge, the protagonist's mind and feelings fail him, and he lets his life be ruled by chance encounters and momentary impulses in order to solve his problems.

Homicidal/suicidal pairings. Several times the hero meets "sexual adventurer" counterparts of himself, whom his actions push toward death (pianist, woman "savior"), or ones who make *his* more likely (HIV prostitute, orgiasts).

Obsessed hero. Dr. Harford must decide what to feel and think about his wife's revelations, by following his impulses and opportunities.

Odyssey toward freedom and knowledge. Harford's dream journey leads to at least one lesson: couples had best tell each other their sexual fantasies, not act on them, and use their erotic energy to enrich the marriage.

15
Summing Up

Man has been turned loose from religion and has hailed the death of his gods; the imperative loyalties of the old nation-states are dissolving and all the old social and ethical values are disappearing. Man in the twentieth century has been cut adrift in a rudderless boat on an uncharted sea; if he is going to stay sane throughout the voyage, he must have something to care about, something that is more important than himself
—Stanley Kubrick, 1968[3]

WITH THE DEATH of Stanley Kubrick on March 7, 1999, a number of interesting metatheories have been proposed to explain all his films. I'd like to categorize and sum up these ideas before giving my own.

One set of theories sees Kubrick as purely an innovator. Anthony Lake sees innovation itself as Kubrick's great strength and weakness: "He wanted to make everything new—the plushiest costume drama ever, the most baroque s.f., the war to end all wars—but for all his erudition, he rarely paused to ponder what might lie in the bedrock of the old, or the ordinary, or the much loved . . . if Kubrick had acknowledged that (the truth may already be slipping through your hands), his films might have been funnier. . . . We should honor and remember Kubrick for having followed his fanatical instincts to the limit."[5]

The *New York Times* editorial page proposed the same idea more elegantly: "What Kubrick's choice of projects reveals is a keen literary sense—he drew after all, from Anthony Burgess and Vladimir Nabokov—and a taste for the extremes of logic, the conclusions our culture's unexamined premises lead us to . . . Strangelove himself . . . a one-man embodiment of the arms race. . . . Humbert Humbert, who is equally besotted with his pubescent Lolita. The visions that get at difficult truths are not usually the ones that soothe us, and those were Kubrick's vision.[8]

A second group, in a way overlapping, see Kubrick's basic characteristic as seeking to disturb or deliver a warning of hidden dangers. Janet Maslin of the *New York Times* writes. "His body of work was unified not only by its bizarre brilliance, but also by its rare ability to disturb. He anticipated, even prophesied, all manner of assaults on the soul of mankind, and he gave voice to its most insidious fears. . . . The Kubrick style was defiantly, mesmerizingly feeling strange . . . if Kubrick told one story, it was a cautionary tale, laced with doomsday thoughts but brightened by wild outrageous humor . . . a truly poetic imagination is gone."[6]

Jean-Pierre Coursodon views this disturbing, warning quality as mainly simply negative: "The past, either distant *(Spartacus)* or recent *(Paths of Glory)* is the realm of injustice, cruelty, indifference to suffering, senseless massacres. The present *(Lolita)* is nightmarish, a world of ludicrous couplings and inexplicable, destructive sexual urges. With a cultural wasteland for its backdrop, the near future is dominated by nauseating violence and pornography *(A Clockwork Orange),* or headed for nuclear holocaust *(Dr. Strangelove).* While in the distant future of *2001: A Space Odyssey,* man is so dehumanized as to become all but indistinguishable from his machinery. As for *The Shining,* it suggests that the present is condemned to endlessly repeat the evils of the past. . . . Kubrick's films . . . are first and foremost sensory experiments, to be enjoyed and if possible discussed as such."[3]

A third approach, exemplified by Godfrey Cheshire, proposes that Kubrick, at least in his later work, tried to systematically explore various categories of experience in order to transcend them: "Kubrick's own drama was not about making firm, sensible judgments, but about escaping from them; every one of his films is about a man or Man slipping the hard grasp of rationality. . . . *Dr. Strangelove* and *2001,* Kubrick's two greatest films, imagine two possible outcomes to humanity's technological precocity: species extinction and species transcendence. . . . *Eyes Wide Shut* comes off as a de facto companion piece to *The Shining.* Both treat home as a metaphor for marriage, both use the constraints of marriage as the pretext for a psychological odyssey by the male partner. . . . *The Shining* points toward despair and death; *Eyes Wide Shut* aims at romantic reconciliation."[2] (I would personally add

Lolita and *A Clockwork Orange* as sexual obsession, singular and plural, and *Paths of Glory* and *Full Metal Jacket* as military discipline, flawed respectively above and below.)

Finally, several writers have proposed so-called antitheories: that Kubrick was overwhelmed by forces and processes as well as ideas beyond his control and understanding. Michael Atkinson, for example, writes: "Why he made the films he made, no one knows—which makes a convincing case for Kubrick as a befuddled artist whose befuddlement worsened with age and sovereignty, and whose galvanic visual sense made it not matter. The stories of his filmmaking methods—the massive and self-insured overruns, the millions spent while Kubrick wandered his set, requesting hundreds of identical takes, or often not shooting anything at all, the years of editing room tinkering—added decaying glamour to his image, but often the films themselves bore out too much lethargy, indecision, suface, and a fascination with gadgets. Perfunctory motives aside, Kubrick's films share only his clinical, indifferent, godlike POV, and many of the movies turn out to be secretly autobio portraits of a monarchical ego struggling for control of its universe."[1]

Stanley Kauffmann also proposes Kubrick lost his way: "'The formalist' says Rudolph Arnheim, 'emancipates the medium from the content it is supposed to serve.'" . . . [Kubrick] became centered on the solution of problems, technical and narrative, rather than on creating works aimed at the response of the viewers. . . . Everything in Kubrick that has been worming through his career, through his ego, and through his extraordinary talent swells and devours this last film . . . the preening pride of being figuratively alone and literally imperial. Perforce there had to be stories and actors, but seemingly they were only necessary nuisances for Kubrick."[4]

Each of these theories makes important points, which I find consistent with my own final, but I believe more clear and precise view of Kubrick's films. I see them each as a story of a heroic protagonist whose conflict with the "modern" world becomes so devilishly and comically total that in the end Kubric's heroes are slyly, completely opposed to everything they once supported and believed. Each film is a total, witty, and profound comic paradox of the modern and postmodern condition.

This is obvious in *Fear and Desire,* where two opposing military teams are played by the same actors, as in his other first films, which have protagonist and antagonist counterparts. With more freedom, this idea became the core of each film.

A good early example of how the idea develops and exfoliates is *Paths of Glory.* The idealist-lawyer Dax is assigned to a military trial that is a complete sham, planned by the authorities—three randomly chosen soldiers are to be executed for cowardice to publicly "excuse" a military-command blunder. Gradually Dax realizes his superiors are all against him, and there is no way to appeal for justice: even resorting to blackmail fails. The film is filled with exquisite ironies. For example, each human sacrifice is chosen by a different form of modern government: fascism (a political enemy); socialism (a social undesirable); and democracy (random lot). In the end the honorable officer continues the empty masquerade of "decent leadership."

Kubrick's subsequent films each deal with this paradigm in other contexts. Lolita's lover is in conflict with a more successful competitor who uses the same sly, manipulative, irrational romantic devices of the first suitor, only more charmingly and ruthlessly. *Lolita* is a comic nightmare of passion reorchestrated against itself.

Dr. Strangelove and *2001* use the identical theme touchstone. In *Dr. Strangelove,* an all-American flying hero from World War II gradually finds himself in a death struggle against the USSR, the US high command, and all his own now betraying technologies, which lead to total annihilation. In *2001,* brilliant-highly trained technologists, kept ignorant like their computers, are soon engaged in a life-and-death struggle against their own super-intelligent technology.

Kubrick's next three films turn inward, to explore the mind itself, "programmed" but challenging its own limits. *A Clockwork Orange* shows a criminal, if bright, mind made helpless by society, only to have society's irrational leaders make it ruthless again. *Barry Lyndon* shows past society similarly turning a decent mind against itself, until the last, when it finds its own way forward once more. *The Shining* dissects the artistic impulse, its total frustration causing the creator to make over his real life into a perverse timeless nightmare "art"—his self-critical faculty interweaving "life" and "entertainment."

In *Full Metal Jacket,* the soldierly virtues ("The Marine Corps wants killers—indestructible men—men without fear!") are pushed to their own paradoxical opposite. One turns on his programmer, the others have no freedom nor understanding themselves, even executing a supremely skillful enemy counterpart without feeling, and marching on to childish TV songs.

Finally, in *Eyes Wide Shut,* Kubrick films a marriage's elaborate, many-leveled structure of temptations and loyalties: the husband drifting through a labyrinth of erotic opportunities and dangers as his wife becomes aware of her own counterpart sexual dreamscape. They turn on their phantasms and rejoin each other.

Kubrick used this paradoxical approach to story telling to explore various aspects of the human condition—political, social, psychological, economic, and creative. If his films have not been as popular or critically acknowledged as they might have been, it is because, I think, their visions have not been adequately understood and illuminated.

Kubrick once told Gene Siskel, "You don't have to make Frank Capra movies to like people." I think Kubrick did like people very much. But rather then feeding their illusions with ideas he did not even believe, as Capra and others apparently did and still do today, Kubrick chose another path. If he could not really solve the modern world's problems, he was able to frame and illuminate them with precision, with wit, and with delight.

Stanley Kubrick made his life an artist's odyssey, a search for new patterns, meanings, and understandings that would illuminate the world. "The very meaningless of life," he said, "forces man to create his own meanings. . . . However vast the darkness, we must supply our own light."

NOTES

(Numbers below include both footnoted material and suggested supplementary readings.)

QUOTATION ON PAGE vii

1. Macklin, F. Anthony. "Sex and Dr. Strangelove." *Film Comment,* Vol. 3, No. 3, p. 55.

CHAPTER 1

1. Gelmis, Joseph. *Film Director as Superstar.* New York: Doubleday, 1970.
2. Kubrick, Stanley. Interview in *Eye,* August 1968, pp. 84–86.
3. ———. Interview in *Newsweek,* December 2, 1957, p. 38.
4. ———. Interview in *The Observer* (London), December 4, 1960.
5. ———. "Words and Movies." *Sight and Sound* (London), Winter 1961, p. 14.
6. Stang, Jonathan. "Film Fan to Film Maker." *The New York Times Magazine,* October 12, 1958.
7. Tournabene, Lyn. "Contradicting the Hollywood Image." *The Saturday Review,* December 28, 1963, pp. 19–21.

CHAPTER 2

1. Agel, Jerome, ed. *The Making of Kubrick's 2001.* New York: New American Library, 1970.
2. Brustein, Robert. "Out of This World." *The New York Review of Books,* February 6, 1970.
3. Burstyn, Joseph, Inc., Synopsis of *Fear and Desire.*
4. Gurnseley, Otis L., Jr. Review of *Fear and Desire* in the New York *Herald Tribune,* April 1, 1953.
5. Kubrick, Stanley. Letter to Joseph Burstyn dated November 16, 1952.
6. ———. Letter to Norman Kagan dated March 23, 1970.
7. McLartten. "Films." *The New Yorker,* April 11, 1953, p. 128.
8. Review of *Fear and Desire* in *Time,* April 3, 1953.
9. Review of *Fear and Desire* in *Variety,* April 2, 1953.
10. Weiler, A. "The Screen in Review." *The New York Times,* April 1, 1953.

CHAPTER 3

1. Gilbert. Review of *Killer's Kiss* in *Variety*, September 29, 1955.
2. Kubrick, Stanley. Interview in *The Observer* (London), December 4, 1960.
3. Lambert, Gavin. "*Killer's Kiss.*" *Sight and Sound* (London), Spring 1956, p. 198.
4. Review of *Killer's Kiss* in *Film Daily*, September 29, 1955.

CHAPTER 4

1. Beckley, Paul V. Review of *The Killing* in the New York *Herald Tribune*, May 21, 1956.
2. Kael, Pauline. *Kiss Kiss Bang Bang*. Boston: Little, Brown, 1968.
3. Kubrick, Stanley. Interview in *The Observer* (London), December 4, 1960.
4. Kubrick, Stanley. Interview in *The Observer* (London), December 4, 1960.
5. ————. "Words and Movies." *Sight and Sound* (London), Winter 1961.
6. Lambert, Gavin. "*The Killing.*" *Sight and Sound* (London), Autumn 1956, p. 95.
7. Weiler, A. H. "*The Killing.*" *The New York Times,* May 21, 1956.
8. White. "*The Killing.*" *Variety,* May 23, 1956.
9. White, Lionel. *Clean Break*. New York: Gold Medal Books, 1950.

CHAPTER 5

1. Alpert, Hollis. "War and Justice." *The Saturday Review,* December 21, 1957, p. 31.
2. Cobb, Humphrey. *Paths of Glory*. New York: Grosset & Dunlap, 1953.
3. Crowther, Bosley. "Shameful Incident of War." *The New York Times,* December 27, 1957.
4. Lambert, Gavin. "*Paths of Glory Reviewed.*" *Sight and Sound* (London), Winter 1957–58, p. 144.
5. Review of *Paths of Glory* in *Time,* December 9, 1957, p. 108.
6. Review of *The Killing* in *Time,* June 4, 1956, p. 106.
7. Stang, Jonathan. "Film Fan to Film Maker." *The New York Times Magazine,* October 12, 1958.

8. Zinsser, William K. Review of *Paths of Glory* in the *New York Herald Tribune,* December 26, 1957

CHAPTER 6

1. Alpert, Hollis. "The Day of the Gladiators." *The Saturday Review,* October 12, 1960.
2. Beckley, Paul V. Review of *Spartacus* in the *New York Herald Tribune,* October 7, 1960.
3. Crowther, Bosley. "Spartacus Enters the Arena." *The New York Times,* October 7, 1960.
4. Dyer, P. J. "*Spartacus* Review." *Sight and Sound* (London), Spring 1961, p. 38.
5. Fast, Howard. *Spartacus.* New York: Modern Library, 1951.
6. Gelmis, Joseph. *Film Director as Superstar.* New York: Double-day, 1970.
7. Kauffmann, Stanley. Review of Spartacus in *The New Republic,* November 14, 1960.
8. Kubrick, Stanley. Interview in *Eye,* August 1968.
9. ———. Interview: "Twenty-nine and Running, the Director with Hollywood by the Horns . . . Dissects the Movies." *Newsweek,* December 2, 1957.
10. ———. Interview in *The Observer* (London), December 4, 1960.
11. Pry. Review of *Spartacus* in *Variety,* October 12, 1960, p. 6.
12. Stang, Jonathan. "Film Fan to Film Maker." *The New York Times Magazine,* October 12, 1958, p. 38.
13. Review of *Spartacus* in *Time,* October 24, 1960.

CHAPTER 7

1. Anby. "*Lolita.*" *Variety,* June 22, 1962.
2. Beckley, Paul V. "*Lolita:* The New Movies." The New York *Herald Tribune,* June 14, 1962.
3. Croce, Arlene. "*Lolita.*" *Sight and Sound* (London), Autumn 1962, p. 191.
4. Gelmis, Joseph. *Film Director as Superstar.* New York: Double-day, 1970.
5. Kael, Pauline. "*Lolita.*" *I Lost It At The Movies.* Boston: Little, Brown, 1965.
6. Kubrick, Stanley. Interview in *Eye,* August 1968.

7. ———. "Words and Movies," *Sight and Sound* (London), Winter 1961.
8. Nabokov, Vladimir. *Lolita.* New York: Putnam's, 1955.
9. "Nymphet Found." *Time,* October 10, 1960, p. 92.
10. Sarris, Andrew. "Movie Journal." *The Village Voice,* July 5, 1962.
11. Stang, Jonathan. "Film Fan to Film Maker." *The New York Times Magazine,* October 12, 1958.
12. Walker, Alexander. *Sex in the Movies.* London: Penguin, 1968.

CHAPTER 8

1. Agel, Jerome, ed. *The Making of Kubrick's 2001.* New York: New American Library, 1970.
2. Brustein, Robert. "Out of This World." *The New York Review of Books,* February 6, 1970.
3. Crist, Judith. "*Dr. Strangelove:* Committed, Bitter, One of the Best." The New York *Herald Tribune,* January 30, 1964.
4. George, Peter. *Dr. Strangelove.* New York: Bantam Books, 1963.
5. Gelmis, Joseph. *Film Director as Superstar.* New York: Doubleday, 1970.
6. Kauffmann, Stanley. *A World on Film.* New York: Harper & Row, 1966.
7. Kael, Pauline. *I Lost It at the Movies.* Boston: Little, Brown, 1965.
8. Kubrick, Stanley. Interview in *Newsweek,* December 2, 1957.
9. Macklin, F. Anthony. "Sex and Dr. Strangelove." *Film Comment,* Vol. 3, No. 3, p. 55.
10. Sarris, Andrew. "Come Now, Dr. Strangelove." *The Village Voice,* January 3, 1964, p. 13.
11. Simon, John. *Private Screenings.* New York: Macmillan, 1967.

CHAPTER 9

1. Agel, Jerome, ed. *The Making of Kubrick's 2001.* New York: New American Library, 1970.
2. Burgess, Anthony. *A Clockwork Orange.* New York: Norton, 1962.
3. Clarke, Arthur C. *2001: A Space Odyssey.* New York: New American Library, 1968.
4. Daniels, Don. "*2001:* A New Myth." *Film Heritage,* Vol. 3, No. 4, Summer 1968.

5. Delaney, Samuel R. "Review of *2001: A Space Odyssey*." In *Best SF: 1968*, edited by Harry Hairison. New York: Putnam's, 1969.

6. Gilliatt, Penelope. "After Man." In *The Making of Kubrick's 2001*, edited by Jerome Agel. New York: New American Library, 1970.

7. Gelmis, Joseph. *Film Director as Superstar*. New York: Doubleday, 1970.

8. Hamilton, Edith. *Mythology*. New York: Mentor Books, 1940.

9. Hunter, Tim et al. "*2001: A Space Odyssey*." *Film Heritage*, Vol. 3, No. 4, Summer 1968, p. 12.

10. Kosloff, Max. "*2001*." *Film Culture*, No. 48–49, Winter & Spring 1970.

11. Kubrick, Stanley. Interview in *Eye*, August 1968.

12. ———. "*Playboy* Interview." In *The Making of Kubrick's 2001*, edited by Jerome Agel. New York: New American Library, 1970.

13. Macklin, F. A. "The Comic Sense of *2001*." *Film Comment*, Vol. 5, No. 4, Winter 1969.

14. Ordway, Frederick I. "Comments on *2001*." In *The Making of Kubrick's 2001*, edited by Jerome Agel. New York: New American Library, 1970.

15. Sarris, Andrew. "Films in Focus." *The Village Voice*, May 7, 1970.

16. Stackhouse, Margaret. "Reflections on *2001*." In *The Making of Kubrick's 2001*, edited by Jerome Agel. New York: New American Library, 1970.

CHAPTER 10

1. Alpert, Hollis. "Milk Plus and Ultra Violence." *The Saturday Review*, December 25, 1971.

2. Bailey, Andrew. "A Clockwork Utopia." *Rolling Stone*, January 20, 1972.

3. Burgess, Anthony. *A Clockwork Orange*. New York: Norton, 1962.

4. Canby, Vincent. "*A Clockwork Orange* Dazzles the Sense and Mind." *The New York Times*, December 20, 1971.

5. ———. "*Orange*—Disorienting But Human Comedy . . ." *The New York Times*, Sunday, January 9, 1972.

6. Crist, Judith. "A Feast, and About Time." *New York,* December 20, 1971.

7. Cocks, Jay. "Kubrick's Degrees of Madness." *Time,* December 20, 1971.

8. Houston, Penelope. "Kubrick Country." *The Saturday Review,* December 25, 1971.

9. Hughes, Robert. "The Decor of Tomorrow's Hell." *Time,* December 27, 1971.

10. Kael, Pauline. "Stanley Strangelove." *The New Yorker,* January 1, 1972.

11. "Kubrick's *Clockwork Orange.*" *Playboy,* January, 1972, p. 200.

12. McDonough, Scott. "England's Actor of the Seventies." *Show,* January, 1972.

13. Murf. *"A Clockwork Orange." Variety,* December 16, 1971.

14. Riley, Clayton. ". . . Or 'A Dangerous, Criminally Irresponsible Horrorshow'?" *The Sunday New York Times Drama Section,* January 9, 1972.

15. Sarris, Andrew. "Films in Focus." *The Village Voice,* December 30, 1971.

16. Walker, Alexander. *Stanley Kubrick Directs.* New York: Harcourt, Brace & Jovanovich, 1971.

17. Weiler, A. H. *"Clockwork Orange* Wins Critics' Prize." *The New York Times,* December 29, 1971.

18. Weinraub, Bernard. "Kubrick Tells What Makes *Clockwork Orange* Tick." *The New York Times,* December 31, 1971.

19. Zavatsky, Bill. "Malcolm McDowell: A Sensitive Thing." *The Herald,* December 19, 1971.

20. Zimmerman, Paul. "Kubrick's Brilliant Vision." *Newsweek,* January 3, 1972.

CHAPTER 11

1. Alcott, John. "Photographing *Barry Lyndon*" in *American Cinematographer,* 1976.

2. Canby, Vincent. "Kubrick's Latest Has Brains and Beauty." *New York Times,* December 21, 1975, Theatre Arts section, p. 1.

3. Corliss, Richard. "Great Pretender, True King, or Some Such." *New Times,* January 23, 1976, p. 27.

4. Dempsey, Michael. "Barry Lyndon." *Film Quarterly,* Fall 1976, vol. 30, no. 1, p. 49.

5. Feldman, Hans. "Kubrick and His Discontents." *Film Quarterly,* Fall 1976, vol. 30, no. 1, p. 12.
6. Kael, Pauline. "Kubrick's Golden Age." *New Yorker,* December 27, 1975, p. 68.
7. "Kubrick's Greatest Gamble." *Time,* December 15, 1975, p. 72.
8. Moscowitz, Ken. "Clockwork Violence." *Sight and Sound,* Winter 1976–77, vol. 46, no. 1, p. 22.
9. Rosenbau, Jonathan. "The Pluck of Stanley Kubrick." *Film Comment,* vol. 12, no. 2, March–April 1976, p. 26.
10. Sarris, Andrew. "What Makes Barry Run?" *Village Voice,* Dec. 25, 1976, pp. 111–12.
11. Silber, Irwin. "Film: Barry Lyndon Finds History Meaningless." *Guardian,* March 17, 1976, p. 19.
12. Thackeray, W. M. *Barry Lyndon.* New York: Grove Press, Inc., 1975.

CHAPTER 12

1. Alberson, Jim. *"The Shining."* Cinefantastique, Fall 1980, p. 74.
2. Boyum, Joy Gould. "The Sheen Is Off Kubrick's New Horror Movie." *Wall Street Journal,* May 30, 1980, p. 21.
3. Clarens, Carlos. "All Work and No Play." *Soho News,* May 28, 1980, p. 43.
4. Cook, David A. "American Horror: The Shining." *Literary Film Quarterly,* 1984, no. 1, p. 2.
5. Denby, David. "Death Warmed Over." *New York Magazine,* June 9, 1980, p. 60.
6. "Har." "The Shining." *Variety,* May 28, 1980, p. 14.
7. Harmetz, Aljean. "Kubrick Films *The Shining* in Secrecy of English Studio." *New York Times,* May 20, 1977.
8. Hofsess, John. "Kubrick: Critics Be Damned." *Soho News,* May 28, 1980, p. 41.
9. Hoile, Christopher. "The Uncanny: The Fairy Tale in Kubrick's *The Shining." Literary Film Quarterly,* 1984, no. 1, p. 20.
10. Kael, Pauline. "Devolution." *New Yorker,* September 6, 1980, p. 130.
11. Kroll, Jack. "Stanley Kubrick's Horror Show." *Newsweek,* May 26, 1980, p. 96.
12. Leogrande, Ernest. "The Shining a No Glow Show." *Daily News,* May 23, 1980, p. 39.
13. Maslin, Janet. "Screen: Nicholson and Shelley Duvall in Kubrick's *The Shining." New York Times,* May 23, 1980.

14. Meisel, Myron. "Why *The Shining* is a Fourteenth Century Film." *Los Angeles Reader,* May 13, 1980, p. 4.
15. Peary, Gerald. "The Dimming." *Real Paper,* June 14, 1980, p. 20.
16. Reed, Rex. "Shining a Tainted Turkey—Empire an Epic." *Daily News,* June 6, 1980.
17. Schickel, Richard. "Red Herrings and Refusals." *Time,* June 2, 1980, p. 42.
18. Shiff, Stephen. "The Shining." *Boston Phoenix,* June 17, 1980.
19. Simon, John. "Horrible Visu." *National Review,* June 27, 1980, p. 39.
20. Wolf, William. "The Dream Master." *New York,* June 9, 1980, p. 62.

CHAPTER 13

1. Canby, Vincent. "Film: Kubrick's *Full Metal Jacket,* on Viet Nam." *New York Times,* June 26, 1987, p. C-3.
2. "Cart." *"Full Metal Jacket."* *Variety,* June 12, 1987, p. 12.
3. Clines, F. X. "Stanley Kubrick's Vietnam." *New York Times,* June 21, 1987, Arts section, p. 1.
4. Cooper, Marc. "Light at the End of the Tunnel." *American Film,* July 1987, p. 10.
5. Corliss, R. "Welcome to Vietnam, the Movie." *Time,* June 29, 1987, p. 66.
6. Harmetz, Aljean. " 'Jacket' Actor Invents His Dialogue." *New York Times,* June 30, 1987.
7. Hasford, Gustav. *The Short-Timers.* New York: Bantam Books, 1980.
8. Hoberman, J. "Dressed to Kill." *Village Voice,* July 7, 1987, p. 72.
9. Kroll, Jack. "Movies—1968: Kubrick's Vietnam Odyssey." *Newsweek,* June 29, 1987.
10. Rabe, David. "Admiring the Unpredictable Mr. Kubrick." *New York Sunday Times,* Arts section, June 21, 1987, pp. 34, 36.
11. Sterritt, David. *"Full Metal Jacket:* Kubrick's View of Viet-Nam." *Christian Science Monitor,* June 26, 1987, p. 19.

CHAPTER 14

1. Booth, Cathy. "Three of a Kind." *Time,* July 5, 1999, p. 30.
2. Chesire, Godfrey. "The Photographer's Final Frames." *NYPress,* July 21, 1999, p. 8.
3. Chronenberg, David. "Amy Taubin Interview." *Village Voice,* April 27, 1999, p. 56.

4. Denby, David. "Kubrick's Dark Orgy." *The New Yorker,* July 26, 1999, p. 50.
5. Dreher, Rod. "Eyes Glaze Over." *New York Post,* July 16, 1999, p. 32.
6. Ginna, Robert E. "The Odyssey Begins." *Entertainment Weekly,* April 9, 1999, p. 16.
7. Glieberman, Owen, "The Temptations." *Entertainment Weekly,* July 23, 1999.
8. Herr, Michael, "Kubrick." *Vanity Fair,* August 1999, p. 89.
9. Hoberman, J. "I Wake Up Dreaming." *The Village Voice,* July 27, 1999.
10. Holden, Stephen. "Tickets to Fantasies of Urban Desire." *New York Times,* July 20, 1999.
11. Klawans, Stuart. "Old Masters.", The *Nation,* August 9, 1999.
12. Lipman, John. "Can Kubrick's 'Eyes' Open Wide?" *Wall Street Journal,* July 14, 1999, p. B-1.
13. Maslin, Janet. "Bedroom Odyssey." *New York Times,* July 16, 1999, B-1.
14. McCarthy, Todd. "Kubrick Casts a Gripping Spell." *Variety,* July 11, 1999, p. 37.
15. Menano, Louis. "Kubrick's Strange Love." *New York Review of Books,* August 12, 1999, p. 34.
16. Rainer, Peter. "Strangelove." *New York Magazine,* July 26, 1999, p. 49.
17. Raphael, Frederick. *Eyes Wide Open: A Memoir of Stanley Kubrick.* New York: Ballantine Books, 1999.
18. Schickel, Richard. "All Eyes on Them." *Time,* July 5, 1999, p. 68.
19. Seiler, Andy. "Nudity Isn't New on Cruise, Kidman Rresumes." *USA Today,* July 16, 1999.
20. Svetkey, Benjamin. "Eyes of the Storm." *Entertainment Weekly,* July 23, 1999, p. 32.
21. Topping, Dana. "Tom and Nicole Go for the Bold." *US Magazine,* July, 1999, p. 18.
22. Weinraub, Bernard. "At the Movies." *New York Times,* July 16, 1999, p. 20.

CHAPTER 15

1. Atkinson, Michael. "Path of Glory." *Village Voice,* March 16, 1999.
2. Cheshire, Godfrey. "The Photographer's Final Frames." *New York Press,* July 21, 1999.

3. Coursodon, Jean-Pierre, *American Directors.* New York: McGraw Hill, 1982, p. 141.
4. Kauffmann, Stanley. "Kubrick, A Sadness." *The New Republic,* August 16, 1999, p. 30.
5. Lane, Anthony. "The Last Emperor." *The New Yorker,* March 22, 1999.
6. Maslin, Janet. "Visionary, a Mind Blower, Kubrick Never Failed to Stun." *New York Times,* March 14, 1999, p. 30.
7. Menand, Luis. "Kubrick's Strange Love." *New York Review of Books,* August 12, 1999, p. 7.
8. *New York Times.* Editorial, March 18, 1999.

KUBRICK FILMOGRAPHY

1951   *Day of the Fight*   RKO. Documentary short Kubrick wrote, directed, produced.

1952   *Flying Padre*   RKO. Documentary short Kubrick wrote, directed, produced.

1953   *Fear and Desire*   Released by Joseph Burstyn, Inc. Produced, directed, photographed and edited by Stanley Kubrick. Associate Producer, Martin Perveler. Screenplay by Howard O. Sackler. Music, Gerald Fried. Unit Manager, Bob Dierks. Assistant Director, Steve Hahn. Make-up, Chet Fabian. Art Director, Herbert Lebowitz. Title Design, Barney Ettengoff. Dialogue Director, Toba Kubrick. With Frank Silvera (Mac), Kenneth Harp (Corby), Paul Mazursky (Sidney), Steve Coit (Fletcher), Virginia Leith (the Girl), David Allen (Narrator). Running time: 68 minutes.

1955   *Killer's Kiss*   United Artists release of Minotaur. Stanley Kubrick and Morris Bousel production. Directed, written, photographed and edited by Stanley Kubrick. Music, Gerald Fried. With Frank Silvera (Vincent Rapallo), Jamie Smith (Davy Gordon), Irene Kane (Gloria Price), Jerry Jarret (Albert, the Fight Manager), Mike Dana, Felice Orlandi, Ralph Roberts, Phil Stevenson (Hoodlums), Julius Adelman (Owner of Mannequin Factory), David Vaughan, Alec Rubin (Conventioneers). Running time: 67 minutes.

1956   *The Killing*   United Artists release of a James B. Harris production. Directed by Stanley Kubrick. Screenplay by Stanley Kubrick from Lionel White's novel, *Clean Break*. Camera, Lucien Ballard. Editor, Betty Steinberg. Music, Gerald Fried. With Sterling Hayden (Johnny Clay), Coleen Gray (Fay), Vince Edwards (Val Cannon), Jay C. Flippen (Marvin Unger), Marie Windsor (Sherry Peatty), Ted De Corsia (Randy Kennan), Elisha Cook (George Peatty), Joe Sawyer (Mike O'Reilly), Tim Carey (Nikki), Jay Adler (Leo), Joseph Turkel (Tiny), Kola Kwarian (Maurice). Running time: 64 minutes.

1957   *Paths of Glory*   Presented by Bryna Productions and released through United Artists. Produced by James B. Harris. Directed by Stanley Kubrick. Screenplay by Stanley Kubrick, Calder

Willingham, and Jim Thompson based on the novel by Humphrey Cobb. Music, Gerald Fried. With Kirk Douglas (Colonel Dax), Ralph Meeker (Corporal Paris), Adolphe Menjou (General Broulard), George Macready (General Mireau), Wayne Morris (Lieutenant Roget), Richard Anderson (Major Saint-Auban), Joseph Turkel (Private Arnaud), Timothy Carey (Private Ferol), Peter Capell (Colonel Judge), Susanne Christian (German Girl), Bert Freed (Sergeant Boulanger), Emile Meyer (Priest), Ken Dibbs (Private Lejeune), Jerry Hausner (Private Meyer), Frederic Bell (Shell-Shocked Soldier), Harold Benedict (Captain Nichols), John Stein (Captain Rousseau). Running time: 86 minutes.

1960 *Spartacus* Universal release of Bryna Productions. Executive producer Kirk Douglas. Produced by Edward Lewis. Directed by Stanley Kubrick. Screenplay, Dalton Trumbo, based on the Howard Fast novel. Camera (Technicolor), Russell Metty. Editor, Robert Lawrence. Music, Alex North. Assistant director, Marshall Green. With Kirk Douglas (Spartacus), Laurence Olivier (Crassus), Jean Simmons (Varinia), Charles Laughton (Gracchus), Peter Ustinov (Batiatus), John Gavin (Caesar), Nina Foch (Helena), Herbert Lom (Tigranes), John Ireland (Crixus), John Dall (Glabrus), Charles McGraw (Marcellus), Joanna Barnes (Claudia), Harold J. Stone (David), Woody Strode (Draba), Peter Brocco (Ramon), Paul Lambert (Gannicus), Robert J. Wilke (Guard Captain), Nicholas Dennis (Dionysius), John Hoyt (Roman Officer), Frederick Worlock (Laelius), Tony Curtis (Antonius). Running time: 196 minutes.

1962 *Lolita* Metro-Goldwyn-Mayer presentation in association with Seven Arts. James B. Harris production. Directed by Stanley Kubrick. Screenplay, Vladimir Nabokov, based on his novel. Camera, Oswald Morris. Music, Nelson Riddle. "Lolita" theme, Bob Harris. Editor, Anthony Harvey. Assistant directors, Rene Dupont, Roy Millichip, John Danischewsky. With James Mason (Humbert Humbert), Shelley Winters (Charlotte Haze), Peter Sellers (Clare Quilty), Sue Lyon (Lolita Haze), Marianne Stone (Vivian Darkbloom), Diana Decker (Jean Farlow), Jerry Stovin (John Farlow), Gary Cockrell (Dick), Suzanna Gibbs (Mona Farlow), Roberta Shore (Lorna), Eric Lane (Roy), Shirley Douglas (Mrs. Starch), Roland Brand (Bill), Colin Maitland (Charlie), Cee Linder (Physician),

Irvin Allen (Hospital Attendant), Lois Maxwell (Nurse Mary Lore), William Greene (Swine), C. Denier Warren (Potts), Isobel Lucas (Louise), Maxine Holden (Receptionist at Hospital), Marion Mathie (Miss Lebone), Craig Sams (Rex), John Harrison (Tom), James Dyrenforth (Beale Senior), Cee Linder (Dr. Keygee). Running time: 152 minutes.

1964 *Dr. Strangelove* Columbia Pictures. Directed by Stanley Kubrick. Produced by Stanley Kubrick. Screenplay by Stanley Kubrick, Terry Southern and Peter George, based on the book, *Red Alert,* by Peter George. With Peter Sellers (Group Captain Lionel Mandrake, President Muffley, Dr. Strangelove), George C. Scott (General "Buck" Turgidson), Sterling Hayden (General Jack D. Ripper), Keenan Wynn (Colonel "Bat" Guano), Slim Picken (Major T. J. "King" Kong), Peter Bull (Ambassador De Sodesky), Tracy Reed (Miss "Foreign Affairs"), James Earl Jones (Lieutenant Lothor Zogg), Jack Creley (Mr. Staines), Frank Berry (Lieutenant H. R. Dietrich), Glenn Beck (Lieutenant W. D. Kivel), Shane Rimmer (Captain G. A. "Ace" Owens, Co-Pilot), Paul Tamarin (Lieutenant Goldberg), Gordon Tonner (General Faceman), Robert O'Neil (Admiral Randolph), Roy Stephens (Frank). Running time: 93 minutes.

1968 (G.B.) *2001: A Space Odyssey* Metro-Goldwyn-Mayer. Directed by Stanley Kubrick. Screenplay by Stanley Kubrick, Arthur C. Clarke. Based on the story *The Sentinel* by Arthur C. Clarke. Photography, Geoffrey Unsworth. Additional photography, John Alcott. Special photographic effects designed and directed by Stanley Kubrick. Special effects, Wally Veevers, Douglas Trumbull, Con Pederson, Tom Howard. Production designers, Tony Master, Harry Lange, Ernie Archer. Art Director, John Hoesli. Produced by Stanley Kubrick. Music, Richard Strauss, Johann Strauss, Aram Khachaturian, György Ligeti. Sound, Winston Ryder. With Keir Dullea (David Bowman), Garry Lockwood (Frank Poole), William Sylvester (Dr. Heywood Floyd), Daniel Richter (Moonwatcher), Douglas Rain (Voice of HAL 9000), Leonard Rossiter (Smyslov), Margaret Tyzack (Elena), Robert Beatty (Halvorsen), Sean Sullivan (Michaels), Frank Miller (Mission Control), Penny Brahms (Stewardess), Alan Gifford (Poole's Father), Edward Bishop, Glenn Beck, Edwina Carroll, Mike Lovell, Peter Delman, Danny Grover, Brian Hawley. Running time: 141 minutes.

1971   *A Clockwork Orange* Warner Brothers release of a Stanley Kubrick production. Produced, directed, and written by Stanley Kubrick from the novel by Anthony Burgess. Executive Producers, Max L. Raab, Si Litvinoff. Camera (color), John Alcott. Production design, John Barry. Art direction, Russell Hagg, Peter Shields. Music, Walter Carlos. Editor, Bill Butter. Sound, John Jordan. Assistant directors, Derek Cracknell, Dusty Symonds, Bill Welch. Reviewed at Warner Bros. studios, Burbank, December 13, 1971 (MPAA rating: X). With Malcolm McDowell (Alex), Patrick Magee (Mr. Alexander), Michael Bates (Chief Guard), Warren Clarke (Dim), John Clive (Stage Actor), Adrienne Corri (Mrs. Alexander), Carl Duering (Dr. Brodsky), Paul Farrell (Tramp), Clive Francis (Lodger), Michael Gover (Prison Governor), Miriam Karlin (Cat Lady), James Marcus (Georgie), Aubrey Morris (Deltoid), Godfrey Quigley (Prison Chaplain), Shela Raynor (Mum), Madge Ryan (Dr. Branom), John Savident (Conspirator), Anthony Sharp (Minister), Phillip Stone (Dad), Pauline Taylor (Psychiatrist), Margaret Tyzack (Conspirator). Also: Steven Berkoff, Lindsay Campbell, Michael Tarn, David Prowse, Barrie Cookson, Jan Adair, Gaye Brown, Peter Burton, John J. Carney, Vivienne Chandler, Richard Connaught, Prudence Drage, Carol Drinkwater, Lee Fox, Cheryl Grunwald, Gillian Hills, Craig Hunter, Shirley Jaffe, Barbara Scott, Virginia Weatherell, Neil Wilson, Katya Wyeth. Running time: 137 minutes.

1975   *Barry Lyndon* Peregrine Production distributed by Warner Brothers. Directed, written, and produced by Stanley Kubrick, adapted from the novel by William Makepeace Thackeray. Executive producer, Jean Harian; production designer, Ken Adam. Director of Photography, John Alcott. Editor, Tony Lawson. Music adapted and conducted by Leonard Rosenman. With Ryan O'Neal (Barry Lyndon), Marisa Berenson (Lady Lyndon), Patrick Magee (Chevalier), Hardy Kruger (Captain Potzdorf), Gay Hamilton (Nora), Marie Kean (Barry's Mother), Diane Koerner (German girl), Murry Melvin (Reverend Run), Frank Middlemass (Sir Charles Lyndon), Arthur O'Sullivan (Highwayman), Godfrey Quigley (Captain Grogan), Leonard Rossiter (Captain Quin), Leon Vitali (Lord Bullingdon), Michael Hordern (Narrator). Running time: 185 minutes.

1980   *The Shining* Warner Brothers release. Produced and directed by Stanley Kubrick, in association with the Producers Circle Co. Executive Producer, Jan Harlan. Screenplay Stanley Kubrick and Diane Johnson, based on the novel by Stephen King. Camera

John Alcott, Editor, Ray Lovejoy. Sound, Ivan Sharrock, Richard Daneil. Production design, Roy Walker. Art direction, Les Tomkins. Assistant director, Brian Cook. Makeup, Tom Smith. Costumes, Milena Canonero. Music, Béla Bartók. With Jack Nicholson (Jack Torrance), Shelley Duvall (Wendy Torrance), Danny Lloyd (Danny), Scatman Crothers (Halloran), Barry Nelson (Ullman), Philip Stone (Grady), Joe Turkel (Lloyd), Ann Jackson (Doctor), and Tony Burton (Durkin). Running time: 146 minutes.

1987   *Full Metal Jacket*   Warner Brothers release. Produced and directed by Stanley Kubrick. Executive Producer, Jan Harlan. Coproducer, Philip Hobbs. Screenplay, Kubrick, Michael Herr, Gustav Hasford, based on the novel *The Short-Timers* by Hasford. Camera (Rank color), Douglas Milsome. Editor, Martin Hunter. Music, Abigail Mead. Production Design, Anton Furst. Art Direction, Rod Stratford, Les Tomkins, Keith Pain. Costume Design, Keith Denny. Sound, Edward Tise. Special Effects Supervisor, John Evans. Technical Advisor, Lee Ermey. Associate Producer, Michael Herr. Assistant Director, Terry Needham. Casting, Leon Vitali. With Matthew Modine (Private Joker), Adam Baldwin (Animal Mother), Vincent D'Onofrio (Private Pyle), Lee Ermey (Gunnery Sergeant Hartman), Dorian Harewood (Eightball), Arliss Howard (Cowboy), Kevyn Major Howard (Rafterman), Ed Ross (Lieutenant Touchdown). Also with: John Terry, Kirk Taylor, Ian Tyler, Papillon Soo Soo, Tan Hung Francione, Costas Dino Chimino Peter Merrill, Kierson, Jecchinis, John Stafford, Cary Landon Mills, Ngoc Lee, Leanne Hong, Gil Kopel, Herbert Norville, Bruce Boa, Tim Colceri, Sal Lopez, Peter Edmund, Marcus D'Amico, Keith Hodiak, Nguyen Phong. Running Time: 116 minutes.

1999   *Eyes Wide Shut*   Warner Brothers release of a Pole Star production made by Hobby Films, Ltd. Produced and directed by Stanley Kubrick. Executive Producer, Jan Harlan. Coproducer, Brian W. Cook. Screenplay, Kubrick, Frederic Raphael. Inspired by the novella *Traumnovelle* (Dream story) by Arthur Schnitzler. Camera (Deluxe London color), Larry Smith. Editor, Nigel Galt. Music, Jocelyn Pook. Production Designers, Les Tomkins, Roy

Walker. Supervising Art Director, Kevin Phipps. Art Director, John Fenner. Set Decorators, Terry Wells, Sr.; Lisa Leone. Costume Designer, Marit Allen; Sound (Dolby/DTS/DDS), Edward Tise. Supervising Sound Editor, Paul Conway. Assistant Director, Brian W. Cook. Second Unit Camera, Patrick Turley, Malik Sayeed, Arthur Jaffa. Casting, Denise Chamian, Leon Vitali. With Rom Cruise (Dr. William Harford), Nicole Kidman (Alice Harford), Sydney Pollack (Victor Ziegler), Marie Richardson (Marion), Rade Sherbedgia (Milich), Todd Field (Nick Nighingale), Vinessa Shaw (Domino), Alan Cumming (Desk Clerk), Sky Dumont (Sandor Szavost), Fay Masterson (Sally), Leelee Sobieski (Milich's Daughter), Thomas Gibson (Carl), Madison Eginton (Helena Harford), Louise Taylor (Gayle), Stewart Thorndike (Nuala), Julienne Davis (Mandy), Carmela Marner (Waitress at Gillespie's). Running time 159 minutes.